DEMOGRAPHIC STATISTICS OF HAWAII: 1778-1965

DEMOGRAPHIC STATISTICS OF HAWAII: 1778-1965

Robert C. Schmitt

UNIVERSITY OF HAWAII PRESS

Honolulu 1968

Manufactured in the United States of America

Library of Congress Catalog Card Number 67-30840

ACKNOWLEDGMENTS

Three of the chapters in this book originally appeared, in somewhat different form, as articles in the Hawaii Historical Review. Chapter II was published in two parts, the first (as "Population Estimates and Censuses of Hawaii, 1778-1850") in the July 1964 issue and the second (as "Population Characteristics of Hawaii, 1778-1850") in the April 1965 issue. Chapter VI was published (as "Birth and Death Rates in Hawaii, 1848-1962") in the January 1964 issue. Chapter VII appeared (as "Migration Statistics of Hawaii, 1823-1962") in July 1963. All three chapters have been extensively revised since their initial appearance. The author is grateful to Richard A. Greer, Editor of the Review, for permission to reprint these articles in their new form.

Chapter V and the appendix on intercensal estimates are based in part on studies made by the author for the State Department of Planning and Economic Development.

Many librarians and archivists assisted with the historical portions of this monograph. Janet E. Bell, Curator of the Hawaiian and Pacific Collection, Sinclair Library, University of Hawaii, and Agnes Conrad and her staff at the Archives of Hawaii were particularly helpful. Assistance was obtained also from the librarians of the Bernice P. Bishop Museum, the Hawaiian Historical Society, the Library of Hawaii, and the Honolulu Municipal Reference Library.

Dr. Paul Bruyere, Charles G. Bennett, George H. Tokuyama, Lillian Louis, Myrna Sen, and Marie Viele, all of the Research, Planning and Statistics Office of the State Department of Health, provided many of the statistics on births, deaths, migration, marriages, and divorces.

Special acknowledgment is due Dr. Andrew W. Lind, Senior Professor of Sociology at the University of Hawaii. Dr. Lind's profound knowledge of Hawaiian demography, shared with the author over a span of nearly twenty years, is reflected in many of the pages that follow. His critical review of both the initial draft and a subsequent revision of the manuscript contributed greatly to the final book.

Other persons providing information, assistance, or encouragement included Dr. Bernhard L. Hormann of the University of Hawaii, Dr. Kenneth P. Emory and his colleagues at the Bishop Museum, members of the Population and Geography Divisions of the U. S. Bureau of the Census, and Rose C. Strombel.

Contents

FOREWORD

The New England missionaries who came to Hawaii early in the nineteenth century have been credited with the introduction of many things, both good and bad, but rarely, if ever, have they been either praised or blamed as the innovators of social science. The fact remains, however, that well within the first decade after their arrival in 1820, these Protestant pioneers had become deeply distressed about the population problem in their island community and were initiating the use of census methods in determining what was actually happening in this regard. Just three years after the first company of missionaries had appeared, they prepared an estimate of the population on each of the islands and of the entire chain, and in 1832 they took a census, with the assistance of native school teachers, on each of the five more important islands. A second census four years later, supplemented by the enumeration of births and deaths within some of the districts, testifies to the genuine concern of the missionaries for the population trends among the native Hawaiians. Thus, it was only natural that a few years later, when the pressure for an official governmental census had mounted sufficiently, a Protestant missionary educator should have been placed in charge, and that beginning in 1860, an official count of the population, in increasing detail and accuracy, should have been conducted every six years, instead of at the ten year intervals common in most of the advanced countries of the world.

Considering the wealth of detailed information regarding the nature of the population in Hawaii over more than a century of time, probably unrivaled in any other developing region of the world, it may seem strange that these rich resources have not been more adequately exploited by students of society, particularly in view of the growing interest in the experience of the so-called "under-developed" areas of the world. This is doubtless largely a consequence of the very limited circulation of the data in published form. Copies of the published reports of the census counts prior to 1900 are available in only a few of the rare-book collections of libraries in Hawaii and scarcely at all outside of the Islands. Moreover, even for the occasional serious student of population trends, the task of unraveling the mystery of Hawaiian terms and definitions and the inconsistencies between returns of one census and the next has been sufficient to discourage significant research efforts except by a very few.

Romanzo Adams was the first social scientist to penetrate deeply into the intricacies of Hawaiian demography, and prior to his death in 1942 he was still busily engaged in the preparation of a manuscript that he referred to as an "attempt to psycho-analyze the census." He meant simply that he was seeking to disentangle some of the obvious inconsistencies and to present more meaningfully some of the census findings. Unfortunately Adams was unable to complete this task, and no one else has thus far ventured to undertake the formidable task in which he was so enthusiastically engaged.

The author of the present volume has accepted a more modest, and perhaps more prosaic, but no less useful assignment. Robert Schmitt has first of all brought together within the confines of a single volume the basic population data derived from the ten different reports of censuses conducted by the Hawaiian government prior to Annexation and from the seven decennial reports by the United States Bureau of the Census during the present century. Nowhere else in published form has so much essential population data for the entire period of Hawaii's experience since Captain Cook's discovery of the Islands been brought together. The author wisely refrains from attempting to extract the full significance of these data, which would have required not one but many volumes to complete, but he performs the more immediately useful function of providing the data themselves and of indicating how they hold together from one period to another. Similarly Mr. Schmitt has brought together for the first time, from obscure and little-known government files, the basic vital statistics of births, deaths, marriages, and divorces, dating back to the early days of the Hawaiian monarchy. He fortunately calls attention to the inadequacies in the early recording of vital statistics and alludes to the distorted conclusions which may result from the calculation of crude rates, but he also presents the meaningful findings of rates adjusted for under-registration and for the abnormalities in the age and sex structure of the population.

Within the covers of this book are the raw and semi-refined demographic materials with which the students of Hawaiian society will have to grapple for many years to come and for the gathering and refinement of which they should be grateful.

Andrew W. Lind

DEMOGRAPHIC STATISTICS OF HAWAII: 1778-1965

I. INTRODUCTION

The demographic history of Hawaii is long, complex, and well documented. Its statistical record is broad in scope and rich in detail, offering important insights for a number of disciplines. Yet, surprisingly, this record sometimes seems poorly understood or appreciated even by historians and students of Hawaiiana.

Hawaiian population, as a field for study, began with the arrival of the first Polynesian settlers more than a thousand years ago and came to world attention with the visit of Captain James Cook and his men in 1778-1779. The origin, size, distribution, and characteristics of this Island people were matters of immediate interest to Cook and his officers. Their impressions became the earliest recorded population statistics on Hawaii.

For the next forty-five years, the only new information on the population of the Islands was that recorded and published by seafaring men and other occasional visitors. Casual observations and the roughest kinds of estimates appeared at wide intervals in a variety of journals, logs, and formal narratives. A little was known about the total population and its geographic distribution, but virtually nothing about the composition of the population, fertility, mortality, or migration.

This period, extending from Cook's visit to the arrival of the missionaries, was a critical one in Hawaii's demographic history. When it began, perhaps 300,000 persons were living in the Islands. In less than half a century the population fell by 50 percent, the result of wars, disease, sterility, and infanticide. The crucial character of these years makes the lack of statistics particularly frustrating.

Estimates and partial censuses by the American missionaries soon began filling this gap. In 1823, only a few years after their arrival, the missionaries were responsible for the first reasonably reliable estimates of the population of the kingdom by island. They took censuses of five of the larger islands in 1831-1832 and 1835-1836. Many kept accurate records of births, deaths, and marriages. Missionaries like William Ellis were joined by educated natives like David Malo in documenting demographic change. Their statistics did much to influence population policy during this period.

The first official censuses, and the earliest deemed complete in coverage, were undertaken in mid-century. The count made in January 1850 was a statistical landmark: it combined an accurate enumeration of all inhabited islands with information on age, sex, and nationality. It was followed by other official censuses in 1853, 1860, and thereafter at regular six-year intervals until 1896. The man responsible for the 1850 count was Richard Armstrong, a missionary who became an educator and public official. His successors greatly expanded the Hawaiian Census in both scope and detail.

The official registration of births, deaths, marriages,

divorces, and immigration all began about the same time as the first censuses. Combined with periodic census tabulations on age, sex, and nativity, these annual series--unfortunately marred by considerable underregistration--provide a useful index of trends in the components of population change.

It is fortunate that the second half of the nineteenth century is well covered by demographic statistics, because the period was one of significant change. Total population, plummeting disasterously at the beginning of the period, finally leveled off in the 1870's and then climbed almost as steeply as it had formerly dropped. The first indentured laborers arrived in 1852. They were followed by massive infusions of new blood, mainly young males from China, Portugal, and Japan, who by 1896 greatly outnumbered the native Hawaiians. Drastic changes occurred in population composition: older persons became a tiny minority, and there were ten single men for each single woman. Most of the labor force worked on sugar plantations.

The last census by the Hawaiian Government took place in 1896, and four years later the United States Census Office (now the Bureau of the Census) assumed this function. In consequence, the scope of the official count was greatly enlarged, and its frequency was reduced to once every decade. Planning of the census became the responsibility of Federal officials, who sometimes lacked sufficient knowledge of the Islands to obtain the most meaningful results. After 1900, allowance was usually made for the unique characteristics of the Territory, but, with the advent of Statehood, Hawaii was again forced into the mold of the Mainland states.

The period covered to date by the U.S. Censuses, 1900 to 1960, was, like earlier statistical periods, marked by major changes. The pure Hawaiian population continued to decline as a result of low fertility, high mortality, out-migration, and intermarriage. Part Hawaiians increased rapidly. Large numbers of laborers continued to move to Hawaii, with Filipinos succeeding the Chinese and Japanese as the major source of new workers. By 1940, however, the direction of movement had been reversed; instead of peasant peoples from Asia, most of the new arrivals were soldiers and sailors, defense workers and other civilians from the Mainland. Plantation employment declined, to be replaced by jobs at Pearl Harbor or in Waikiki hotels. Oahu boomed, while the Neighbor Islands lost population.

Since 1960 the record has been filled in by postcensal estimates and sample surveys made by State agencies. Vital events have been tabulated in growing detail by the State Department of Health, the first of the State agencies to employ a nucleus of trained professional statisticians. New sources of information on in- and out-migration have been exploited by the State Department of Planning and Economic Development, often working closely with the Hawaii Visitors Bureau. Creation of the position of State Statistician in 1963 has further encouraged the development of important demographic series. At the University of Hawaii, veteran sociologist Andrew W. Lind has carried forward the pioneering studies of his colleague Romanzo Adams. Both the State Government and the University have taken advantage of new data processing equipment, from the first Hollerith sorter installed by the Health Department in 1931 to the IBM 7040 computer put into operation on the University campus in 1963.

Four major themes have dominated this 189-year history: depopulation of the native Hawaiians, immigration of foreign laborers, intermarriage among the various racial groups, and most recently, movement between Hawaii and the Mainland. The first two themes have now passed into history. The third, interracial marriage, is now being replaced by population exchange with the Mainland as the dominant factor in demographic change in Hawaii.

The history of Hawaiian demographic statistics, summarized in the foregoing paragraphs and described in detail in the pages to follow, is not nearly as well known as it might be. General historians have so far shown little interest in statistical matters. Population studies of national scope have given Hawaii only passing attention. Romanzo Adams, still regarded by many as the leading authority on Hawaiian demography, published relatively little; his The Peoples of Hawaii (1925 and 1933) is tantalizingly brief, and his Interracial Marriage in Hawaii (1937) was largely restricted to a single facet of population research. Except for a few important fragments, most of his unpublished writings are lost or in disarray. Adams's successors have tended to confine themselves to brief articles in professional journals, limited-distribution reports, and similar work of a fugitive nature.

The chief exceptions occur in the publications of Andrew Lind and Irene Taeuber. Lind's An Island Community (1938) and Hawaii's People (1955 and 1967) are major works of high professional competence. Their emphasis, however, is on the charting and interpretation of demographic trends rather than on documentation of sources or methodological evaluation. Irene Taeuber's article on "Hawaii" in the April 1962 issue of Population Index is a brief but highly perceptive, carefully documented account directed toward the interests of professional demographers. Except for the works mentioned, no single study describing the statistics of Hawaiian demography is currently available.

This apparent neglect would cause little concern if the subject were unimportant. Such however is not the case. Hawaii is regarded by authorities as both a demographic laboratory and prototype. Inhabited by a number of differing ethnic groups in varying stages of assimilation, it provides an ideal setting for cross-sectional and historical analyses of social, economic, and biological variables. Moreover, Hawaii has moved from a primitive, preliterate society to a modern, urban, industrial State in less than two centuries. This demographic transition, exhaustively documented by Island statisticians, is in many respects like that now confronting folk and peasant societies throughout the world. These emerging areas could learn much from a study of Hawaii's past. Such study might hold significant implications for population control and policy.

It is the purpose of the following chapters to provide some of the raw material for analyses of this kind. Tables throughout this work summarize trends in total population, geographic distribution, urbanization, population composition, births, deaths, migration, marriages, and divorces. Major trends are further summarized in Tables 1-3. Table 4 indicates, in summary form, the subject matter covered by each census since 1832. Stress is placed throughout this volume on documentation and evaluation of sources, methodology, and manner of tabulation and presentation, rather than on population trends and analyses *per se*.

Table 1.--POPULATION OF HAWAII: 1778 TO 1965

Estimate or census date	Population	Percent annual change[a]	Estimate or census date	Population	Percent annual change[a]
1778...........	300,000	...	1890: Dec. 28....	89,990	1.8
1823...........	134,925	-1.8	1896: Sept. 27...	109,020	3.3
1831-1832.......	124,449	-0.9	1900: June 1.....	154,001	9.4
1835-1836.......	107,954	-3.6	1910: April 15...	191,874	2.2
1850: Jan.......	84,165	-1.8	1920: Jan. 1.....	255,881	3.0
1853: Dec. 26...	73,138	-3.5	1930: April 1....	368,300	3.6
1860: Dec. 24...	69,800	-0.7	1940: April 1....	422,770	1.4
1866: Dec. 7....	62,959	-1.7	1950: April 1....	499,794	1.7
1872: Dec. 27...	56,897	-1.7	1960: April 1....	632,772	2.4
1878: Dec. 27...	57,985	0.3	1965: April 1....	746,650	3.3
1884: Dec. 27...	80,578	5.5			

[a]Computed according to the formula: $r = 100 \log_e(P_1/P_0) / t$.

Source: 1778 and 1823 estimates by Romanzo Adams; 1831-1832 and 1835-1836 estimates by Adams from partial censuses; 1850-1896 censuses by the Hawaiian Government; 1900-1960 censuses by USBC; 1965 estimate by HDPED.

Table 2.--POPULATION DISTRIBUTION AND DENSITY: 1853 TO 1965

Subject	1853	1878	1900	1920	1940	1960	1965
TOTAL POPULATION							
All islands....	73,138	57,985	154,001	255,881	422,770	632,772	746,650
Oahu[a]..............	19,126	20,236	58,504	123,496	257,696	500,409	617,774
Percent..........	26.2	34.9	38.0	48.3	61.0	79.1	82.7
Other islands......	54,012	37,749	95,497	132,385	165,074	132,363	128,876
Urban..............	11,455	14,114	39,306	92,251	264,262	483,961	...
Percent..........	15.7	24.3	25.5	36.1	62.5	76.5	...
Rural..............	61,633	43,871	114,695	163,630	158,508	148,811	...
DENSITY PER SQUARE MILE[b]							
All islands....	11.4	9.0	24.0	39.9	65.9	98.6	116.4
Oahu[a]..............	32.0	33.8	97.7	206.2	430.2	836.8	1,033.1
Other islands......	9.3	6.5	16.4	22.8	28.4	22.8	22.2

[a]Includes outlying islands legally part of the City and County of Honolulu.

[b]Based on land area of 6,415 square miles (598 on Oahu and 5,817 on the other islands) for 1853, 1878, 1960, and 1965 and on 6,416 square miles (599 on Oahu and 5,817 on the other islands) for 1900, 1920, and 1940.

Source: Official censuses, 1853-1960; HDPED, SR 37 (Nov. 19, 1965), p. 5.

Table 3.--CHARACTERISTICS OF THE POPULATION: 1853 TO 1960

Subject	1853	1878	1900	1920	1940	1960
Males per 1,000 females.........	1,131	1,428	2,233	1,443	1,376	1,148
Median age (years)..............	...	27.7	26.9	23.3	23.2	24.3
Race, total (%).................	100.0	100.0	100.0	100.0	100.0	100.0
Hawaiian or part Hawaiian......	98.1	81.9	24.4	16.3	15.2	16.2
Caucasian......................	1.9	6.5	18.7	21.4	26.5	32.0
Other races....................		11.6	56.9	62.3	58.3	51.9
Place of birth, total (%)........	100.0	100.0	100.0	100.0	100.0	100.0
Hawaii.........................	97.5	83.6	38.3	53.3	65.8	66.6
Mainland United States.........	2.5	16.4	2.8	4.3	12.8	21.8
Other Areas....................			58.9	42.4	21.4	11.7
Hawaii-born on mainland[a].........	0.7	2.2	2.2	7.2	7.8	21.5
Married (%): Males[b].............	...	48.0	36.7	50.5	39.1	57.7
Females[b]...........	...	72.8	77.9	75.7	56.3	66.4
Fertility ratio[c]................	...	545	575	781	455	603
Average household size[d].........	...	...	3.7	...	4.5	3.9
In group quarters (%)[d]..........	...	...	28.4	...	8.5	6.3
Attending school (%)[e]...........	52.5	43.8	45.3	62.9	72.4	83.7
Illiterate (%)[f].................	25.0	20.1	35.2	21.2	11.6	5.0
Armed forces (% of labor force)..	...	...	0.3	3.9	14.3	17.8
Males: % in labor force[g]	...	59.4	94.0	91.0	82.7	81.2
Females: % in labor force[g].......	...		19.3	22.8	30.9	39.9
Agricultural workers[h]...........	...	67.1	63.5	52.3	35.5	7.6
Births per 1,000 civ. pop.[i]......	19.8	41.0	13.3	40.4	24.1	29.2
Deaths per 1,000 civ. pop.[i]......	105.1	49.8	19.5	18.1	7.6	6.0
Male life expect. at birth (years)..:....................	...	...	...	47.8	59.5	69.1
Female life expect. at birth (years)......................	...	...	...	47.3	62.6	73.2
Marriages per 1,000 civ. pop.[j]...	25.6	...	8.4	8.4	13.5	8.8
Divorces per 1,000 civ. pop......	0.4	2.0	0.3	2.2	2.4	2.1
Housing units: % owner occupied	...	...	23.1	13.4	25.4	41.1

[a]Hawaii-born persons in Mainland U.S. as percent of Hawaii-born total for Hawaii and Mainland combined. Interpolated for 1853 and 1878.

[b]Based on persons 15 and over through 1920, 14 and over thereafter.

[c]Children under 5 per 1,000 women 15 to 44. Estimated for 1878.

[d]Estimated for 1940.

[e]Based on population 5 to 20. Estimated for 1853 and 1878.

[f]Based on persons over 16 in 1853, 15 and over for 1878, 1900, and 1920, and 14 and over thereafter. Estimated for 1853, 1878, and 1940.

[g]Based on population over 15 in 1878, 14 and over thereafter.

[h]Employment in agriculture, forestry, and fisheries as a percent of total civilian employment.

[i]Rates refer to calendar 1853, 24-month period ended Dec. 31, 1879, calendar 1901, and years ended June 30, 1920, 1940, and 1960.

[j]Rate for 1900 refers to year ended June 30, 1902.

Source: School attendance and illiteracy from HDPED, SR 31 (June 21, 1965), p. 18; other data from official censuses and vital statistics, 1853 to 1960.

Table 4.--SUBJECTS INCLUDED IN PUBLISHED CENSUS TABLES: 1832 TO 1960

Subject	1832	1836	1849	1850	1853	1860	1866	1872	1878	1884	1890	1896	1900	1910	1920	1930	1940	1950	1960
Geographic distribution:																			
Islands	✓	✓	✓	✓	✓	✓	✓	✓	✓	✓	✓	✓	✓	✓	✓	✓	✓	✓	✓
Judicial districts		✓			✓	✓	✓	✓	✓	✓	✓	✓	✓	✓	✓	✓	✓	✓	✓
Cities and towns under 5,000																✓	✓	✓	✓
Wards, precincts, or neighborhoods							✓			✓	✓					✓			
Census tracts																	✓	✓	✓
City blocks																			✓
Demographic characteristics:																			
Age and sex			✓	✓	✓	✓	✓	✓	✓	✓	✓	✓	✓	✓	✓	✓	✓	✓	✓
Race			✓	✓	✓	✓	✓	✓	✓	✓	✓	✓	✓	✓	✓	✓	✓	✓	✓
Nativity			✓	✓	✓	✓	✓	✓	✓	✓	✓	✓	✓	✓	✓	✓	✓	✓	✓
Country of birth					✓			✓	✓	✓	✓	✓	✓	✓	✓	✓	✓	✓	✓
Citizenship													✓	✓	✓	✓	✓	✓	
Marital status					✓	✓	✓	✓	✓	✓	✓	✓	✓	✓	✓	✓	✓	✓	✓
Households													✓	✓	✓	✓	✓	✓	✓
Household relationship																		✓	✓
Families and unrel. individuals																		✓	✓
Children ever born											✓	✓						✓	✓
Physical or mental handicaps			✓	✓	✓														
Social characteristics:																			
School attendance											✓	✓	✓	✓	✓	✓	✓	✓	✓
Years of school completed																	✓	✓	✓
Literacy										✓	✓	✓	✓	✓	✓	✓			
Mother tongue																✓			✓
Ability to speak English													✓	✓	✓	✓			
Length of residence					✓								✓	✓	✓	✓			✓
Place of residence 5 years earlier																		✓	✓
Religion					✓					✓		✓							
Voting registration											✓								
Veteran status																			✓
Economic characteristics:																			
Occupation or industry							✓	✓	✓	✓	✓	✓	✓	✓	✓	✓	✓	✓	✓
Unemployment																✓	✓	✓	✓
Income																	✓	✓	✓
Transportation to work																			✓
Automobiles available																			✓
Real estate ownership							✓	✓	✓	✓	✓	✓							
Housing:																			
Tenure												✓	✓	✓	✓	✓	✓	✓	✓
Persons in unit													✓				✓	✓	✓
Other characteristics											✓	✓					✓	✓	✓

II. ESTIMATES AND PARTIAL CENSUSES: 1778-1850

The seventy-two year period from 1778 to 1850 was one of sweeping changes in the demographic statistics of Hawaii. The first population estimates of the Islands were made by Captain Cook and his men in 1778-1779. American missionaries prepared estimates during the 1820's and conducted censuses of the larger islands in 1831-1832 and 1835-1836. Government censuses were initiated in 1847. By 1850 officials could report a complete and accurate count of the population, tabulated by age, sex, race, and geographic area and supplemented by data on births, deaths, marriages, and divorces. This growing body of information measured the vast changes occurring throughout the kingdom. Catastrophic depopulation was accompanied by the birth of urban centers at Honolulu, Hilo, and Lahaina. Declining birth rates and high infant mortality altered the age distribution of the people. Young men went to sea and never returned. Foreigners began to take up residence in the Islands, and at the end of the period Hawaii was on the threshold of its first influx of indentured laborers.

Sources

Many individuals and groups contributed statistics on the population of Hawaii before 1850. Their work, unfortunately, appeared piecemeal in widely scattered accounts, often missed by later historians. The following pages present an effort to bring together and summarize these little known sources.

No statistical record of pre-contact population still

exists, unless we include the legendary census of Umi.

> Umi became king of Hawaii about the year 1500, and established his court in Kona. On one occasion he is said to have collected all the people of Hawaii at a small plain between the cones on the inner side of Hualalai, to number them, and this is called the Plain of Numbering to this day, by the older Hawaiians. Two small hills are said to have been the seats of the king and queen, with their retainers, while the census was being taken. Later all the people went down on the plain, where each deposited a stone, the strongest the largest, making huge stone-pile memorials around the heiau, one for each district and on the sides toward the districts. Thus the piles showed the relative size of the population of the districts.[1]

The earliest surviving contemporary estimates of population are those devised by Captain Cook and his officers. Cook himself recorded an estimate for the island of Kauai in January 1778. Captain James King, who completed Cook's account of his voyage after the latter's death, offered island-by-island estimates for the entire archipelago as of 1779. An alternative series was recorded by William Bligh, Cook's Master during the voyage. Captain George Dixon, who visited the Islands in 1787, suggested still a different total for the date of contact.

Contemporary estimates are almost completely lacking for the critical years between 1779 and 1822. The only exception is a series prepared by George Youngson, an English carpenter who lived in Hawaii around 1805. Later writers, such as Adams, have had to resort to interpolation and non-statistical sources to reconstruct the demographic history of this period.[2]

Estimates by the American missionaries are available for

1823 and later dates. Unlike the rough approximations published by early navigators, these estimates were usually based on intimate knowledge of the area, house counts, and even partial enumerations. Even so, it was possible for Adams to characterize their efforts as "not very accurate, but nevertheless, valuable."[3]

The missionaries conducted censuses of five of the larger islands in 1831-1832 and 1835-1836. Careful preparations were made to obtain vital data as well as population counts:

> Considering the important bearing which the probable decrease of the population of these islands has upon our work,
>
> Resolved 1. That a register be kept at each station of all the births and deaths, as far as they come within our knowledge, to be embodied in the annual report of the stations.
>
> 2. That we take the best means in our power for obtaining a correct census of the people throughout the whole group, including both natives and foreigners, in separate lists. And that each station obtain the cooperation of the chiefs, or teachers or other persons, who shall, as far as practicable, visit and number the people at their houses. And that some missionary, at each station, shall receive the returns, add them, and forward the account, with the names of the districts, to the Printing Committee as early as the first of November next.[4]

Field work was undertaken in late 1831 and again in late 1835. The data were tabulated, estimates were added for the three missing islands (Molokai, Lanai, and Kahoolawe), and the island totals were published in 1836. The missionaries admitted, "There is some reason to believe that the population in 1832 was somewhat over-rated, and we think it may be a little under-rated by the present [1835-1836] enumeration."[5] Users of the reports were sufficiently impressed, however, to urge that the count be repeated annually.[6]

Efforts to complete a general population census in 1840 were apparently successful only on Kauai.[7]

The first census law of the Kingdom of Hawaii was enacted on June 7, 1839 and approved by Kamehameha III on November 9, 1840. This law required the tax officers to "enumerate the people, male and female" by taxation status and to "take a yearly account of the deaths and births."[8] On April 27, 1846, responsibility for conducting the census "including an annual bill of mortality, and of the natural increase" was transferred to the Department of Public Instruction.[9]

The first census under the new act was begun in January 1847. It proved to be reasonably complete for only three districts.[10]

The census of January 1848 was an even greater failure. Neither population, births, nor deaths were accurately compiled.[11]

It was not until January 1849 that the census enumerators managed to obtain a moderately successful count of the population of all the islands. Published results included population totals, annual births, and annual deaths for each island, and for all islands combined, data on age, sex, and race or nationality.[12] Initially acclaimed, the 1849 count was later deemed incomplete and unreliable.[13] Even so, it represented a great stride forward.[14]

Finally, in 1850, the Kingdom of Hawaii secured its first fully acceptable population count. In scope, the 1850 census was identical to the one taken a year earlier. In completeness, however, it appears to have been far superior. The Minister of Public Instruction noted "greater accuracy ... this year than last," a modest evaluation fully accepted by later critics.[15] This census, together with its three immediate predecessors, is described in greater detail in Chapter III.

Publication of the 1850 census provided a bench mark in the seventy-two-year evolution of Hawaii's demographic statistics. It had been a period of constantly increasing scope, refinement, and statistical sophistication in the compilation and analysis of population and vital data.

What did these statistics show?

Total population

Population totals before 1778 are lacking. Radiocarbon dating, supported by linguistic analysis, indicates that the Hawaiian Islands were probably inhabited by 750 A.D., and perhaps much earlier.[16] From a small initial population--"presumably ... not more than a few hundred persons," according to Adams[17]--the Hawaiians increased until "population was pressing against the means of subsistence" and even the more remote or marginal areas were occupied.[18] A few writers have speculated that a peak was reached before 1778. Evidence, however, is lacking:

The exact degree of biological equilibrium achieved by the Hawaiians during the five centuries of their isolation will never be known. It seems difficult to justify the persistent claims that the native population of Hawaii, like that of neighboring archipelagos in Oceania, was in process of degeneration and decline previous to the advent of Europeans.[19]

Numerous estimates are available for 1778-1779, the years of first contact. Cook's officers were responsible for at least three, ranging from 242,200 to 500,000. Later students have usually expressed preferences for totals between 200,000 and 400,000, although one was as low as 100,000.

The highest estimate is one suggested by Captain James King, who completed Cook's narrative of the voyage following the latter's death at Kealakekua in 1779:

In his manuscript log (as yet unprinted), Lieut. King, after discussing the question at considerable length, says, "The above numbers collected together give half a million for the population of these islands. It is mere guesswork, founded principally upon the numbers given to Otaheiti, and the comparative size and cultivation of these (Sandwich) Islands with that."[20]

King's published estimate was 20 percent lower, amounting to 400,000 for the entire archipelago:

... the interior parts of the country are entirely uninhabited; so that, if the number of the inhabitants along the coast be known, the whole will be pretty accurately determined. The other [point] is, that there are no towns of any considerable size, the habitations of the natives being pretty equally dispersed in small villages, round all their coasts. It is on this ground, that I shall venture at a rough calculation of the number of persons in this group of islands.

The bay of Karakakooa, in Owhyhee, is three miles in extant, and contains four villages of about eighty houses each; upon an average, in all three hundred and twenty; besides a number of straggling houses; which may make the whole amount to three hundred and fifty. From the frequent opportunities I had of informing myself on this head, I am convinced, that six persons to a house is a very moderate allowance; so that, on this calculation, the country about the bay contains two thousand one hundred souls. To these may be added, fifty families, or three hundred persons, which I conceive to be nearly the number employed in the interior parts of the country, amongst their plantations; making in all two thousand four hundred. If, therefore, this number be applied to the whole extent of coast round the island, deducting a quarter for the uninhabited parts, it will be found to contain one hundred and fifty thousand. By the same mode of calculation, the rest of the islands will be found to contain the following numbers:

Owhyhee, ------------	150,000
Mowee, --------------	65,400
Woahoo, -------------	60,200
Atooi, --------------	54,000
Morotoi, ------------	36,000
Oneeheow, -----------	10,000
Renai, --------------	20,400
Oreehoua, -----------	4,000
Total of inhabitants	400,000

I am pretty confident, that, in this calculation, we have not exceeded the truth in the total amount.[21]

If King's estimate of 600 inhabitants per mile of coast is applied to a more accurate measurement of "general coastline" (725 miles, excluding the leeward islets), an all-island population of 435,000 is obtained.

Bligh's estimate was 242,200.[22] His basis for this figure is unknown.

Captain George Dixon, a visitor in 1787, deemed King's estimate of 400,000 "greatly exaggerated" and suggested that a 1779 total of 200,000 would "be much nearer the truth." Dixon's all-island total was apparently based on his own observation of

Kauai and the previous estimates for that island by Cook and King.[23] Captain V. M. Golovnin, who visited Hawaii in 1818, likewise preferred 200,000, citing the opinion of European residents as his authority.[24]

Among the many later writers who accepted King's figure, one was Artemas Bishop.[25] Another was the editor of the Pacific Commercial Advertiser.[26] A. O. Forbes published an exhaustive review of the evidence which in balance seemed to support an estimate of 400,000.[27] A number of travel and history books (frequently ascribing the estimate to Cook) quoted it uncritically. Other historians, however, preferred a lower estimate. David Malo, who lived from 1793 to 1853, is said to have guessed the 1778 total at 360,000.[28] Cheever and Elkin inclined toward 300,000.[29] Writing in 1888, S. E. Bishop noted that "later historians have leaned to the more moderate estimate of 250,000."[30] Simpson, Hopkins, and Goodrich voted for 200,000.[31] Dutton indicated a total "over 150,000."[32] Evaluating King's estimate, Marques termed it "loose" and "absolutely devoid of any scientific accuracy and value," while Goodrich called it "a ludicrous exaggeration."[33]

The lowest estimate of all was that proposed by Sir Peter Buck, who was quoted as saying: "I know of no accepted opinion as to what the Hawaiian population was at the time of Cook's visit. It was perhaps 100,000 or more, but not above 150,000."[34] Myerson, after citing Buck's statement, commented: "Probably the true figure lies between 150,000 and 300,000."[35]

These lower figures are given partial support by contemporary evidence for individual islands. Both Dixon and Menzies visited Kauai during the eighteenth century and found King's estimate (and perhaps Cook's) too high.[36] William Bayly hiked over two-thirds of Niihau on January 29, 1778 and reported only one-twentieth the population later estimated by King.[37] Vancouver and Menzies noted that Lehua, said by King to have 4,000 inhabitants, was unpopulated.[38] Emory's archeological survey of Lanai indicated a maximum pre-contact population of 3,150, in contrast to King's estimate of 20,400.[39] The only suggestion that King may have been correct is the finding by Tyerman and Bennet[40] that the population living on Kealakekua Bay when they visited it in 1822 averaged 685 per mile of shoreline, not much less than the 800 estimated by King forty-four years earlier.

In view of the wide range of opinion cited in the foregoing paragraphs, most modern authorities have compromised on a 1778-1779 population total of 300,000. This figure was first seriously proposed by James Jackson Jarves.[41] It has more recently been adopted by Adams, Hormann, Lind, and Emory.[42] It was also the estimate accepted by the present author in compiling the first Statistical Abstract of Hawaii and its historical supplement.[43]

A forty-three year statistical gap followed the departure of Cook's expedition. Although many navigators stopped in the Islands and a growing number of white men settled there, contemporary population estimates for the important period between

1779 and 1822 are virtually non-existent.

The sole exception is an early nineteenth century series attributed to one George Youngson. In his account of his trip around the world from 1817 to 1820, Louis de Freycinet referred to three separate sets of population data for the Sandwich Islands--King's (1779), Stewart's (1825), and Youngson's. Of the latter, he wrote:

> A note believed to date from 1805 indicates that the total population was about 264,160.[44]

And in a footnote to this brief statement:

> This note was submitted by an English carpenter, George Youngson, who settled on Guam after having lived several years in the Sandwich Islands. Although he maintained that he constructed the estimate with care, it hardly seems to be more than an arbitrary approximation.

Youngson's estimate deserves comment. It has been completely ignored in the published literature, and except for Kuykendall (whose notes[45] contain a reference to Freycinet's use of the data), no modern writer appears to be aware of the Youngson figure. Freycinet's footnote sounds skeptical; the methodology, if any, remains a question mark; Youngson's qualifications as a demographer--he is, after all, described as a carpenter--are open to question; and, in fact, no other historical record of Youngson's residence in Hawaii is available locally. Although such considerations would appear to throw some doubt on the validity of Youngson's estimate, the fact remains that it stands the test of reasonableness far better than many others published for the years before 1832. This is particularly true if it is assumed to pertain to 1803 rather than 1805, and thus to represent the population before rather than after the great plague of 1804.[46] It is quite close to Adams's reconstructed figure of 266,000 for 1803.[47] The Youngson figures for individual islands are intermediate between King's 1779 estimates and those computed by the missionaries in the 1820's; except for Molokai, Lanai, and Niihau, in fact, they appear to be remarkably close to what we now judge to have been the correct totals.

Relatively few efforts have been made by later writers to fill the forty-three-year span following King's departure. David Malo was reported to have estimated a population of 240,000 for 1798.[48] A newspaper editor, writing in 1862, suggested all-island totals of 350,000 in 1800 and 175,000 in 1804.[49] Adams proposed estimates for four separate dates between 1778 and 1823: 270,000 to 280,000 in 1796; 266,000 to 280,000 in 1803-1804; 152,000 to 154,000 in 1804-1805; and 144,000 to 145,000 in 1819.[50]

The record is resumed in 1822. In a note dated August 10, 1822, Tyerman and Bennet asserted that the population was "above 200,000."[51] Mathison, who visited Oahu at the same time as Tyerman and Bennet, wrote that he would not put it "at more than 150,000" for the entire chain.[52]

The missionaries tried to estimate the population in 1823. Their "official" figure was 150,000.[53] Stewart reported the same total, but his estimates for individual islands added to little more than 141,000.[54] Ellis gave the all-island total as "130,000 or 150,000"; his data by island, differing from Stewart's in only a few minor details, summed to somewhat above 139,000.[55] The version usually quoted by later writers, with or without credit, was that derived by Jarves from Stewart's figures and labeled "a loose estimate for 1823." In this form, the island data added to 142,050.[56] Adams's revision put the total at 134,925.[57]

The missionary census of 1831-1832, supplemented by estimates for the unsurveyed islands, showed a population usually reported as 130,313, although one source gave the count as 129,814.[58] Findings of both this census and the count made four years later were eventually revised by Adams. "He did this by checking earlier figures against later ones, the figures with one island with those of another over a period of time .... He came to the point where he was able to evaluate the relative reliability of individual enumerators."[59] He even uncovered some double-counting.[60] Adams concluded: "Accepting the data of the census, revising the estimates on the basis of later and more adequate information and adding, I find the population in 1832 to have been 124,449."[61]

The missionaries published estimates for both 1833-1834 and mid-1834, but neither report amounted to more than a rounding or slight adjustment of the 1831-1832 census counts.[62]

The missionary census of 1835-1836, like its predecessor limited to five islands and supplemented by estimates for the other three, indicated a population usually given as 108,579,[63] although one source reported 108,393.[64] Adams revised this total downward to 107,954.[65]

Several estimates are available for the early and middle 1840's. The abortive census of 1840 suggested a total in the neighborhood of 88,000.[66] Kuykendall later estimated the native population at 103,790 in 1840 and 99,626 in 1844.[67] Horatio Hale, philologist for the Wilkes Expedition, visited Hawaii in 1840-1841 and reported a figure of 100,000.[68] The 1845 total was later estimated at 90,000.[69]

The official census taken in January 1849 reported 80,641.[70] As noted earlier, this census was marred by considerable underenumeration. The population, birth, and death totals obtained twelve months later suggested a "true" 1849 population of 87,063.

The census of January 1850 reported an Island population of 84,165.[71]

The trend indicated by the foregoing data is summarized in Table 5.

Geographic distribution

Major population shifts occurred between 1778 and 1850. Although all islands suffered serious losses, rates of decline varied greatly by geographic area. Villages with particularly strategic locations slowly struggled toward urban status. By the end of the period, Oahu, once third most populous of the islands, was vying with Hawaii for first place, and Honolulu had become an undisputed city.

Early population statistics could be compiled for a variety of geographic areas. The eight major islands provided obvious natural units for such breakdowns. (The entire archipelago contains 124 named islands, but most of them are tiny offshore specks close to the major islands. The leeward group, from Nihoa to Kure, was unpopulated during the first half of the nineteenth century.) The major land divisions recognized by the ancient Hawaiians, the moku (today's judicial districts), likewise were used as statistical areas, first in the legendary census of Umi and later in the missionary enumerations. Each moku, in turn, consisted of one or more ahupuaa (land divisions usually extending from the uplands to the sea), which were sometimes used for small-area head counts. Still another statistical area was the village or town, often defined on an ahupuaa basis.

Estimates by island go back as far as 1778-1779. Both King and Bligh compiled systematic geographic series covering all of the major islands. Cook published an estimate (30,000 in January 1778) for Kauai,[72] Bayly recorded one (500, also in January 1778) for Niihau, and Ledyard reported a figure ("almost or quite 100,000" in January 1779) for the island of Hawaii.[73] Golovnin, who visited Hawaii in 1818, quoted older residents who thought King's 1779 estimates were triple the actual total for Molokai and double the true number on the other islands. Both Malo and Emory subsequently revised King's estimates in the light of later knowledge.

Totals by island for post-contact dates are available for 1798, 1805, 1823, 1831-1832, 1835-1836, 1849, and 1850. The 1798 estimates were reportedly prepared by Malo; those for 1805, by Youngson; 1823, by Jarves from previously published missionary estimates. Data for 1831-1832 and 1835-1836 consisted of census counts for five islands and estimates for the other three, all made by the American missionaries.[74] Government censuses were conducted in 1849 and 1850. Estimates for individual islands have been issued from time to time; examples include a 1798 estimate for the island of Hawaii by Townsend ("not ... over a hundred thousand"), an 1821 estimate for Oahu by the missionaries (20,000), 1822 estimates for Oahu by Tyerman and Bennet (20,000), Mathison (8,000), and others.[75]

Nine of the series described above are presented in Table 6.

Data were compiled by _moku_ or _ahupuaa_ in several of the missionary counts. Geographic distributions were shown most consistently in the 1835-1836 census. In other missionary enumerations, however, small-area data were restricted to only part of the kingdom.

Population counts or estimates were frequently published for cities and towns, but the value of these figures is limited by uncertainty regarding the boundaries ascribed to each community. The name "Honolulu," for example, was sometimes applied to the urban nucleus immediately behind Honolulu Harbor, sometimes to the entire _ahupuaa_ (which adjoined Kapalama on one side and Waikiki on the other), and sometimes to the entire _moku_ (which extended from the Halawa-Moanalua boundary to Koko Head).[76] Similar confusion is possible regarding the boundaries of Hilo, Lahaina, or Hana.

Honolulu was apparently the largest urban concentration in the kingdom. On December 13, 1831, Bingham wrote:

> Phelps has been taking the census of the village of Honolulu. He makes 5,522 inhabitants, including 180 foreigners. The inhabitants living on the plantations of Honolulu are not included. These, when added, will probably make from 7,500 to 8,000.[77]

Two years later, in an estimate of the population "within a few miles" of each missionary station in the Islands, a report to the American Board of Commissioners for Foreign Missions (ABCFM) showed 6,000 in Honolulu proper, 4,500 in Honolulu _aina_ ("in the rear of Honolulu"), and 3,000 in Waikiki.[78] The census of 1835-1836 reported 12,994 in the _moku_ of "Honolulu a me Waikiki."[79] Honolulu estimates for which the geographic boundaries were unspecified included those of Tyerman and Bennet and Mathison (2,000-3,000 in 1822), an unidentified missionary (4,000 in 1822 or 1823), Ellis (6,000-7,000 in 1823), Duhaut-Cilly (6,000 in 1828), Chapin (6,000-7,000 in the mid-1830's), Diell (6,400 in "Honolulu proper" and 9,000 in "the Ahupuaa, or whole district" in 1838), Hines (10,000 in 1840), Simpson (8,400 in "town and neighborhood" in the early 1840's), and the _Friend_ (8,000-10,000 in 1845).[80]

Other important towns included Hilo, Kailua, Lahaina, and

Hana. Hilo had a population of "not less than 2,000" in 1823 and 4,181 in 1833-1834.[81] Kailua, Kona numbered "two or three thousand" in 1820.[82] Lahaina, variously (and broadly) defined, was estimated at 4,000 in 1833-1834, 3,175 in 1835-1836, and 5,000 in 1841-1842.[83] Hana had 2,858 inhabitants in 1835-1836.[84]

Cook estimated Waimea (Kauai) to have a population of 500 in January 1778; fourteen years later, Vancouver found only one-third of that number.[85] Waikiki showed similar signs of decline when visited by Vancouver in 1792, but eventually it recovered, and by 1833-1834 had a population of 2,571.[86]

Much geographical shifting about occurred between 1778 and 1850. Some of the decline in specific areas can be attributed to warfare and epidemics. Other areas lost population through out-migration, as residents sought new jobs or experiences or followed their chiefs to new locations. Richards and Stewart, writing from Lahaina on March 6, 1824, observed that the population had increased from 2,500 to 4,000 since their arrival nine months earlier, largely because many chiefs had moved to the community. Consequently, the "number of common people has exceedingly increased." But such increases were seldom permanent:

> In one month more, the inhabitants may be reduced to their former number and all the new houses may be demolished. Such are the changes which are constantly taking place at the Sandwich Islands. All that is necessary to produce such changes is merely a whim of some person of distinction, occasioned, perhaps, by the scream of a child, or the prediction of a maniac.[87]

Composition of the population

Relatively little is known regarding the composition of the population before 1850. Comprehensive statistics on age, sex, and race were first compiled in the 1849 census. Data on marital status, household relationship, school enrollment, educational attainment, labor force status, occupation, industry, family income, and many other subjects included in modern censuses were not collected until long after the middle of the nineteenth century.

The 1850 census reported more males than females and a relatively low proportion of children. These data (which excluded the blind and deaf as well as foreigners and their dependents) indicated a median age of 32.2 years. Persons under 18 years of age accounted for less than three-tenths of the population. There were 110.1 males per 100 females. Detailed statistics appear in Table 7. The picture was similar to the one which had emerged from the incomplete 1847 and 1849 counts.[88]

Both the high sex ratio and high median age may have been nineteenth century developments. Turnbull, who visited Hawaii in 1802-1803, wrote that "the women, according to Mr. Young's account, are said to be more numerous than the men."[89] Two decades later, however, Ellis observed: "The number of males is much greater than that of females in all the islands, in consequence of the girls being more frequently destroyed in infancy ... We do not know the exact proportions ...."[90] Later writers mentioned, with increasing frequency, the declining percentage of children.

By 1849 it was clear that depopulation had become most severe among young persons and females.

The ethnic composition of the kingdom was likewise undergoing change. In 1778 Cook found a homogeneous Polynesian population. By 1850 the number of full-blooded Hawaiians had dropped by more than two-thirds, to 82,035; part Hawaiians totalled 558, not counting those who either did not know or failed to report an admixture of non-Hawaiian blood; and 1,572 Americans, Europeans, and other foreigners lived in the Islands. Trends in racial composition are traced in Table 8.

Estimates of average household size vary widely. The lowest figure was 3 1/3 persons per house, reported by Maui missionaries.[91] Cook, in his Kauai estimate, allowed five persons per house. So did Loomis, Tyerman and Bennet, Ellis, and Emory.[92] King had allowed for six persons per house, and another early writer had assumed an average of eight.[93] The average probably declined during the nineteenth century, as a result of the decreasing proportion of children.

Fertility and mortality

Population growth or decline is the net result of four distinct forces: births, deaths, in-migration, and out-migration. Births and deaths, in combination, provide natural increase or decrease. The difference between in-migration and out-migration is referred to as net migration. Until 1852, when immigrant labor was first brought to Hawaii, natural decrease greatly outweighed migration in its importance to demographic change in the Islands.

The first statistical information ever assembled on fertility and mortality in Hawaii was that compiled by the missionaries. Even before passage of the 1835 General Meeting resolution "that a register be kept at each station of all the births and deaths," many missionaries were keeping records of the vital events occurring in their districts. Although uniform coverage of all islands was apparently never attained under missionary auspices, coverage was sufficient to provide a general idea of fertility and mortality levels. Records kept by the Rev. William P. Alexander for Halelea, Kauai, from September 1834 to September 1835, for example, revealed crude birth and death rates of 25.7 and 52.8 per 1,000 population in that district.[94] Projected by Alexander to the entire kingdom, these rates suggested some 6,838 annual deaths but only 3,335 births.[95]

Birth and death statistics were next compiled as part of the official census enumerations undertaken during the late 1840's. As noted earlier, the 1847 and 1848 counts were unsuccessful. The 1849 census, while somewhat incomplete, presumably underenumerated vital events in the same degree as population, and consequently it produced approximately correct rates for the preceding year: 18 births and 98 deaths per 1,000.[96] Corresponding rates for 1849, based on the 1850 census, were respectively 17 and 51.[97] Additional information appears in Table 9.

Although neither vital events nor population totals of the 1850 census were reported in sufficient detail to permit computation of reliable life table values, broad inferences can be derived from later statistics. The situation in mid-century was certainly no better, and probably even worse, than that evident toward the end of the century. Concerning the latter period, Taeuber has written:

> If the relevant proportions of the part-Hawaiians are combined with the Hawaiians and the analysis limited to women, there is an approximation to a closed population. The age ratios and the age structures of the populations of 1890 and 1896 suggest birth rates of 50 or more per 1,000 total population. If birth rates were at this level and population was declining, death rates must have been above 50. These rates suggest the combination of a gross reproduction rate above 3.0 with an expectation of life at birth of less than 20 years.
>
> The age structures of 1890 and 1896 and the rates of decline in the late nineteenth century sustain the argument that fertility and mortality were high, and that depopulation resulted from a normally high mortality and episodic decimation. A recurrent or localized low fertility associated with venereal disease, epidemics, or malnutrition is not inconsistent with this interpretation. Physiological sterility need not imply altered reproductive mores. There is a further and more hypothetical extension of the argument. If the fertility of the pre-contact period was high, the precarious ecological balances can have been preserved only by a level of mortality that was also high.[98]

Precise measurement of fertility and mortality levels for earlier periods of Island history is impossible. Noting "the abnormally high death rates and the correspondingly low birth rates which must have prevailed during the first half of the last century in Hawaii," Lind has written: "As a matter of fact, the data are not available with which to compute vital rates for this period ...."[99]

Despite such difficulties, Adams has made a valiant effort to reconstruct the birth and death rates of the native (that is, Hawaiian and part Hawaiian) population as far back as 1778. His method was to estimate the native population, including those absent at sea, at significant points in the demographic history of Hawaii, and then to devise average birth and death approximations consistent with his population estimates. Adams divided the years from 1778 to 1850 into ten natural periods. He wrote:

> The history of each period is examined for data relating to factors that might be supposed to influence birth rates and death rates....
>
> The early records for limited areas and periods kept by missionaries have been used in making some of the earlier estimates and the earliest are based on the general health history of the time so far as it is available.... The population figures are wholly matters of estimate for 1825 and earlier dates. While they are based on a consideration of the accounts and estimates of early explorers and residents and also on information that became available at later dates, they cannot be regarded as more than approximations--closer approximations, probably, than were made, commonly, by the men of that time.[100]

Adams encountered particularly great difficulty with two points: the total population on contact, and the loss resulting from an epidemic a quarter of a century later. He noted: "While some students who are entitled to an opinion would modify the figures considerably for 1778 and in smaller measure for the other dates, such modifications would not affect the character of the population trend seriously."[101] Regarding the epidemic--later thought to have been cholera or bubonic plague--David Malo had written in 1839: "In the reign of Kamehameha, from the time I was born until I was nine years old, the pestilence (mai ahulau) visited the Hawaiian Islands, and the majority (ka pau nui ana) of the people from Hawaii to Niihau, died."[102] Levi Chamberlain had heard much the same story from the natives he talked to when he toured Oahu in February 1828.[103] Kuykendall, who dated this epidemic at 1804, contended that the statement that it "carried off more than half the population" was "probably the result of legendary exaggeration."[104] Even so, Adams "credited Malo's estimate as not far from correct, but ... estimated the loss a little lower than he did."[105] Adams eventually prepared two different sets of estimates (arbitrarily labeled A and B by the present author), which differ chiefly in the date assigned to the plague described by Malo and the degree of depopulation estimated for the quarter of a century preceding it.

Adams's estimates of birth and death rates are shown in Table 10.

However speculative these estimates, it is evident that mortality was high throughout this period, and from time to time reached appalling levels. Venereal disease, introduced by Cook's crew in 1778, quickly spread through the population and adversely affected fertility as well as mortality rates; Forbes, in fact, regarded syphilis as the greatest single cause of population decline during the century following contact.[106]

Warfare, often exceedingly bloody, continued until 1795. The men who collected sandalwood for the China trade suffered physically and neglected cultivation and fishing. The *mai okuu* (epidemic), described by Malo and others, struck sometime between 1802 and 1807, probably in 1804. There was an influenza epidemic in 1826. Four devastating epidemics occurred in rapid succession in 1848 and 1849: measles, whooping cough, diarrhea, and influenza. Together, these four diseases killed more than 10,000 of the perhaps 87,000 persons in little more than a twelve-month period.[107]

The roles of abortion, infanticide, and infant mortality are difficult to assess. Artemas Bishop, writing in 1838, noted that "the great majority of children born in the islands die before they are two years old."[108] Some students attributed the frequent barrenness, still births, and infant deaths to venereal disease. Abortion and infanticide, known to have existed in pre-contact times, reached new highs in 1819-1825 and 1832-1836.

Social and economic disorganization likewise contributed to population decline. Nineteenth century writers frequently mentioned alcohol, tobacco, sexual promiscuity, idolatry, *kahunas*, and landlessness as important factors. Adams has referred to still others, such as limited knowledge of treatment for certain diseases, poor infant care, breakdown of the old moral order, incapacitation of entire villages by disease and the resulting disruption of important economic activities, and "disorder and excesses" following the death of a ruler.[109]

Taeuber added:

> The early diversions of activity from local to market production resulted in the main in a conspicuous consumption among the elite. Social disorganization and individual demoralization were cumulative under the impact of such diverse factors as alcoholism, permissive codes of sex behavior, the erosion and abolition of tabu, and the declining securities in feudal land and labor relations. Then, too, there are persuasive arguments about psychological lethargies and a will to death.[110]

Migration

Migration, while not as significant as natural increase or decrease, nevertheless was an important force in both the growth and decline of Hawaii. Unfortunately, compilation of migration statistics did not begin until 1852, when the first organized importation of foreign labor was undertaken.

The first Hawaiian migration, of course, was that which initially peopled the Islands. Emory wrote of it in 1962:

> Now ... it begins to look as if the first settlers came from the Marquesas, and long ago, and that about the 12th century, Tahitian influence overwhelmed the islands. In any case, we are now sure of at least two migrations from central East Polynesia (if you can use the term migration for a canoe-load of migrants): (1) the migration which resulted in first settling the islands, and (2) a much later one which resulted in bringing from the Society Islands changes that had taken place after the branching migration to New Zealand.[111]

Adams had observed earlier:

> Probably the immigrant ancestors of the Hawaiians numbered not more than a few hundred persons ... The comparatively large population at that time [1778] was the result of natural increase plus a few canoe loads of later immigrants.[112]

Not long after foreign ships started to call at Island

ports, Hawaiians began to enlist as seamen. At first they served in the fur trade: "As early as 1788, though, sea captains were being advised to pick up a Hawaiian or two before leaving for the Northwest Coast."[113] Many Islanders died abroad. Kittelson adds:

> Although the fur trade had fallen off by the middle 1820's, there was no reduction in the demand for skilled Hawaiian sailors. American whalers had been calling at Honolulu for several years already, and the stage was set for a dangerously large emigration of island sailors and laborers.[114]

The number of Hawaiians at sea and abroad continued to increase through the 1830's and 1840's. Not all returned; all 479 who left on Boki's expedition on December 2, 1829 perished.[115] Some found work and homes in foreign countries, where they formed small Hawaiian communities. Concern mounted. The number absent, as estimated by Adams, increased from 200 in 1823 to 300 in 1825, 400 in 1832, 600 in 1836, 3,500 in 1848, and 4,000 in 1850.[116] The latter figure amounts to almost 5 percent of the total Hawaiian and part Hawaiian population at that time, and 12 percent of all Hawaiian males 18 years of age or more. According to Kuykendall:

> The nation undoubtedly suffered an appreciable loss [of population] through the enlistment of Hawaiian youths as sailors on whaling vessels, but it is impossible to get any conclusive statistical measure of the extent of the loss. During the three years 1845-1847, nearly two thousand Hawaiians enlisted as seamen on foreign ships, and during those years there was some discussion of the subject. It was pointed out that many of these native seamen never returned to live in Hawaii and the population was thereby reduced ....[117]

Many of the out-migrants moved to California. Even before "the California excitement led to an emigration of young Hawaiians from the islands,"[118] some were living on the Coast. An article on "Statistics of San Francisco," initially published in August 1847, stated that the population of that city consisted of 375 whites, 34 Indians, 10 Negroes, and 40 Hawaiians. The latter group consisted of 39 males and one female, "mostly employed as boatmen in navigating the Bay ...."[119] By 1850, some 588 Hawaii-born persons were living on the Mainland, including 319 in California.[120]

This out-migration was offset to only a limited extent by in-migration. Over the years, the population had been augmented by sailors who had jumped ship, missionaries, foreign consuls, businessmen, professional men, and others. Some, particularly the missionaries, brought dependents. Numerically they remained few: in 1850, only 1.9 percent of the population was foreign born.[121]

Hawaii, in 1850, had reached the end of an era. Statistically, future censuses and vital data tabulations would show increasing detail and sophistication. Demographically, the Island nation was about to embark on a course of imported labor, declining mortality, ethnic change, and urbanization. Its seventy-two-year apprenticeship was completed.

Table 5.--TOTAL POPULATION: 1778 TO 1850

Date	Population		Date	Population
	Series A[a]	Series B[a]		
1778..........	300,000	300,000	1823...............	134,925
1796..........	280,000	270,000	1831-1832..........	124,449
1803..........	...	266,000	1835-1836..........	107,954
1804..........	280,000	154,000	Jan. 1849..........	87,063
1805..........	152,000	...	Jan. 1850..........	84,165
1819..........	145,000	144,000		

[a]Adams's alternate estimates, here arbitrarily designated A and B.

Source: 1778-1836, Adams's estimates and census adjustments; 1849, figure implied by 1850 census rather than actual 1849 count; 1850, official census count.

Table 6.--POPULATION BY ISLAND: 1779 TO 1850

Island	1779			1805 (Youngson)	1823 (Jarves)	1831-1832 (Census)	1835-1836 (Census)	1849 (Census)	1850 (Census)
	King	Emory	Bligh						
All islands...	400,000	300,000	242,200	264,160	142,050	130,313	108,579	80,641	84,165
Hawaii........	150,000	120,000	100,000	100,000	85,000	45,792	39,364	27,204	25,864
Maui..........	65,400	75,000	40,000	48,000	20,000	35,062	24,199	18,671	21,047
Kahoolawe.....	...	...	...	160	50	80	80	...	...
Lanai.........	20,400	3,500	1,000	7,000	2,500	1,600	1,200	528	604
Molokai.......	36,000	10,000	20,000	25,000	3,500	6,000	6,000	3,429	3,540
Oahu..........	60,000	60,000	40,000	40,000	20,000	29,755	27,809	23,145	25,440
Kauai.........	54,000	30,000	40,000	40,000	10,000	10,977	8,934	6,941	6,956
Niihau........	10,000	1,500	1,000	4,000	1,000	1,047	993	723	714
Lehua.........	4,000	...	200	...	...	...	...	...	...

Sources: Estimates for 1779, 1805 and 1823; missionary censuses for 5 islands and estimates for Kahoolawe, Lanai and Molokai for 1831-32 and 1835-36; and official censuses for 1849 and 1850: Emory estimates from unpublished lecture notes.

Table 7.--POPULATION BY AGE AND SEX: JANUARY 1850

(Excludes 754 blind or deaf persons and 2,872 foreigners or dependents of foreigners)

Sex	All ages	Under 18	18 to 30	31 to 52	53 and over	Median (years)
Both sexes...	80,539	23,366	15,747	22,065	19,361	32.2
Males..........	42,203	12,983	7,995	11,018	10,207	31.2
Females........	38,336	10,383	7,752	11,047	9,154	33.1

Source: Polynesian, May 4, 1850.

Table 8.--POPULATION BY RACE: 1778 TO 1850

Race	1778	1823	1832	1836	1850
All races.....	300,000	134,925	124,449	107,954	84,165
Hawaiian........	300,000	134,750	124,049	107,354	82,035
Part Hawaiian...	...	...	...	...	558
Non-Hawaiian....	...	175	400	600	1,572

Source: Adams, Interracial Marriage in Hawaii, p. 8.

Table 9.--VITAL STATISTICS: 1834 TO 1849

Year	Population	Number			Rate per 1,000		
		Natural decrease	Births	Deaths	Natural decrease	Births	Deaths
1834-35...	129,540	3,503	3,335	6,838	27	26	53
1848......	80,641	6,465	1,478	7,943	80	18	98
1849......	84,165	2,898	1,422	4,320	34	17	51

Source: Alexander's estimates for 1834-35; official census data for 1849 and 1850.

Table 10.--ESTIMATED BIRTH AND DEATH RATES OF HAWAIIANS AND PART HAWAIIANS: 1778 TO 1850
(Includes persons absent at sea)

Series and period	Length of period (years)	Decrease in population	Annual rates per 1,000		
			Natural decrease	Births	Deaths
Series A:					
1778-1796......	18	20,000	4	35	39
1796-1804......	8	...	...	33	33
1804-1805......	1	128,000	457	25	482
1805-1819......	14	7,000	3	29	32
1819-1823......	4½	10,050	17	25	42
Series B:					
1778-1796......	18	30,000	6	34	40
1796-1803......	7	4,000	2	33	35
1803-1804......	1	112,000	421	20	441
1804-1819......	13	10,000	5	28	33
1819-1823......	4	9,000	17	25	42
Both series:					
1823-1825......	2	3,950	15	25	40
1825-1832......	7	6,551	7	29	36
1832-1836......	4	16,495	35	25	60
1836-1848......	13	12,498	9	30	39
1848-1850......	2	8,863	48	22	70

Source: Series A, Adams, MS, p.113 (quoted in part by Hormann, p. 228); Series B, Adams, MS, p. 458.

III. THE HAWAIIAN CENSUSES: 1847-1896

The Hawaiian Government conducted twelve population censuses during its century-long existence. The first of these censuses, taken in 1847, was rudimentary and seriously incomplete; the last, made in 1896, was sophisticated, accurate, and comprehensive to a remarkable degree. The twelve enumerations charted a period of profound demographic transformation, during which a precipitous decline was arrested and turned into an equally rapid rise, and the composition of the population--in age, sex, race, marital status, and countless other ways--was drastically and irrevocably altered.

The Hawaiian censuses can be discussed under four headings: legislation, operations, findings, and evaluation.

Legislation

As Hawaii neared the middle of the nineteenth century, its leaders expressed growing concern over demographic matters. Population estimates made by Captain King in 1779 and the American missionaries in 1823 and censuses taken by the missionaries in 1831-1832 and 1835-1836 clearly revealed the extent of the decrease of native Hawaiians over the sixty-year period since contact. Unfortunately, the missionary censuses offered little of the detailed information needed in this time of demographic crisis: they were limited to five of the eight major islands and took no account of age, race, sex, nativity, occupation, marital status, or detailed geographic distribution (see Chapter II). Better statistics were obviously needed.

This concern led to the first census law, enacted June 7, 1839 and approved by the king on November 9, 1840:

> Let the tax officers ... enumerate the people, male and female, together with the children who pay the yearly tax; and make a separate enumeratien [sic] of the old men and women and those children who do not pay taxes--let them take a yearly account of the deaths and births, by which it may be ascertained whether the people of the kingdom are really diminishing in numbers or not, and by that means the amount of taxes can be known.[1]

This legislation failed to produce usable results, and it was accordingly replaced by a new law, approved on April 27, 1846:

> The minister of public instruction shall be charged with the stated enumeration of the inhabitants of this kingdom, of whom it shall be his duty to make a complete census to be laid before His Majesty in privy council. The census to be taken shall comprise, in distinct columns, the inhabitants in each district, between such ages as the privy council shall direct, specifying also the proportional number of each sex, and shall, as far as practicable, indicate their avocations [sic] and such other particulars as the privy council shall direct, including an annual bill of mortality, and of the natural increase.[2]

Although the 1846 law specified no exact dates or intervals for the census, annual counts were taken in January 1847, 1848, 1849, and 1850. The law was thereupon amended to require the Minister of Public Instruction to conduct a "complete census" every third year, beginning in 1853.[3] This amendment was passed on June 18, 1851 and signed on July 11, 1851.

Further legislative changes were instituted in 1859. The new law required the President of the Board of Education to make, in 1860 and every sixth year thereafter, a complete population census, showing population by district, sex, "and other such particulars." A five-dollar penalty was imposed for refusal to answer, and appropriations for taking the census were authorized. This act was approved on May 17, 1859.[4]

These provisions were substantially repeated in the census act passed by the 1864-1865 legislative assembly. This act, approved by King Kamehameha V on January 10, 1865, required the Board of Education, every sixth year counting from 1860, "to make a complete census of the inhabitants of the Kingdom ...; every census shall comprise, in distinct columns, the number of inhabitants in each district, the number of each sex, and such other particulars as the Board of Education may direct, and shall show the increase or decrease of the population." Persons refusing to answer census queries could be fined as much as five dollars. The Minister of Finance was directed to pay census expenses upon order of the Board of Education, out of any monies appropriated by the Legislature for that purpose.[5] The 1865 act was the basis for the remaining six censuses undertaken by the Hawaiian Government.

A final example of legislative concern occurred in 1888, when the Legislature passed a resolution noting the need for "fuller statistics regarding all questions of social and economic importance" and urging the appointment of a three-member commission to study possible changes in census practice, to report back to the 1890 session. The commission was duly appointed. Its report, submitted two years later, was considered by the Legislature, but no changes were made in the existing law.

Operations

Adequate understanding of the Hawaiian censuses requires a knowledge of the census operations--schedule development, enumeration procedures, supervision, editing, tabulation, publication, and expenditures. These considerations greatly influenced the completeness, comprehensiveness, accuracy, and ultimate value of the various enumerations.

Little appears to have been done to implement the 1840 census act. Its mandate was heeded by only a few of the tax officials entrusted with the enumeration, and no systematic effort was made to compile their results. Evidence of this abortive census appears in several handwritten account books for the years 1840-1843, preserved in the Archives of Hawaii. The earliest of these books lists the names of a large number of residents of Waialua District, Oahu, with their sex and place of residence. A tabular summary presents, separately for Kawailoa, Paalaa, Mananui, and Mokuleia, the number of persons in each of the following categories: males, females, male children, female children, and parents subject to taxation; mothers; fathers, mothers, male children, and female children exempt from taxation; old men; old women; new born children, by sex; diseased persons, by sex; teachers; and male criminals.[6] No record exists, however, of similar data for other districts.

The 1846 census act gave new impetus to this effort at

enumeration. On November 20, 1846, William Richards, the Minister of Public Instruction, recommended in Privy Council that a "census of the people as provided by the Constitution" be taken. His motion was carried,[7] and preparations were soon begun. "In the month of December, circular letters were sent to all the general superintendents of schools, giving instructions to take the census of the islands, at the commencement of the present year [1847]. The manner and form of its taking was prescribed, and blanks for the purpose were forwarded."[8]

The circular of December 1, 1846 revealed a good deal of insight and knowledge regarding census procedures. The instructions warned against getting information from others than household heads and spoke of the dangers of either missing persons or double-counting. Avoiding underenumeration of infants was especially stressed. In a pioneering effort to establish a vital-statistics registration system, census takers were instructed to include "all the newly born babes of this year and all the births from the time of the death of Hoapili wahine. And on the right line, insert again those who were born this year 1846." If blanks proved too short, enumerators were to "attach additional length of paper to the original by pasting it with poi."[9]

Unfortunately, the 1847 count proved little better than its predecessors. "The returns are not full from either of the larger islands and only about one half of the whole are complete," reported Mr. Richards. Tabulations were published for

Kau, Lanai, and Niihau.[10] The amount of detail obtained in one district is revealed by a handwritten table for Kauai District No. 3, which extended from Kalalau to Kealia. Population counts were shown by sex and age, using five- and ten-year age groups to age 70; totals were given as well for the blind, the deaf, births, and deaths.[11] Returns were so sketchy from other districts, however, that the effort had little value.

A similar effort was made a year later, in January 1848. Keoni Ana, Minister of the Interior acting provisionally as Minister of Public Instruction, was in charge. His annual report concluded: "The efforts ... to secure a correct census ... have not been successful ...."[12]

A third annual census was announced for the first week in January 1849.[13] This was the first of three taken under the direction of Richard Armstrong, who had just been appointed Minister of Public Instruction. The printed schedule called for information on place of residence (both ahupuaa and the smaller ili maloko), age, sex, nationality, blindness or deafness, and births and deaths occurring during 1848. Age was to be obtained by reference to well-known events: the birth of Liholiho (1797), the death of Kamehameha I (1819), and the death of Kaahumanu (1832). The question on nationality provided space for foreigners without wives, foreigners with foreign wives, foreign children, foreigners with Hawaiian wives, and hapa haole (half-foreign) children.[14] These categories were used in the final tabulations, published in November 1849.[15] Costs of the 1849 count were modest. "My plan has been to make each district, as far as possible, bear its own expenses," wrote Armstrong.[16] On March 10, 1849, he asked the Privy Council "for a small sum to meet the expenses of taking the census according to law" and was granted a sum "not to exceed $200.00"--less than 1/4¢ per capita![17]

The results, while still imperfect, far surpassed those of earlier efforts. An editorial writer hailed it as "probably the most accurate census which has ever been made."[18] A year later, however, the Minister of Public Instruction admitted some under-enumeration: "It was then taken at a time of general sickness. The measles and whooping cough prevailed throughout the islands, and it is propable [sic] that the [enumerators] ... were unable, in many cases, to attend properly to their duty."[19] Modern authorities have alternatively called the 1849 census "incomplete to a moderate extent" and "wholly unreliable."[20] If we accept the population count and birth and death data reported by the 1850 census, the 1849 population total would appear to have been 87,063, not 80,641.

The fourth official census of the kingdom was conducted in January 1850. Like its predecessor, it called for information on place of residence, sex by broad age groups, nationality, blindness and deafness, and births and deaths. Results were released in May 1850,[21] and some of the original completed schedules are still extant.[22] Armstrong wrote: "This has been taken under my general superintendence, both in Jan. 1849 and

1850, and I give the result as I have received them [sic] from the School Superintendents of the several districts. They, together with the school teachers, assisted by the Am. Missionaries, were the immediate agents of the work."[23] Armstrong claimed "greater accuracy ... this year than last," a statement generally agreed to by later authorities. Adams, discussing the 1850 census and its successors, noted that "the data on numbers, sex and geographical location are believed to be reasonably accurate," although "the age data are not to be relied upon in the earlier censuses."[24] Kuykendall thought that the 1850 figures "may be used with some corrections."[25]

The 1850 census was the last to be made on an annual basis. On October 31, 1850, "Mr. Armstrong stated to His Majesty in Council, that it is not his intention to take the Census of the Islands during the year 1851, unless ordered to do so by the King. His Majesty signified his approbation of this intention."[26]

The next official population count was made during the last week of 1853, just in time to stay within the three-year period specified by law. Instructions were hurriedly prepared and sent out.[27] According to R. Armstrong:

> The Census was taken on the 26 of December last, under the general supervision of the American Missionaries, E. P. Bond Esq., of Lihue, Kauai, and Wm. Ap. Jones of Lahaina, to all of whom the government is under obligation. ... The native school teachers were employed as the subordinate agents in the work ... For the entire accuracy of the work I cannot vouch, but in my opinion, it is as correctly done as is possible with native

agents. The sum total is probably not far from the truth. The gross amount and the numbers of the sexes are the most reliable part of the returns. Not much dependence can be placed on those for ages, as few natives know what their ages are.[28]

The 1853 census showed far more detail than its predecessors. Geographically, data were presented for each of the twenty-four judicial districts (moku) of the kingdom, instead of merely by island as in 1849 and 1850. The native population was classified by sex, marital status (two categories), age (under 20 and over 20), religion (three categories), race mixture, and whether blind, deaf, or "insane and idiotic." Foreigners were classified by sex, marital status, race of spouse, age (four classes), length of residence in Hawaii, and place of birth (26 areas). These tabulations were published in three forms: as single broadside sheets, as part of the separate biennial report of the Minister of Public Instruction, and in the newspaper reprint of the biennial report.[29] The completed schedules are apparently no longer extant. According to Armstrong's report, "The cost of taking the census has been kept within the appropriation of $1200 ...." This came to 1.64¢ per capita.

The sixth official census of Hawaii was taken during the last week of December 1860.[30] It was under the direction of M. Kekuanaoa, President of the Board of Education, and J. Fuller, Superintendent of the Census. The scope of this census was somewhat more limited than that of 1853, a fact which resulted in adverse editorial comments.[31] Information was obtained on sex, marital status (two categories), age (under 20, between 20 and 60, and over 60), and nativity (natives and foreigners). Unfortunately, Chinese residents were classified as natives in Honolulu and as foreigners elsewhere in the kingdom.[32] Population characteristics were tabulated for each of the twenty-four judicial districts. Results were published in broadside form, in the newspaper, and in the biennial report of the Board of Education.[33] The completed schedules have presumably been lost. Fuller thought that the census was taken as "accurately as ever could be, with the limited means at the disposal of the Board." Out of the original appropriation of $2,000 (or 2.87¢ per capita),[34] only $1,489.50 (or 2.13¢ per capita) was expended.

The next census was conducted as of December 7, 1866. As in 1860, M. Kekuanaoa was in charge. This count was much more ambitious than the 1860 one, utilizing a far more detailed and explicit schedule.[35] Information was compiled on sex, marital status (two categories), nationality or race (native, half-caste, Chinese, and other foreigners), age (under 15, between 15 and 40, and over 40), number of freeholders, occupation (four categories), and number of cattle, sheep, and goats. In addition to tabulations by judicial district, a table was prepared reporting data for fifteen smaller areas in Honolulu District. The earlier practice of publishing results in broadside, newspaper, and biennial report form was continued.[36] A few of the original completed schedules are still in existence.

Kekuanaoa regarded this census "as fully reliable and correct as possible." Out of $3,500 appropriated for the work,[37] $3,465 was spent. The per capita appropriation was 5.56¢; the per capita expenditure, 5.50¢.

The 1866 census was followed by one taken on December 27, 1872. H. R. Hitchcock, Inspector-General of Schools, was director on this occasion. Except for deletion of the questions on cattle, sheep, and goats, the same items as in 1866 were carried on the schedule. However, the number of age categories was increased to four (under 6, between 6 and 15, between 15 and 40, and over 40), the number of nationality groups to ten (including, for the first time, a class for those Hawaii-born of foreign parents), and the number of occupational categories to eight. Statistics were tabulated by judicial district but not for Honolulu neighborhoods. As before, results were published in three different media.[38] Original completed schedules are apparently no longer extant. Costs of the 1872 census were $3,515 (or 6.18¢ per capita) out of an appropriation of $3,600 (or 6.33¢ per capita).[39]

Hitchcock seemed satisfied with the results. He wrote:

> Extraordinary pains were taken at the Department Office. ... The great majority of returns bear evidence of having been filled out as required ... and are reasonably accurate, when the confusing nature of statistical tables, on the Hawaiian mind, is duly considered. ... I am satisfied that the statistics contained in the census table, are as reliable as the census returns of older, and more enlightened nations.[40]

The ninth of the twelve Hawaiian censuses was conducted as

of December 27, 1878, under the general direction of Charles R. Bishop, President of the Board of Education. It was carefully planned, and enumeration schedules were detailed and explicit.[41] Like all of the Hawaiian population counts, it was a de facto census, referring to all persons who slept on the considered premises on the night of December 27. Schedules were left in advance at each dwelling, where the "head, or chief person of the house" was to write in the requested information for each occupant. Sub-agents later called for the completed forms and checked them for omissions or inaccuracies. Except for a reduction in the number of occupational categories from eight to four, the contents and class intervals used in the schedule and in the published tabulations were identical to those of 1872.[42] Many of these completed schedules, perhaps all, survive. The usual threefold method of publication was followed.[43] Costs of the census were defrayed by an appropriation of $4,000 (or 6.90¢ per capita).[44]

The next census took place on December 27, 1884. F. L. Clarke, Superintendent of Census, was in charge. Enumeration procedures were much the same as those in 1878, when schedules, left in advance at each dwelling, were to be completed by household heads and picked up later by the agents. Several new questions were added to those asked previously, and more detailed answers were sought. The number of age categories was increased to five (under 6, between 6 and 15, between 15 and 30, between 30 and 50, and over 50), the breakdown on race and nationality was increased to thirteen groups, and data were obtained for four broad and 139 detailed occupational categories. Other questions concerned sex, marital status (married or not), religion (Protestant or Catholic), number of freeholders, and literacy. Tabulations for 1884 were much more detailed than for previous years. Population totals and characteristics were reported for Honolulu "health and fire wards" as well as for each of the judicial districts in the kingdom. Data on age, sex, occupation, and literacy were cross-tabulated by race or nationality in several tables, albeit with varying detail or coverage. For the first time, census results appeared in a separately issued bulletin.[45] The original completed schedules were apparently discarded or lost.

Despite its many virtues, the 1884 census met with criticism. On August 27, 1888, the Legislature adopted a resolution calling for appointment of a three-member commission to consider the need for "fuller statistics regarding all questions of social and economic importance," study possible changes in census practice, and report back to the 1890 Legislature. H. S. Townsend, W. O. Smith, and A. Jaeger were appointed and given $250 to do their work.[46] The committee, after due consideration, concluded that "the last census was probably more inaccurate than its predecessors for many years; and the changed condition of society abundantly accounts for the fact." Noting the importance of detailed cross-tabulations, they added that "the Superintendent of the census of 1884, was allowed no clerical aid whatever, and was paid less than seven hundred dollars for his own services. The only wonder is that he ever reported at all."[47] The total census appropriation for 1884 had been $7,000, of which $6,821.82 was spent.[48] Per capita appropriation was 8.69¢; per capita expenditure, 8.47¢ (including 6.54¢ for supervisors and enumerators).[49]

The 1888 Census Committee offered a number of excellent suggestions, many of which were disregarded. Among other things, they suggested extending the enumeration period beyond a single day, having enumerators ask all questions directly rather than picking up already-completed census forms, increasing lead time for planning the census, choosing enumerators and supervisors more carefully, and checking results against other information (such as voting registers, tax assessors' books, and plantation personnel records) to ascertain completeness. The committee recommended using three separate census schedules--the first for population, the second for agriculture, and the third for mortality data. Items recommended for inclusion in future population schedules included age, sex, nationality (individual and each parent), citizenship, years of residence in Hawaii, marital status, employment status (whether self-employed, full-time or part-time), occupation (for those over 15), amount of wages earned, school attendance (for those under 15), literacy (for those over 20), religion, home ownership, and mortgage status. The committee added that "the most important changes proposed consist in specifying the minimum ages of those whose occupations and literacy are to be reported and in an effort to find out about the mortgages on homes." The mortality schedule, to cover all persons who had died during the preceding twelve months, was intended to check on and supplement the existing death registration system, which the committee deemed "notoriously incomplete." Employment of specialists to develop additional data on crime, insanity, pauperism, agriculture, commerce, insurance, and the balance of payments was urged. The estimated cost of such a census was $15,300, including the $150 monthly salary proposed for the superintendent.[50] These recommendations, submitted to the 1890 Legislature, were mostly disregarded.

The last census of the Kingdom of Hawaii was taken as of Sunday night, December 28, 1890, under the direction of C. T. Rodgers, General Superintendent of the Census. As usual, lead time was quite short; Rodgers was not appointed until November 6. He managed to find 156 enumerators, interpreters, and helpers, most of whom had "limited education and lack of experience." Individual work loads ranged from less than 100 persons (on windward Molokai) to 2,729 (in Honolulu's Chinatown). The population count was on a de facto basis. Inter-island ships afloat on the night of the census were assigned to Honolulu District, a provision which added 196 passengers and crew members to the Honolulu total.

The 1890 census surpassed all of its predecessors in scope and detail. Information was compiled on age, sex, nationality, occupation, marital status, school attendance, literacy, real estate ownership, voter registration, number of children ever born and number surviving (asked of females over 15), and the number of inhabited buildings by type and the number of occupants for each category. Although the number of nationality categories was left unchanged at thirteen, notable improvements were made in the classification of age (increased from five groups to eight), occupation (now eleven), and marital status (with four classes instead of only two). Seven kinds of inhabited buildings were recognized, including private residences, plantation quarters, and five varieties of group quarters. Although a few series were still tabulated by judicial district (and the five representative districts of Honolulu were shown in one table), emphasis was shifted to cross-tabulations of nationality with various social or demographic characteristics. Numerous derived rates were shown, usually on a specific age base: school attendance was related to the population between 6 and 15, literacy to persons over 6, and marital status, maternity rates, and employment status to the population over 15. An appendix summarized important statistics from sources outside the census, statistics bearing chiefly on mortality, government finance, assessed valuation, imports and exports, shipping, and plantations.

The 1890 census results appeared in a separately published bulletin.[51] Bound volumes containing the original completed schedules are filed in the State Archives. The Legislature appropriated $12,000 (or 13.33¢ per capita) to take the 1890 census.[52] Per capita expenditure for personnel was 6.56¢.

Except for a few items, the census was regarded as reasonably accurate. Data obtained on school attendance and voter registration closely approximated corresponding totals from other official sources, but statistics on real estate ownership were termed "very unsatisfactory."[53] Moreover, "a casual query to illiterate women as to the numbers of children they had borne did not provide useable data on levels of fertility."[54]

The last census undertaken by the Hawaiian Government, and the only one made by the Republic, was conducted as of Sunday, September 27, 1896. Alatau T. Atkinson was superintendent. He employed 158 enumerators, many of whom had sub-assistants, and three tabulation clerks. His report notes that census procedures were largely modeled on those of New Zealand.

The 1896 census added a number of refinements to the 1890 program, expanding it in both scope and detail. Information was compiled on age, sex, nationality, marital status, occupation, children ever born and children surviving (asked of females over 15), literacy by language, school attendance by type of school, real estate ownership, home ownership, religion, livestock ownership, and type, exterior material, number of rooms, and occupancy of buildings. Age classes were increased to ten, from "under 1" to "over 100." Fifteen occupational groups were listed. For the first time, tabulations on nationality included the Hawaii-born children of foreign-born parents in the parents' nationality group, thus initiating the concept of "race" (or ethnic stock) still used in U. S. Census reports for Hawaii and in statistical reports of the State Department of Health and other official agencies. Data were shown for twelve such ethnic groups, including Hawaiian, part Hawaiian, Americans, Portuguese, four different North European groups, Chinese, Japanese, South Sea Islanders, and a miscellaneous category. As in 1890, only a few items were tabulated by judicial district, and greatest emphasis was given to ethnic characteristics. Housing statistics were shown in considerable detail, although not to the extent desired by Atkinson. He outlined several needed cross-tabulations, precluded by lack of funds, "for showing where the over-crowding occurred, and where legislation might step in."[55]

Along with its many improvements over earlier censuses, the 1896 count retained one of their more obvious defects, namely, ambiguous age intervals. Age classes were described as "under 1 year," "1 to 6," "6 to 15," "15 to 30," "30 to 45," and so on. This practice left unclear the treatment of a six-year-old (that is, a child who has reached his sixth birthday but not his seventh) and others at age-breaks in the categories. The census instructions offer no clue. Without indicating his source, Romanzo Adams wrote: "In 1890, the age-class, 1-6, included no persons who had reached the end of the sixth year, but in 1896 children 6 years of age and under seven were also included under this caption."[56]

The 1896 census was published in a separate bulletin.[57] The original completed schedules are filed in the State Archives. The legislative appropriation for this census amounted to $12,000.[58] Expenditures for personnel came to $6,909.50. Per capita figures were 11.01¢ for the entire census and 6.34¢ for personnel.

No further population censuses were taken by the Hawaiian Government. The next one would have been conducted in 1902, but annexation, achieved in 1898, made Hawaii eligible for inclusion in the regular decennial U. S. Census. The Territory appeared in the Twelfth Census of the United States, taken as of June 1, 1900, and in every decennial count thereafter.

Findings

Some idea of the scope, content, and classifications of the Hawaiian censuses can be obtained from the accompanying statistical tables. The data presented in these tables chart demographic trends in the Islands from 1850 to 1896.

Intercensal changes in the number and geographic distribution of inhabitants are described in Tables 11, 12, and 13. Frequent changes in judicial district boundaries during the nineteenth century make it necessary to use considerable caution in interpreting small area data, particularly for Maui and Kauai.[59]

Tables 14 and 15 report age and sex distributions. Class intervals for age were changed frequently during this half-century span. As noted earlier, age data were probably more subject to misreporting than any other subject covered by the Hawaiian censuses.

Race and nationality trends are traced in Tables 16 and 17. As noted previously, the ethnic breakdowns used in these counts differed in many respects from those adopted after annexation. Both Adams and Lind have consequently published adjusted racial totals for these years based on the 1910-1930 classification system. These adjustments included correcting for the misclassification of Chinese in 1860 and part Hawaiians in 1900, distributing the Hawaii-born children of foreign parents by race for 1866-1890, preparing estimates for groups not yet listed in 1860 and 1866, and grouping nationalities by ethnic equivalents. Adams published two versions of his estimates; in the second, he added an 1850 breakdown, revised his 1900 estimates, and omitted detail for the non-Hawaiian segment.[60] Lind's adjustments generally followed those of Adams, differing only in the provision of greater detail and in minor variations for several of the years, chiefly 1853, 1860, 1866, and 1900.[61]

Marital status, religion, and freeholders are covered in Table 18. These subjects appeared only sporadically in the Hawaiian censuses.

Table 19 reports occupational data. Amount of detail, definitions, and terminology varied greatly from census to census, making the charting of trends extremely difficult. Intercensal changes indicated by this table should therefore be treated with great caution.

School attendance, literacy, fertility, and housing trends are traced in Table 20. Except for literacy, these subjects first appeared on Hawaiian census schedules in 1890.

The ten tables given here can only summarize some of the more important findings of the census reports. They may prove useful in indicating the general contents of the censuses and their comparability over time. The original publications present comprehensive cross-tabulations by geographic area, age, sex, nationality, and other subjects. Works by Adams, Lind, and Taeuber have discussed and interpreted these data at considerable length. Their studies, cited in the Bibliography, should be consulted by anyone interested in detailed substantive findings.

An evaluation

A modern demographer reviewing the history of the Hawaiian censuses cannot fail to be impressed by the foresight and intelligence of the men who planned and conducted these enumerations and by the breadth and apparent quality of the data they collected. They succeeded in the face of many handicaps. Census procedures were still rudimentary and primitive during the 1840's and 1850's, even in the more civilized nations. Honolulu was remote, in time and distance, from the centers of demographic knowledge; parts of the kingdom, in turn, were remote from Honolulu. Most of the census directors were missionaries or educators; none was a trained demographic statistician.

Receiving little pay, they worked with ludicrously small budgets, inexperienced supervisors and enumerators, and little or no clerical staff. Lead time for planning was invariably short, and tabulation deadlines (to judge from census publication dates) were little better.

All of the important series were included: age, sex, nationality, marital status, fertility, school attendance, literacy, occupation, and housing. Tabulations were often rich in analytic detail, charting historical trends, geographic distributions, and interrelationships.

The Hawaiian censuses contributed several major innovations. The first United States Census of Housing did not take place until 1940, fifty years after the initial compilation of comprehensive housing statistics in a Hawaiian census. A question on the number of children ever born was first tabulated by the U. S. Census in 1950, sixty years after its first appearance in the Hawaiian reports. Self-enumeration using census questionnaires distributed in advance of the census date was tried in the Islands at least as early as 1878, eighty-two years before its cautious, limited adoption on the Mainland.

Underenumeration, double-counting, and misclassification problems appear to have been no greater in Hawaii than in more developed areas at the time; however, this judgment admittedly rests on inadequate grounds, as no post-enumeration surveys designed to check census accuracy were ever taken. Except for school attendance and voter registration, neither of which was included prior to 1890, alternative sources for comparison with census findings were unavailable. The inadequacy of birth, death, and migration records precluded construction of an independent estimate of net intercensal change. Comparison of cohort totals from successive censuses showed little, chiefly because of broad age classes and the importance of migration.

Any final appraisal of census quality under such conditions must be based on the comments of contemporaries, notably those of the superintendents, and the overall consistency and reasonableness of the results. The census directors were, perhaps surprisingly, perceptive, objective, and candid in their remarks. They regarded their work before 1850 as incomplete and inaccurate, and until 1872, were apologetic for the quality of their enumerators. Age statistics were treated with suspicion until late in the century. An editorial criticized the limited scope of the 1860 count, and a legislative committee damned the 1884 census as "inaccurate." Even so, it is evident that the Hawaiian censuses were planned with great care. Findings were usually consistent with what is known of the general social and economic conditions of the period. Notwithstanding their limitations, the censuses contributed greatly to knowledge of the demography of Hawaii.

Table 11.--POPULATION OF HAWAII: 1850 TO 1896

Census date	Population	Annual change	
		Amount	Percent[a]
January 1850..........	84,165	...	...
December 26,1853.......	73,138	-2,771	-3.5
December 24, 1860......	69,800	-478	-0.7
December 7, 1866.......	62,959	-1,150	-1.7
December 27, 1872......	56,897	-1,002	-1.7
December 27, 1878......	57,985	181	0.3
December 27, 1884......	80,578	3,766	5.5
December 28, 1890......	89,990	1,569	1.8
December 27, 1896......	109,020	3,310	3.3

[a]Computed by the formula for continuous compounding.

Table 12.--POPULATION BY GEOGRAPHIC AREAS: 1850 TO 1896

Year	Total	Hawaii	Maui	Lanai	Molokai	Oahu			Kauai	Niihau
						Total	Honolulu	Other Oahu		
1850...	84,165	25,864	21,047	604	3,540	25,440	(a)	...	6,956	714
1853...	73,138	24,450	17,574	600	3,607	19,126	11,455	7,671	6,991	790
1860...	69,800	21,481	10,400	646	2,864	21,275	14,310	6,965	6,487	647
1866...	62,959	19,808	14,035	394	2,290	19,799	13,521	6,278	6,299	325
1872...	56,897	16,001	12,334	348	2,349	20,671	14,852	5,819	4,961	233
1878...	57,985	17,034	12,109	214	2,581	20,236	14,114	6,122	5,634	177
1884...	80,578	24,991	16,970	2,614		28,068	20,487	7,581	8,935	
1890...	88,990	26,754	17,557	2,826		31,194	22,907	8,287	11,859	
1896...	109,020	33,285	17,726	105	2,307	40,205	29,920	10,285	15,228	164

[a]Not shown in the official reports, but later given as 14,484 (The New Era and Weekly Argus, Honolulu, Jan. 12, 1854).

Table 13.--POPULATION BY ISLAND AND DISTRICT: 1853 TO 1896

Island and District[a]	1853	1860	1866	1872	1878	1884	1890	1896
All islands....	73,138	69,800	62,959	56,897	57,985	80,578	89,990	109,020
Hawaii............	24,450	21,481	19,808	16,001	17,034	24,991	26,754	33,285
Puna............	7,748	2,158	1,932	1,288	1,043	944	834	1,748
Hilo............		4,742	4,655	4,220	4,231	7,988	9,935	12,878
Hamakua..........	3,874	2,230	2,050	1,516	1,805	3,908	5,002	5,680
South Kohala.....		1,321	1,089	892	718	589	538	558
North Kohala.....	3,395	2,632	2,345	2,086	3,299	4,481	4,303	4,125
North Kona.......	4,110	3,488	3,268	2,218	1,967	1,773	1,753	3,061
South Kona.......	3,113	2,683	2,449	1,916	1,761	1,825	1,812	2,327
Kau.............	2,210	2,227	2,020	1,865	2,210	3,483	2,577	2,908
Maui...............	17,574	16,400	14,035	12,334	12,109	15,970	17,357	17,726
Hana............	5,331	4,509	3,501	2,760	2,067	2,814	3,270	3,792
Makawao[b]........	2,947	3,310	2,653	2,512	3,408	5,073	5,266	5,464
Wailuku..........	4,463	3,695	4,300	4,060	4,186	5,814	6,708	6,072
Lahaina..........	4,833	4,886	3,581	3,002	2,448	2,269	2,113	2,398
Lanai.............	600	646	394	348	214	2,614	2,826	105
Molokai...........	3,607	2,864	2,299	2,349	2,581			2,307
Oahu..............	19,126	21,275	19,799	20,671	20,236	28,068	31,194	40,205
Honolulu.........	11,455	14,310	13,521	14,852	14,114	20,487	22,907	29,920
Koolaupoko.......	2,749	2,318	2,195	2,028	2,402	2,621	2,499	2,753
Koolauloa........	1,345	1,187	1,163	1,269	1,082	1,321	1,444	1,835
Waialua..........	1,126	1,309	1,136	851	939	1,265	1,286	1,349
Waianae..........	2,451	2,151	1,784	1,671	1,699	2,374	903	1,281
Ewa.............							2,155	3,067
Kauai and Niihau...	7,781	7,134	6,624	5,194	5,811	8,935	11,859	15,392
Hanalei..........	1,998	1,641	2,186	1,558	1,597	1,807	2,472	2,775
Koolau...........						...	...	...
Kawaihau.........	...	...	...	...	...	1,882	2,101	2,762
Puna............	1,615	1,738	1,478	1,301	1,832	...	...	...
Lihue...........	...	...	...	...	...	1,984	2,792	3,425
Koloa...........	1,296	1,324	1,084	833	1,008	1,500	1,755	1,835
Waimea..........	2,082	1,784	1,551	1,269	1,197	1,762	2,739	4,431
Niihau..........	790	647	325	233	177			164

[a]For changes in judicial district boundaries, see Robert D. King, "Districts in the Hawaiian Islands," in John Wesley Coulter, comp., A Gazetteer of the Territory of Hawaii, pp. 214-230. Major shifts were made on Kauai in 1878, 1880, 1886, and 1887.

[b]Hamakua before 1866.

Table 14.--AGE AND SEX: 1850 TO 1896

<table>
<tr><th>Census date and age (in years)</th><th>Male</th><th>Female</th></tr>
<tr><td>1850, total[a]...</td><td>42,203</td><td>38,336</td></tr>
<tr><td>Under 18.....</td><td>12,983</td><td>10,383</td></tr>
<tr><td>18 to 31.....</td><td>7,995</td><td>7,752</td></tr>
<tr><td>31 to 53.....</td><td>11,018</td><td>11,047</td></tr>
<tr><td>Over 53......</td><td>10,207</td><td>9,154</td></tr>
<tr><td>1853, total....</td><td>38,810</td><td>34,328</td></tr>
<tr><td>Under 20.....</td><td colspan="2">30,306</td></tr>
<tr><td>Over 20......</td><td colspan="2">42,518</td></tr>
<tr><td>Not reported.</td><td colspan="2">314</td></tr>
<tr><td>1860, total....</td><td>37,499</td><td>32,301</td></tr>
<tr><td>Under 20.....</td><td colspan="2">21,476</td></tr>
<tr><td>20 to 60.....</td><td colspan="2">42,378</td></tr>
<tr><td>Over 60......</td><td colspan="2">5,861</td></tr>
<tr><td>Not reported.</td><td colspan="2">85</td></tr>
<tr><td>1866, total....</td><td>34,395</td><td>28,564</td></tr>
<tr><td>Under 15.....</td><td>8,721</td><td>7,957</td></tr>
<tr><td>15 to 40.....</td><td>14,702</td><td>11,495</td></tr>
<tr><td>Over 40......</td><td>10,972</td><td>8,812</td></tr>
<tr><td>1872, total....</td><td>31,650</td><td>25,247</td></tr>
<tr><td>Under 6......</td><td>3,574</td><td>3,295</td></tr>
<tr><td>6 to 15......</td><td>4,803</td><td>4,128</td></tr>
<tr><td>15 to 40.....</td><td>12,282</td><td>10,279</td></tr>
<tr><td>Over 40......</td><td>9,991</td><td>7,545</td></tr>
<tr><td>1878, total....</td><td>34,103</td><td>23,882</td></tr>
<tr><td>Under 6......</td><td>3,823</td><td>3,785</td></tr>
<tr><td>6 to 15......</td><td>4,761</td><td>3,897</td></tr>
<tr><td>15 to 40.....</td><td>15,540</td><td>9,595</td></tr>
<tr><td>Over 40......</td><td>9,979</td><td>6,605</td></tr>
<tr><td>1884, total....</td><td>51,539</td><td>29,039</td></tr>
<tr><td>Under 6......</td><td>5,130</td><td>5,060</td></tr>
<tr><td>6 to 15......</td><td>6,574</td><td>5,759</td></tr>
<tr><td>15 to 30.....</td><td>16,823</td><td>9,010</td></tr>
<tr><td>30 to 50.....</td><td>18,683</td><td>6,788</td></tr>
<tr><td>Over 50......</td><td>4,329</td><td>2,422</td></tr>
<tr><td>1890, total....</td><td>58,714</td><td>31,276</td></tr>
<tr><td>Under 1......</td><td>955</td><td>930</td></tr>
<tr><td>1 to 6.......</td><td>4,881</td><td>4,653</td></tr>
<tr><td>6 to 15......</td><td>6,297</td><td>5,802</td></tr>
<tr><td>15 to 30.....</td><td>19,348</td><td>9,770</td></tr>
<tr><td>30 to 45.....</td><td>18,373</td><td>5,764</td></tr>
<tr><td>45 to 60.....</td><td>5,898</td><td>2,740</td></tr>
<tr><td>60 to 75.....</td><td>2,338</td><td>1,095</td></tr>
<tr><td>Over 75......</td><td>624</td><td>522</td></tr>
<tr><td>1896, total....</td><td>72,517</td><td>36,503</td></tr>
<tr><td>Under 1......</td><td>1,215</td><td>1,294</td></tr>
<tr><td>1 to 6.......</td><td>6,810</td><td>6,596</td></tr>
<tr><td>6 to 15......</td><td>7,694</td><td>6,592</td></tr>
<tr><td>15 to 30.....</td><td>26,781</td><td>11,888</td></tr>
<tr><td>30 to 45.....</td><td>19,883</td><td>6,311</td></tr>
<tr><td>45 to 60.....</td><td>7,248</td><td>2,558</td></tr>
<tr><td>60 to 75.....</td><td>2,462</td><td>940</td></tr>
<tr><td>75 to 90.....</td><td>382</td><td>277</td></tr>
<tr><td>90 to 100....</td><td>33</td><td>37</td></tr>
<tr><td>Over 100.....</td><td>9</td><td>10</td></tr>
</table>

[a]Data exclude 754 blind and deaf persons and 2,872 foreigners.

Table 15.--AGE AND SEX RATIOS: 1866 TO 1896

Sex and age (in years)	1866	1872	1878	1884	1890	1896
Both sexes..........	62,959	56,897	57,985	80,578	89,990	109,020
Under 15..........	16,678	15,800	16,266	22,523	23,518	30,201
Over 15...........	46,281	41,097	41,719	58,055	66,472	78,819
Male................	34,395	31,650	34,103	57,539	58,714	72,517
Under 15..........	8,721	8,377	8,584	11,704	12,133	15,719
Over 15...........	25,674	23,273	25,519	39,835	46,581	56,798
Female..............	28,564	25,247	23,882	29,039	31,276	36,503
Under 15..........	7,957	7,423	7,682	10,819	11,385	14,482
Over 15...........	20,607	17,824	16,200	18,220	19,891	22,021
Males per 1,000 females[a]....	1,204	1,254	1,428	1,775	1,877	1,987
Under 15..........	1,096	1,129	1,117	1,082	1,066	1,085
Over 15...........	1,246	1,306	1,575	2,186	2,342	2,579
Percent under 15....	26.5	27.8	28.1	28.0	26.1	27.7
Male..............	25.4	26.5	25.2	22.7	20.7	21.7
Female...........	27.9	29.4	32.2	37.3	36.4	39.7

[a]The ratio was 1,101 in 1850, 1,131 in 1853, and 1,161 in 1860.

Table 16.--RACE: 1853 TO 1896

Census date	All races	Hawaiian ("native")	Part Hawaiian ("half-caste")	Non-Hawaiian ("foreign")		
				Total	Born in Hawaii	Born elsewhere
Number:						
1853.....	73,138	70,036	983	2,119	291	1,828
1860[a]....	69,800	67,084		2,716	...	...
1866.....	62,959	57,125	1,640	4,194	...	...
1872.....	56,897	49,044	2,487	5,366	849	4,517
1878.....	57,985	44,088	3,420	10,477	947	9,530
1884.....	80,578	40,014	4,218	36,346	2,040	34,306
1890.....	89,990	34,436	6,186	49,368	7,495	41,873
1896.....	109,020	31,019	8,485	69,516	13,733	55,783
Percent:						
1853.....	100.0	95.8	1.3	2.9	0.4	2.5
1860[a]....	100.0	96.1		3.9	...	...
1866.....	100.0	90.7	2.6	6.7	...	...
1872.....	100.0	86.2	4.4	9.4	1.5	7.9
1878.....	100.0	76.0	5.9	18.1	1.6	16.4
1884.....	100.0	49.7	5.2	45.1	2.5	42.6
1890.....	100.0	38.3	6.9	54.9	8.3	46.5
1896.....	100.0	28.5	7.8	63.8	12.6	51.2

[a]Chinese living in Honolulu included with the native population.

Table 17.--PLACE OF BIRTH OF THE FOREIGN BORN AND NATIONAL ORIGIN OF THE NON-HAWAIIAN POPULATION: 1853 TO 1896

Subject	Total	Portugal[a]	Other Europe[b]	United States	China	Japan	Other countries[c]
Foreign born:							
1853.......	1,828	35	571	692	364	166	
1872.......	4,517	395	931	889	1,938	364	
1878.......	9,530	436	1,236	1,276	5,916	666	
1884.......	34,306	9,377	3,436	2,066	17,939	116	1,372
1890.......	41,873	8,602	2,675	1,928	15,301	12,360	1,007
1896.......	55,783	8,232	2,741	2,266	19,382	22,329	833
Non-Haw'n:[d]							
1866.......	4,194	...	...	...	1,206	...	...
1890[e]......	49,368	12,719	6,220		29,362		1,067
1896.......	69,516	15,191	4,161	3,086	21,616	24,407	1,055

[a]For 1853, includes Spain, Spanish America, and Brazil.

[b]After 1853, limited to Great Britain, Germany, and France (plus Norway beginning in 1884).

[c]For 1853, includes 22 not reported and 14 omitted from tabulation.

[d]Includes Hawaii-born persons of foreign extraction, distributed by parents' nationality.

[e]Partly estimated (1890 Census, p. 17).

Table 18.--MARITAL STATUS, RELIGION, AND REAL ESTATE OWNERSHIP:

1853 TO 1896

Census date	Percent married[a]		Unmarried: males per 1,000 females[a]	Religion[b]			Free-holders
	Male	Female		Protestant	Catholic	Mormon	
1853...	...	...	...	56,840	11,401	2,778	...
1866...	61.6	75.1	1,919	...	...	...	7,154
1872...	56.2	71.2	1,983	...	...	...	6,580
1878...	48.0	72.8	3,011	...	...	...	6,717
1884...	36.3	70.4	4,714	29,685	20,072	...	5,729
1890...	36.9	72.9	5,452	...	...	...	4,695
1896...	34.4	71.0	5,830	23,273	26,363	4,886	6,327

[a]Based on population over 15.

[b]Data not available for other religions. For 1853, limited to Hawaiian and part Hawaiian population.

Table 19.--OCCUPATION: 1866 TO 1896

Sex and census year	All occupations		Agriculturalists[b]	Laborers[c]	Mechanics	Professional workers[d]	Other occupations
	Number[a]	Percent of pop. over 15					
Both sexes:							
1866....	...	...	8,258	5,025	1,146	512	...
1872....	...	...	9,670	4,772	2,115	582	...
1878....	24,795	59.4	8,763	7,871	2,606	5,555	
1884....	39,541	68.1	10,968	12,351	3,919	12,303	
1890....	41,073	61.8	5,377	25,466	2,802	638	6,790
1896....	55,294	70.2	7,570	34,438	2,265	1,224	9,797
Male:							
1890....	38,930	83.6	5,280	23,863	2,690	483	6,614
1896....	51,705	91.0	7,435	32,027	2,265	942	9,036
Female:							
1890....	2,143	10.8	97	1,603	112	155	176
1896....	3,589	16.3	135	2,411	...	282	761

[a]May include workers under 15.

[b]"Agriculturalists" to 1884; "farmers" and "planters and ranchers" for 1890; and "farmers and agriculturalists," "rice planters," "coffee planters," and "ranchers" for 1896.

[c]"Laborers" in 1866, 1890, and 1896; "plantation laborers" in 1872; and "contract laborers" in 1878 and 1884.

[d]"Professionalists" in 1866; "clergymen," "teachers," "licensed physicians," and "lawyers" in 1872; "professional men and teachers" in 1890; and "doctors," "lawyers," and "other professions" in 1896.

Table 20.--SCHOOL ATTENDANCE, LITERACY, MATERNITY, AND HOUSING: 1884 TO 1896

Subject	1884	1890	1896
Number attending school	...	9,872	13,744
Per 1,000 children 6-15	...	816	962
Able to read and write[a]	39,016	38,380	59,538
Per 1,000 persons over 6	554	488	639
Women ever married	...	16,595	17,969
Mothers	...	10,664	12,391
Per 1,000 women ever married	...	643	690
Children ever born	...	46,100	54,039
Per 1,000 women ever married	...	2,778	3,007
Per 1,000 mothers	...	4,323	4,361
Children surviving	...	28,421	36,569
Per 1,000 children born	...	617	677
Occupants of inhabited buildings	...	89,990	109,020
Private residences	...	60,703	71,809
Plantation quarters	...	26,745	32,244
Group quarters[b]	...	2,542	4,967
Occupants per inhabited building	...	5.73	6.09
Private residences	...	5.05	5.12
Plantation quarters	...	7.82	9.24
Group quarters[b]	...	10.21	12.90

[a]For 1890, "the intention has been to make the expression 'Able to Read and Write,' apply to Hawaiian, English, or some European language only." Literacy in Asiatic languages was apparently included in 1896. Treatment in 1884 was not specified.

[b]Includes hotels and boarding houses, lodging houses, boarding schools, jails and lock-ups, hospitals and asylums, and barracks.

IV. THE U. S. CENSUSES: 1900-1960

Seven decennial population censuses have been made in Hawaii by the United States Bureau of the Census. The first was undertaken in 1900, less than two years after annexation; the most recent, in 1960. The 1900 count marked something of a demographic watershed: it was a time when the native Hawaiian population was near its lowest ebb, three out of five residents were foreign-born, the sex ratio far exceeded 200, and illiteracy rates reached modern highs. By 1960 a striking transformation had occurred in the population and its composition, drastically altering age and sex distribution, data on race and place of birth, and education statistics. This metamorphosis was matched by a corresponding growth and refinement of census procedures and content, from a relatively naive and limited kind of population inventory to a far-ranging, sophisticated survey of social, demographic, economic, and housing characteristics.

General background

The United States Census of Population has been taken decennially since 1790 under authority of the Constitution and a series of special Congressional Acts. Its original purpose was to conduct a head-count for periodic reapportionment of the U. S. House of Representatives. Since 1789, when it was first provided for by the Constitutional Convention, the census has acquired a progressively wider scope and range of application. This expanded function has been given implicit recognition by the enabling legislation usually passed by Congress shortly before each decennial count.

All census work is now conducted by the United States Bureau of the Census. In 1900 and earlier years, the enumeration was made by a special office especially organized for each decennial count and disbanded upon completion of its task. By virtue of the act of March 6, 1902, a permanent Bureau of the Census was created in the Department of the Interior. The bureau was subsequently transferred to the newly formed Department of Commerce and Labor, and still later to the Department of Commerce. The Director of the Census serves under the Secretary of Commerce, a cabinet official.

Decisions regarding the content and format of census schedules, tabulation, and publication are made in Washington by officials and staff members of the bureau. Comments and suggestions by advisory committees of demographers, statisticians, and census users are carefully considered in such work. In defining metropolitan areas, classifying industries, and similar activities, the Bureau of the Census must follow policies and definitions established by the Office of Statistical Standards of the U. S. Bureau of the Budget.

Relatively little allowance is made for regional differences in population composition or statistical needs. Variation in the treatment of different regions is largely precluded by the magnitude of the census effort, machine requirements, and other considerations which demand a high degree of uniformity and systematic cohesion. The chief exceptions in recent years have been in questions on ethnic stock (Aleutians in Alaska, Hawaiians in Hawaii, "persons of Spanish surname" in the Southwest) or citizenship (in New York State). Much greater flexibility has been apparent in the treatment of outlying territories and possessions--a category that included Hawaii before 1960.

Machine tabulation has been an important factor in the U. S. Census for seventy-five years. The first modern punch-card equipment was designed during the 1880's expressly for use in the decennial census. It was used extensively in tabulating results of the 1890 count and, in improved form, for the 1900 and succeeding enumerations. The electronic computer was introduced in the 1950 census.[1] These machines greatly increased the accuracy, speed, and analytic detail possible in mass statistical operations.

Paradoxically, the switch to machine tabulation appears to have adversely affected analysis of data for Hawaii. The censuses taken under the auspices of the Hawaiian Government were presumably tabulated entirely by manual methods, inasmuch as neither adding machine, desk calculator, nor punch-card equipment were available in the Islands during the nineteenth century. (The adding machine arrived in Hawaii around 1903, the rotary calculator in 1912-1916, and the punch card in 1930.)[2] Despite the use of hand methods, the understaffed and underbudgeted Hawaiian census offices managed to complete their field work and tabulation within a few months of the census date, rushing final results into print with minimal delay. The heavily staffed, well financed U. S. Bureau of the Census, in contrast, often took several years for publication of its final reports, in spite of batteries of Hollerith sorters and Univac computers.

The greater delay in tabulation and publication of results was only one of many changes resulting from the transfera of responsibility from the Hawaiian Board of Education to the U. S. Bureau of the Census. Formerly data had been compiled at six-year intervals; now the enumeration was on a decennial basis. Far greater detail became available on age distribution, occupation or industry, and school attendance. In contrast, beginning in 1900 less information was obtained regarding ethnic stock, housing, and religion. In many cases it was impossible to make direct comparisons between results of the U. S. censuses and those taken by the Hawaiian Government. Comparability with census findings for the Mainland United States was of course greatly increased.

At first, the Federal census officials tried to treat Hawaii like the rest of the country. Statistical tables in the 1900 census bulletins listed Hawaii between Georgia and Idaho, and included Honolulu alphabetically with Mainland cities over 25,000. Data on characteristics by race included a conventiona white-nonwhite breakdown, although a special concession was made to local usage in a few tables: "For the purpose of presenting the statistics in the general tables, in a form suitable for comparison with the statistics for the states and territories of the United States proper, the Hawaiians, part Hawaiians, Caucasians, and South Sea Islanders are included in the white population; but in the statements which follow, each of these elements is presented separately."[3] Other territories and possessions--Alaska, Arizona, New Mexico, Oklahoma--were similarly integrated into the national series.

Sentiment apparently changed after 1900. One reason may have been the obvious inapplicability of many Mainland classification schemes to the unique conditions found in the outlying areas. The effort to describe race in Mainland statistical terms in particular may have been regarded as unsuccessful. A second reason for separate treatment of Hawaii and other outlying areas in the 1910 and succeeding counts was probably the changed geographic complexion of the nation. The last two Mainland areas to change their territorial status gained statehood in 1912, just as results of the 1910 census were being published. It thereupon became easier for the census bureau to regard the Mainland (including Arizona and New Mexico) as a homogeneous whole, and to banish Alaska, Hawaii, and Puerto Rico to a sort of statistical limbo. The form and content of census reports for these latter areas no longer followed the Mainland models, and the results were excluded from national totals.[4]

Census operations and content

1900

The Twelfth Decennial Census was taken as of June 1, 1900, under provisions of the census act approved March 3, 1899.

> The present census, that of 1900, has been taken as a part of the work of the Twelfth Census of the United States, the Director of the Census having been authorized and directed by section 7 of the census act to make suitable provisions for the enumeration of the population and products of the Hawaiian Islands, and to employ for the purpose either supervisors and enumerators or special agents, as he should deem necessary.
>
> The census of Hawaii was accordingly taken by special agents, under the supervision of Mr. Alatau T. Atkinson as chief special agent, Mr. Atkinson having previously served as the general superintendent of the Hawaiian census in 1896.[5]

Many subjects were covered by the 1900 enumeration: geographic distribution, sex, age, place of birth, parentage, race or color, citizenship, conjugal condition, school attendance, literacy, ability to speak English, length of residence in the United States, gainful employment, household membership, and tenure of housing.

Geographic distribution was reported by island and judicial district. Honolulu was included in tables for cities and towns; its boundaries, following local (but unofficial) usage, were based on those of Honolulu District, extending from Red Hill to Koko Head. County governments were not organized until 1905, and hence were not included in the geographic data. The lack of statistics on urban places other than Honolulu can be explained by the fact that incorporated municipalities have never been recognized in Hawaii and unincorporated places were not shown separately in census reports. Thus, only judicial districts--land divisions of long standing in Hawaii, despite many minor boundary shifts[6]--remained the basis of small-area statistics.

Tabulations on age were limited to the Territory as a whole and the City of Honolulu. For the Territory, single-year data were reported through age 99; for Honolulu, five-year groups were shown to 34 and ten-year groups to 64. This was an important advance over the Hawaiian censuses, which used fifteen-year groupings past age 15. Unlike most of the Hawaiian censuses, however, the 1900 count omitted all age breakdowns for counties and islands.

For the first time in Hawaii, statistics on "families" were compiled. This term embraced both "private families"--defined in much the same manner as "households" in later censuses--and "families not private." The latter category included groups of persons in barracks, dormitories, institutions, and the like, each of which was treated as housing a single family.

Occupational statistics were based on the number of persons "gainfully employed," a concept similar to that of "experienced labor force" in more recent censuses. Questions on gainful employment were asked of all persons 10 years of age or more.

For the United States as a whole, the Twelfth Decennial

Census bore a per capita cost of 18¢. Hawaii's share was thus about $27,720.[7]

Final census results appeared chiefly in two bound volumes together with data for states and other territories. Volume I presented statistics on geographic distribution, sex, nativity, and citizenship; Volume II, on age, race, conjugal condition, school attendance, illiteracy, gainful employment, and households.[8]

1910

The next decennial census was held as of April 15, 1910. Taken under authority of the census act of July 2, 1909, it presented statistics on agriculture, manufactures, and mines and quarries, as well as data on population. Detailed information was published on its operational aspects, perhaps in partial atonement for its marked statistical limitations:

> The territory of Hawaii has been included within the area of enumeration by the acts of Congress providing for the last two Federal censuses. The peculiar conditions prevailing in this insular territory necessitate a special adaptation of census methods, literature, and schedules, and in addition the remoteness of the territory from the mainland, as well as the remoteness of the several inhabited islands from one another and the infrequency of interisland communication, tend to complicate the organization and supervision of the field work. In certain sections it is difficult to find competent persons who can be induced to undertake this work by the offer of temporary employment at a comparatively low rate of remuneration. Moreover, among certain classes of the population, which for very considerable areas is predominantly Asiatic and non-English speaking, census taking has been popularly regarded with suspicion in the past, and in certain localities enumerators have even encountered violent opposition. Preliminary to the actual enumeration in 1910 it was therefore necessary to prepare and disseminate a considerable

> amount of literature explaining in Oriental and other languages the purposes and methods of the census. Lessons upon the schedules were given in the public schools, instructions and schedules were translated into Chinese, Japanese, and other languages, and agents were specially trained in advance to supervise the actual work of enumeration. Every effort was made to select and train for this work in each district individuals entirely familiar with the local conditions within the districts to which they were to be severally assigned and able to speak the language prevailing therein. Wherever necessary, interpreters were employed to assist the enumerators. As a result of this preliminary work, it is believed that the Thirteenth Census was an accurate and complete enumeration of the population.[9]

The foregoing methodological statement--apparently deemed unnecessary for equally polyglot immigrant areas in Eastern Seaboard cities and in the more remote and suspicious sections of the Kentucky hill country--was accompanied by an extended historical footnote, which contained such value-loaded statements as "Her [Lilioukalani's] governmental policies were distasteful to the progressive element of the population ...."

The 1910 census contained tabulations on geographic distribution, urban places, age, sex, race, place of birth, year of immigration, citizenship, marital status, school attendance, illiteracy, inability to speak English, "families," tenure, and gainful employment. A new "racial" classification, geared to the unique character of the Territory, was adopted and used for a number of cross-tabulations. This system, derived from the breakdown pioneered in the 1896 Hawaiian census, was followed in detail until 1930, and in somewhat telescoped form through the 1960 count. Geographic detail included data for counties (organized in 1905), islands, judicial districts, and the two cities of Honolulu and Hilo. The latter community had been accorded legal boundaries by the 1911 Territorial Legislature, just in time for inclusion in the 1910 census bulletins. Honolulu was still assumed to be coterminous with Honolulu Judicial District, a definition not given legislative confirmation until 1923. Neither Hilo nor Honolulu had separate municipal governments; their boundaries were set chiefly for statistical purposes, zoning controls, and public utility franchises.

The treatment of age was disappointing. For the Territory as a whole, five-year age groups were reported through 99, but single-year data were limited to ages below 25. For counties and cities, the 1910 census showed less detail than its 1866 counterpart. Although six age groups were reported (or could be obtained by subtraction), five pertained to ages of 20 or younger, and the sixth was an open-ended class covering all persons 21 and over. It thus became impossible to determine, for example, the number of females of child-bearing age on Oahu or the number of persons 65 and over in Hilo--the kinds of data needed for computing age-specific birth and death rates, estimating the demand for social welfare services, and similar applications.

Per capita cost of the 1910 census throughout the nation was 17¢, one cent less than in 1900. Hawaii's share was thus $32,619.

Dr. Victor S. Clark was Special Agent in Charge of the 1910 Census in Hawaii.[9a]

Final tabulations for Hawaii appeared in three different bound volumes. Data on the Territory's geographic distribution and population composition were presented in Volume III of the census, along with other state reports, but Hawaii was not included in any of the summary tables. The same material was reprinted as a supplement at the end of the Abstract of the Census. Occupational statistics for the Islands were published in Volume IV.[10]

The 1910 reports began the practice, continued until 1940, of grouping statistics for minor outlying insular possessions with data for the Territory of Hawaii. The Midway Islands, geographically but not politically part of the Hawaiian Archipelago, were thus combined with the Territory in all published tabulations from 1910 to 1940. This practice added 35 persons to the Territorial total in 1910, 31 in 1920, 36 in 1930, and 560 in 1940.

1920

The Fourteenth Decennial Census was taken as of January 1, 1920, under the census act approved March 3, 1919. It included reports on population, agriculture, manufactures, and mines and quarries. Subjects covered by the section on population included geographic distribution, age, sex, race, place of birth, citizenship, year of immigration, inability to speak English, illiteracy, school attendance, gainful employment, housing tenure, and "families."

Statistics on age remained sketchy. For the Territory as a whole, five-year age groups were shown through 95-99, with single-year data limited to ages under 25. For Honolulu, Hilo, and the various counties, the two highest categories were 20-44 and 45 and over.

As in 1910, many cross-tabulations by race were provided. Twelve groups were recognized, following the pattern established by the Thirteenth Census and maintained through 1930: Hawaiian, Caucasian-Hawaiian, Asiatic-Hawaiian, Portuguese, "Porto Rican," Spanish, "other Caucasian," Chinese, Japanese, Korean, Filipino, and Negro and all other.

As before, statistics were compiled for counties, islands, judicial districts, and two urban places, Hilo and Honolulu. The published Honolulu total erroneously included 1,507 residents of Ewa District. This mistake, not caught until 1953, was repeated in recapitulations of 1920 data in all censuses through 1950.

Hawaii's share of the costs of conducting the 1920 census amounted to about $61,411, based on a per capita cost of 24¢ for the nation as a whole.

The identity of the supervisor for Hawaii remains unknown.

Data for Hawaii were published principally in three of the bound census reports. Volume I contained a short table on population trends by island and judicial district; Volume III, more extensive tabulations on composition and characteristics of the population; and Volume IV, detailed statistics on persons engaged in gainful occupations.[11] As in 1910, Hawaii was excluded from state summaries and national totals.

<u>1930</u>

The Fifteenth Census of the United States was conducted as of April 1, 1930, in conformity with the census act, approved June 18, 1929, which provided for this and subsequent decennial censuses. A number of economic censuses were taken concurrently. Subjects included in the population census were geographic distribution, age, sex, race, place of birth, year immigrated, citizenship, mother tongue, ability to speak English, illiteracy, school attendance, marital condition, "families," tenure, gainful employment, and, for the first time, unemployment. This last question was limited to members of the experienced labor force on salary, wage, or commission.

Far greater geographic detail was shown than in previous counts. For the first time, statistics for cities and towns other than Hilo and Honolulu were reported, using ad hoc boundaries laid out for census purposes. There was also a table on election precincts, giving summary data on age, sex, race, and nativity. The value of these small-area statistics is considerably diminished by the lack of suitable reference maps.

Tabular detail on age distribution was increased for small areas but reduced for the Territory as a whole. Age statistics for election precincts, for example, were grouped into eight class intervals, including one for persons 65 and over. At the

Territorial level, however, published detail on age was less specific than ever: single-year data through age 24, five-year groups to 34, and ten-year classes through 74. Fortunately, recapitulations of 1930 data on age presented in the 1940, 1950, and 1960 census reports showed five-year groupings through age 74.

Statistics on nativity and citizenship continued to classify persons born in the Philippines as native-born citizens. This practice was begun in 1900, shortly after annexation of the Philippine Islands, and continued through the 1940 census, six years before the Commonwealth was granted complete independence. The effects of this practice were noted particularly in 1930 statistics on mother tongue and year of immigration, which, being limited to the foreign born, excluded Filipinos.

Based on a per capita cost of 32¢ for the entire country, the cost of the 1930 population census of Hawaii was $117,856.

Starke M. Grogan was chief statistician in charge of the census of outlying territories and possessions. No record could be found of the name of the local supervisor.

Final results of the 1930 enumeration were consolidated into a single bound volume which combined the population and agriculture bulletins for all outlying areas.[12]

1940

The Sixteenth Decennial Census was conducted as of April 1, 1940, under authority of the 1929 census act. The population census was combined with a census of housing, the first of its kind. Censuses of business, manufactures, and similar subjects were made at approximately the same time.

The housing census contained data on vacancy status, tenure, number of dwelling units in structure, exterior material, race of occupants, number of rooms, lighting equipment, toilet facilities, bathing facilities, state of repair, water supply, mortgage status, household size, refrigeration equipment, persons per room, radio, value of owner occupied units, and monthly rent of tenant-occupied units.

Subjects treated in the population count included geographic distribution, age, sex, race, place of birth, citizenship, marital status, school attendance, years of school completed (for persons 25 years of age or older), employment status, class of worker, occupation, industry, wage or salary income in 1939, and months worked in 1939. The questions on years of schooling, class of worker, income, and months worked were new; those on employment status, occupation, and industry represented a new approach to what had formerly been termed "gainful employment." Questions used in 1930 but omitted in 1940 (presumably because of declining importance) concerned illiteracy, inability to speak English, mother tongue, and year of immigration.

Statistics were published for counties, islands, judicial districts, urban places (Honolulu, Hilo, and a number of smaller places defined for census purposes), and census tracts. The latter unit, consisting of 97 relatively small, homogeneous, and permanent statistical areas--42 on Oahu and 55 elsewhere in the Territory--replaced precincts as the smallest type of area reported. The census tract system, following existing land division boundaries, was laid out in the late 1930's by a local committee.[13] Statistics on age, race, sex, and a wide variety of housing items were tabulated by tracts. Housing data for city blocks were published for Mainland cities but not for Honolulu.

For the first time, one of the minor outlying islands legally considered to be part of the City and County of Honolulu appeared in the census; it was Palmyra, with 32 inhabitants. None of the leeward group, extending from Nihoa to Kure, appeared to be populated. Among the islands not under the jurisdiction of the Territory but included with it for census purposes were Baker, Canton, Enderbury, Howland, Jarvis, Johnston, and Midway.

Several changes were made in the classification of race. Asiatic-Hawaiians and Caucasian-Hawaiians were combined as "part Hawaiians," and Portuguese, Spanish, and "other Caucasians" were combined as "Caucasians." Puerto Ricans retained their statistical identity.

Age detail was further restricted. For the Territory as a whole, five-year age groups were reported to 54, and ten-year groups to 74. Census tract statistics showed ten-year groups from age 5 upward. No single-year data were reported.

Statistics on occupied dwelling units replaced the series

on families, which had been compiled in every census since 1900. Barracks, dormitories, institutions, and other group quarters, which had been included in the family totals, were omitted from the count of occupied dwelling units.

The concept of "labor force" replaced that of "gainfully employed." The labor force was defined to include all persons 14 years of age or more who were either working or seeking work. Statistics were shown separately for employed persons, those on public emergency work, and the unemployed. The employed were further classified by occupation, industry, and class of worker. In contrast, the statistics on gainful employment compiled in 1930 and earlier had included persons as young as 10 years of age, generally omitted unemployed persons seeking their first jobs, and had failed to distinguish between the concepts of occupation and industry.

Nationally, per capita cost of the 1940 Censuses of Population and Housing was 42¢. Hawaii's share of the total was thus $177,563.

Fred W. Coil was area supervisor for Hawaii. John F. Child, Jr. was assistant area supervisor.[14]

The 1940 publication program was quite limited, perhaps because of wartime conditions. Findings for Hawaii appeared in three brief bulletins, two on population and one on housing; the first population bulletin was later reissued as part of a bound volume.[15]

1950

The Seventeenth Decennial Census was taken as of April 1, 1950, in accordance with the 1929 census act; the housing census was authorized by the Housing Act of 1949, approved July 15, 1949. A special enumerator's reference manual was published for Hawaii shortly before the census was taken, and census procedures and forms were later reviewed in a separate monograph.[16]

Only a few changes were made in the Census of Housing. Vacant dwelling units classified as dilapidated or not for rent or sale were distinguished from other vacant units; the concept of "dilapidated" replaced that of "needing major repairs"; separate totals were shown for owner-occupied dwelling units on leased land and those on fee-simple property; and owner-occupied units in multi-unit structures or on leased land were excluded from tables on value. Otherwise, the 1940 and 1950 housing statistics were quite similar.

The population census compiled data on geographic distribution, age, sex, race, race mixture, nativity and place of birth, citizenship, school enrollment, years of school completed, marital status, households, married couples, families, unrelated individuals, number of children ever born (for married, widowed, or divorced women 45 years old and over), residence five years earlier, employment status, class of worker, occupation, industry, hours worked during the week, weeks worked during 1949, and income received during 1949 by persons, families, and unrelated individuals. Several of these items, such as race mixture, residence five years earlier, hours worked, and family income, were new; one, number of children ever born, had last appeared in the 1896 Hawaiian census.

Extensive use was made of sampling techniques in 1950. Subject matter surveyed on a sample basis included school enrollment, years of school completed, families and unrelated individuals, married couples, children ever born, residence five years earlier, parents' birthplace, hours worked, weeks worked, and income of persons, families, and unrelated individuals. Questions regarding these subjects were asked only of every fifth person enumerated. This was the first use of sampling in an official U. S. census in Hawaii, although limited use of sampling had already been tried ten years earlier on the Mainland.

Following the practice initiated in 1910, the Bureau of the Census proved highly sympathetic to local needs, even at the expense of direct comparability with Mainland data. In line with this policy, the bureau continued to classify race according to the unique Island tradition, included a question on Territorial citizenship (or eligibility to vote), reported place of birth in a manner most meaningful for the Islands, redefined mobility in a way suggested locally, and in tabulations on industry, added categories for "sugar farms," "pineapple farms," "coffee farms," "sugar processing," and "pineapple canning." On the Mainland, enumerators asked a question regarding place of residence one year prior to the census date; in Hawaii, the question referred to residence on August 14, 1945 (V-J Day) and included a category for "different island."

The 1950 count presented considerable detail for small areas. Separate totals were often shown for counties, islands, urban places and villages, and census tracts. A number of tracts were split into two or more parts, increasing the number on Oahu from 42 in 1940 to 84 in 1950. Many series heretofore limited to larger areas were now published for tracts. Population totals were reported for half a dozen villages with fewer than 100 inhabitants--Hookena (20), Kalapana (60), Keanae (54), Milolii (95), Pukoo (42), and Waipio (95). The outlying islands legally part of the City and County of Honolulu were arbitrarily grouped with tract 29-D; only one, French Frigate Shoals, was inhabited at the time.[17] Honolulu remained the only large American city for which block statistics on housing were not published.

Statistics on age, often inadequate in earlier censuses, were tabulated in considerable detail. For the Territory, single-year data were reported to age 84, and five-year groups, through age 99. For counties, islands, and urban places, five-year classes were published to age 74.

For the first, and so far only, time in a decennial census, data on race mixture were compiled. Prior to 1950, the only mixture recognized in census tabulations had been "part

Hawaiian," a category shown separately since 1849. By official definition:

> Mixtures of Caucasian and other races are classified according to the race of the nonwhite parent. Mixtures of nonwhite races, other than Hawaiian, are classified according to the race of the father.
>
> Race mixture was obtained by asking the question, "Is this person of mixed race?" for every person enumerated. Since mixtures of Caucasian and any other race are classified according to the race of the nonwhite parent, no person classified as Caucasian can, by definition, be of mixed race.[18]

Information was compiled on households, families, unrelated individuals, and married couples. The term "household" referred to persons occupying a dwelling unit and included persons living alone and groups of unrelated individuals sharing a house or apartment. A family, in contrast, was defined as "a group of two or more persons related by blood, marriage, or adoption and living together." This term differed markedly from that of the censuses before 1940, when the count of "families" included both persons living alone and groups in group quarters.

Members of the armed forces were treated in a somewhat different fashion than previously. As in earlier censuses, the final count included all Air Force, Army, Coast Guard, Marine Corps, and Navy personnel either stationed ashore or aboard ships in Hawaii ports on the census date.[19] These men had formerly been classified as "gainful workers" or as "employed" members of the labor force. Statistics on occupation in 1940 and earlier had reported enlisted men under the category of "soldiers, sailors, marines, and coast guards"; commissioned officers were classified with civilian workers in their respective occupations. It was thus impossible to determine the exact number of armed forces--or, conversely, the exact civilian population--in the Islands. In 1950, however, the armed forces were excluded from data on occupation and industry, and their exact numbers could be computed by subtracting published totals for the "civilian labor force" from the corresponding figures for "labor force."

Minor differences were evident between figures for corresponding items in different tables of the 1950 bulletins. As a result of sampling variation, apparent discrepancies were most frequent in cross-tabulations between full-count data and information collected on a sample basis. A second source of apparent error was the editing of comparable items in different operations; the totals for households and occupied dwelling units (by definition identical) seldom agreed. A third reason was the use of a two-stage tabulation program, involving separate machine runs for the "P-B" and "P-C" bulletins. As noted in the latter series:

> The differences between figures for corresponding items in different tables and reports are caused by errors in the tabulation processes. These errors include machine failure, loss of punch cards, and other types.[20]

In some instances as many as four figures were published for the same item. The effect of these differences was usually quite small. The population 25 years old and over, for example, was given as 249,393 in the "P-B" full-count tables, 249,386 in the "P-C" full-count tables, 247,480 in the "P-B" sample statistics, and as 247,410 in the "P-C" sample data. Both of the "P-B" figures were repeated in the 1960 bulletins.

Further changes sometimes occur when data are recapitulated in a later census. Minor adjustments may be made to eliminate the "no answer" group or to compensate for lost cards; for example, the number of males employed as "craftsmen, foremen, and kindred workers" in 1950 was given as 25,320 in the "P-B" report, as 25,251 in the "P-C" bulletin, and as 25,300 in the table repeating 1950 data in the 1960 report. Changes in definition may also be a factor; persons on public emergency work were treated as a separate category in the 1940 bulletin but were combined with the unemployed in recapitulations of 1940 labor force data in the 1950 report. A third cause of change may be simple error, such as occurred when the 1950 total for unrelated individuals (57,230 in the 1950 reports) was incorrectly shown as 49,270 in one of the 1960 tables while appearing correctly in another.

Per capita cost of the Seventeenth Census for the entire nation was 60¢, an increase of 43 percent in only ten years. Hawaii's share of the total cost was about $299,876. Data for both 1940 and 1950 covered both the population and housing censuses.

Joel Williams, Chief, Territories and Possessions Section, visited Hawaii in 1948 to help plan the census. Robert B.

Mueller was Hawaii Census Supervisor.[21]

Final results for Hawaii appeared in a series of bulletins and bound volumes. Paperback bulletins were issued on number of inhabitants, general characteristics, detailed characteristics, housing characteristics, and census tract statistics.[22] The first of these bulletins was later combined in a bound volume with the corresponding releases for other states and outlying areas. It was also bound in a single volume with the second and third population bulletins for Hawaii and the corresponding bulletins for other territories and possessions. The same procedure was followed with the single housing bulletin for Hawaii.[23] Only the census tract report was left unbound.

1960

The Eighteenth Decennial Census of the United States was conducted as of April 1, 1960. Legal provision for the 1960 Censuses of Population and Housing was made in the Act of Congress of August 31, 1954 (amended August 1957), which codified Title 13, United States Code. Information on census organization, forms, and procedures was published in an enumerator's reference manual, various census monographs, and other reports.[24]

Changes in the housing census were largely definitional. The "dwelling unit" concept used in 1940 and 1950 was replaced by one based on the "housing unit," defined as follows:

> A house, an apartment or other group of rooms, or a single room, is regarded as a housing unit when it is occupied or intended for occupancy as single living quarters. Separate living quarters are those in which the occupants do not live and eat with any other persons in the structure and in which there is either (1) direct access from the outside or through

a common hall, or (2) a kitchen or cooking equipment for exclusive use of the occupants.[25]

This definition included many quarters in rooming houses and hotels which were classified as "nondwelling-unit quarters" in 1950. Inasmuch as a "household" was defined as the persons occupying a dwelling unit in 1950 and the persons occupying a housing unit in 1960, this change tended to increase totals on households as well as on housing, and somewhat reduced average household size.

Several new items were added to the housing schedule, and at least one important question was dropped. For the first time in Hawaii, statistics were compiled on television ownership, air conditioning equipment, heating equipment (!), number of automobiles available, length of time vacant, and gross (as well as contract) monthly rent. Unfortunately, the distinction between owner-occupied housing units on leased land and those on land owned in fee simple was abandoned, thereby terminating an exceptionally useful series and reducing validity of all data on the value of owner-occupied housing. A second omitted housing item was the question on exterior material.

Subject matter covered by the population census included geographic distribution, age, sex, color or race, marital status, household relationship, state or country of birth, parents' nativity, mother tongue, residence five years prior to the census date, year moved into present house, school enrollment (public and private), years of school completed, veteran status, married couples, families, and unrelated individuals, children ever born, employment status, weeks worked, hours worked, class of worker, occupation, industry, place of work, means of transportation to work, earnings, and income of persons, families, and unrelated individuals. Several of these items, such as year moved into present house and place of work, were new, and one, mother tongue, was appearing for the first time since 1930. Two items covered in 1950, race mixture and citizenship, were dropped.

Numerous changes were made in the treatment of small areas, not all of them improvements. The 84 census tracts in the City and County of Honolulu were extensively revised and renumbered, from 1 to 114 (with the last of these consisting of the outlying islands legally part of the city). Over strong objections voiced by local census users, all Neighbor Island census tracts were abolished and replaced by a system of "Census County Divisions" with similar boundaries. Only a few statistical series were published for these CCD's. For the first time, housing data were published for city blocks not only in Honolulu but also in Hilo, Hawaii, and Lahaina and Wailuku, Maui.

Other changes in the treatment of geographic data included the definition of a Honolulu Urbanized Area, limited use of the island as a statistical unit, and the suppression of all data for judicial districts and villages under 300. Although data for CCD's could be grouped to approximate judicial districts and islands, the information obtainable was restricted to only a few items. The Honolulu Urbanized Area consisted of the City of Honolulu plus the built-up area extending through Halawa, Aiea, Waimalu, and Pearl City to Waipahu. Since, under Bureau of the Census policy, no unincorporated places under 10,000 within an urbanized area are shown separately in census reports, both Pearl City and Waipahu were omitted from the 1960 tables on cities and towns. No exact comparison could be made of the 1950 and 1960 data on urban and rural populations as a result of this treatment of the built-up parts of the Pearl Harbor rim.

Statistics on race or ethnic stock were largely replaced by data on color, in accordance with Mainland practice. The traditional classification by race was used only in a tabulation of age, sex, marital status, and household relationship, shown for the State as a whole and for the Honolulu Standard Metropolitan Statistical Area (City and County of Honolulu).[26] An abbreviated breakdown, presenting totals by sex for "white," Negro, Indian, Japanese, Chinese, Filipino, and "all other" residents, was used for cities over 10,000 and counties. Virtually all demographic, social, economic, and housing characteristics were reported separately for "whites" and "nonwhites," however, and a few statistics were later shown for Chinese, Filipinos, Japanese, and Negroes.[27] Census tract totals using the older racial classification system were subsequently tabulated at the request and expense of the State Government.[28]

Many of the population and housing questions in the 1960

census were asked on a sample basis. One-fourth of all housing units (and hence households) and one-fourth of all persons in group quarters were included in the population sample. In the housing census, between 5 percent and 25 percent of all units were sampled.

Census officials visiting Hawaii to help plan the 1960 count included Wayne F. Daugherty, Chief, Housing Division, and William T. Fay, Chief, Geography Division. Charles W. Churchill was Hawaii Census Supervisor,[29] and his assistant was B. David Swenson.

Per capita cost of the 1960 Censuses of Population and Housing was 57¢, or three cents less than in 1950. On a pro rata basis, Hawaii's share was $360,680.

As in past years, census results for Hawaii were issued in a series of press releases, preliminary and advance bulletins, preprints of the final reports, bound volumes, and special subject reports. First returns, which appeared in a newspaper story on May 24, 1960, gave a State population of 621,405. Revised preliminary figures (620,385 for the State), still based on unedited field counts, were issued in a press release on June 9, 1960. Two "Preliminary Reports," one for the Honolulu Standard Metropolitan Statistical Area and the other for the State, were released in June and July 1960. The second of these gave the State total as 620,346. The final State figure (632,772) was published first in an "Advance Report" dated November 10, 1960. An "Advance Report" on general population characteristics was released on March 30, 1961.[30] These leaflets were followed successively by preprints of the final reports on number of inhabitants, general population characteristics, general social and economic characteristics, and detailed characteristics. These four preprints were combined in a bound volume issued in 1963.[31] A separate census tract bulletin was published, presenting both population and housing statistics.[32] About the same time, Census of Housing bulletins appeared on area statistics, metropolitan housing, and block statistics for Hilo, Honolulu, Lahaina, and Wailuku.[33] Various subject reports presented data for Hawaii.[34] In 1965 the State published the results of a special tabulation by military status.[35]

Findings

Major trends revealed by the seven U. S. censuses so far conducted in Hawaii are charted in the accompanying statistical tables.

Tables 21-24 present data on overall growth rates, geographic distribution, and urbanization. Although most of the changes shown by these tables resulted from births, deaths, and migration, a few reflected shifting boundaries. Wahiawa Judicial District, for example, was created in 1913 from parts of Waialua and Waianae Districts. Hilo, first granted official boundaries in 1911, was greatly expanded thirty years later, thereby annexing 893 persons and many square miles. Smaller cities and towns, such as Lahaina and Lihue, were first reported separately in 1930, although they had existed as population centers for many decades.

Table 25 reports data on age and sex. Far greater detail is given in the original census bulletins.

Statistics on ethnic stock (or "race") and place of birth appear in Tables 26 and 27. The classification systems used for race in 1900 and 1960 differed somewhat from those for intervening years, thereby affecting comparability.

Tables 28 and 29 show data on mobility. The series on Hawaii-born persons living on the Mainland goes back to 1850.

Trends in marital status, families, and average household size are charted in Tables 30 and 31. Changes in definitions and varying treatment of the population in group quarters seriously hinder any effort to follow decennial shifts in average household size.

Table 32 reports statistics on school attendance or enrollment, years of school completed, illiteracy, and ability to speak English. The series on median educational attainment, shown here for all persons 25 years of age or older, was initiated in 1940. It replaced two older series, one on illiteracy (defined as the inability to write, regardless of reading ability) and the other on ability to speak English. The Bureau of the Census later published estimates of illiteracy by state for 1950 and 1960, based on national survey results and state data on years of school completed.

Data on the fertility ratio and completed fertility rate

appear in Table 33. The fertility ratio is the number of children under the age of 5 per 1,000 women of childbearing age. Its value as an index of long-term changes in natality levels is limited by its sensitivity to the high infant mortality rates that prevailed early in the century. The completed fertility (or birth) rate is the number of children ever born per 1,000 women past the childbearing age.

Statistics on persons engaged in gainful occupations, 1900 to 1930, and the labor force, 1940 to 1960, are cited in Table 34. As noted in an earlier section, the data on "gainful workers" compiled through 1930 are not exactly comparable to the figures on "labor force" first collected in 1940. Although it was possible to limit the 1910-to-1930 data to the same age groups used in later censuses, no adjustment was possible for changes in the treatment of seasonal workers or unemployed persons.

Income statistics are given in Table 35. Wage and salary data were compiled for members of the experienced labor force, including armed forces, in both 1940 and 1950. The most nearly comparable data for 1960 included total earnings and omitted the armed forces. Data on total family income first appeared in the 1950 census. The medians shown in this table reflect increases in consumer prices as well as growth in true buying power.[36]

Table 36 reports data on housing characteristics. Information available prior to 1940 was limited to tenure. Beginning in 1940, however, the Bureau of the Census obtained statistics on structural characteristics, occupancy, equipment, rent or value, and similar aspects of housing. Important definitional changes occurred in 1910 (when group quarters were included), 1940, and 1960.

These tables present only a highly abbreviated overview of demographic-trend data available for Hawaii in the decennial U. S. Census reports. For a full appreciation of the mass of information contained in the census--its scope and depth, together with the many definitional problems involved--it is necessary to go to the original volumes.

Accuracy of the census

Any evaluation of the quality of the U. S. Census must necessarily be incomplete. Although an assessment of definitions, classification schemes, tabular detail, and publication programs can be made without undue difficulty, determining the extent of underenumeration, double-counting, or misclassification--equally important matters--requires much greater skill and far more information. An evaluation of the first type has already been offered, at least implicitly, in the preceding pages. Mention has been made of the failure to provide data on urban places before 1930, the lack of satisfactory tabular detail on age until 1950, the greatly improved labor force, household, and housing definitions introduced in 1940 and thereafter, and the ill-advised substitution of color (meaningless in Hawaii) for race in 1960.

Questions of accuracy are another matter. Although the Bureau of the Census undertook post-enumeration surveys in both 1950 and 1960 in order to estimate the extent of under- or over-enumeration, neither survey was adequate for showing results at the State level. A comparison of cohort totals from one census to the next often provides clues to defects in coverage, at least in relatively "closed" populations; in Hawaii, however, large-scale in- and out-migration seriously reduces the value of such comparisons. Comparing census data on net intercensal change with a corresponding figure independently derived from birth, death, and migration statistics is similarly fruitless; any apparent discrepancy (or "error of closure") is more likely to reflect deficiencies in the migration data than a poor census count.

Errors in editing are sometimes uncovered by reviewing unpublished enumeration-district tallies or obtaining a special tabulation. In 1920, as previously noted, part of Ewa Judicial District was inadvertently included with Honolulu in published totals. Forty years later, the crews of two ships berthed in Pearl Harbor were erroneously added to the population of Waikiki as census tract 19CV, a tract designation intended for persons aboard yachts and houseboats moored in Ala Wai Yacht Harbor. The latter group, meanwhile, was included with the population ashore.[37] The same census greatly overstated the number of pure Hawaiians, partly because of editing procedures for ascribing race when it is not reported on the census schedule.[38]

Re-enumeration of selected areas sometimes provides insight into the question of census accuracy. Urban redevelopment areas in central Honolulu were enumerated by three different agencies in as many years: the Bureau of the Census in 1950, the Honolulu City Planning Commission a few months later, and the Honolulu Redevelopment Agency in 1953. The Census and Agency counts were quite close, but the Planning Commission totals were distinctly lower. The origin-destination survey of Oahu, conducted late in 1960 by the State Department of Transportation, reported dwelling units by census tract, and its totals differed widely from some of the corresponding U. S. Census counts.[39] In all of these cases, however, differences in coverage, definitions, and survey dates make any exact comparison impossible.

Payroll statistics routinely compiled by various government agencies often provide a useful standard for gauging the accuracy of census data on the labor force. In 1940, for example, the number of persons reported in the census as on public emergency work in Hawaii was 2,326, whereas the number recorded on the Work Project Administration (WPA), National Youth Administration (NYA), and Civilian Conservation Corps (CCC) payrolls at that time was 3,568.[40] Estimates of employment and unemployment, prepared by the State Department of Labor and Industrial Relations in part from returns required by the State Employment Security Law, differed markedly from the corresponding 1960 Census figures. Despite valiant efforts to remove them, obvious discrepancies remained.[41] At least some appear to be the result of underenumeration, double-counting, or misclassification in the census.

There is considerable evidence that the 1960 count understated the number of armed forces and dependents in the Islands. According to a special tabulation of census data, there were 47,267 officers and enlisted men and 56,576 members of families with head in the armed forces (excluding the head) in Hawaii as of April 1, 1960.[42] In computing a base for its postcensal population estimates, however, the Bureau of the Census has used an April 1, 1960 armed forces figure of 54,000 obtained directly from the Department of Defense.[43] Records of the latter agency showed 35,400 shore-based personnel in Hawaii, 6,646 Naval afloat and mobile activities temporarily based ashore, and 62,608 military dependents located in the State.[44] Local commanding officers, meanwhile, reported a State total of 52,881 armed forces (41,927 ashore and 10,954 aboard ships homeported in Hawaii) and 60,057 military dependents.[45]

Statistics on race have been notoriously subject to classification errors. Mention has already been made in the previous chapter of Adams's two efforts to correct the published 1900 ethnic totals, which obviously included many part Hawaiians in the pure Hawaiian and Caucasian categories. This "passing" of part Hawaiians as pure-blooded Hawaiians has become progressively more evident in recent decades. In 1930, according to Adams, 9,780 persons classified as Hawaiian were actually part Hawaiian; the number of unmixed Hawaiians in the Islands was 12,856 instead of 22,636, and the number of part Hawaiians was 38,004 rather than 28,224.[46] There is a good deal of evidence that most of the 11,294 Hawaiians (and a sizeable number of the non-Hawaiians) reported in 1960 were in reality part Hawaiian. Similar errors may have occurred in classifying non-Hawaiians of mixed ancestry (sometimes called "Cosmopolitan" in local parlance), in view of the somewhat arbitrary and complex rules for such cases. The problems of racial classification have inspired a rather wide literature in recent years.[47]

Although the errors and discrepancies cited above sometimes involve thousands of persons, their net effect is often insignificant in relation to the total population. For all their limitations, the U. S. Census reports offer an unequalled statistical picture of the social, demographic, and economic development of Hawaii since 1900.

Table 21.--POPULATION, URBAN AND RURAL: 1900 TO 1960

Census date	Hawaii			Urban[a]		Rural[a]	
	Population	Annual change: Number	Annual change: Percent[b]	Places	Population	Population	Percent of Total
June 1, 1900......	154,001	...	...	1	39,306	114,695	74.5
April 15, 1910....	191,874	3,837	2.2	2	58,928	132,946	69.3
January 1, 1920...	255,881	6,592	3.0	2	92,251	163,630	63.9
April 1, 1930.....	368,300	10,968	3.6	12	197,937	170,363	46.3
April 1, 1940.....	422,770	5,447	1.4	17	264,262	158,508	37.5
April 1, 1950.....	499,794	7,702	1.7	17	344,869	154,925	31.0
April 1, 1960.....	632,772	13,298	2.4	19	483,961	148,811	23.5

[a]Data before 1930 limited to places with legally established boundaries (Honolulu and Hilo).

[b]Computed according to the formula: $r = 100\,[\log_e (P_1/P_o)]/t$.

Table 22.--POPULATION BY ISLAND: 1900 TO 1960

Island	1900	1910	1920	1930	1940	1950	1960
All islands..	154,001	191,874	255,881	368,300	422,770	499,794	632,772
Oahu[a]...........	58,504	81,993	123,496	202,887	257,696	353,020	500,409
Honolulu[a].....	39,306	52,183	81,820	137,582	179,358	248,034	294,194
Rest of Oahu..	19,198	29,810	41,676	65,305	78,338	104,986	206,215
Other islands...	95,497	109,881	132,385	165,413	165,074	146,774	132,363
Hawaii........	46,843	55,382	64,895	73,325	73,276	68,350	61,332
Maui.......... } Lanai......... }	25,416	28,623	36,080	48,756	46,919	40,103	35,717
Lanai.........		131	185	2,356	3,720	3,136	2,115
Kahoolawe.....	...	2	3	2	1	...	...
Molokai.......	2,504	1,791	1,784	5,032	5,340	5,280	5,023
Kauai.........	20,562	23,744	29,247	35,806	35,636	29,683	27,922
Niihau........	172	208	191	136	182	222	254
Percent of total							
Oahu............	38.0	42.7	48.3	55.1	61.0	70.6	79.1
Honolulu......	25.5	27.2	32.0	37.4	42.4	49.6	46.5
Rest of Oahu..	12.5	15.5	16.3	17.7	18.5	21.0	32.6
Other islands...	62.0	57.3	51.7	44.9	39.0	29.4	20.9

[a]Data for Island of Oahu and City of Honolulu include minor outlying islands legally part of the City: 32 in 1940 (all in Palmyra), 14 in 1950 (all on French Frigate Shoals), and 15 in 1960 (all on French Frigate Shoals). Excludes Midway, never part of the Territory or State of Hawaii but sometimes reported with Hawaii for census purposes. Palmyra was detached in 1959.

Table 23.--POPULATION BY DISTRICT: 1900 TO 1960

County and district[a]	1900	1910	1920	1930	1940	1950	1960
Total..........	154,001	191,874	255,881	368,300	422,770	499,794	632,772
Hawaii County.......	46,843	55,382	64,895	73,325	73,276	68,350	61,332
Puna..............	5,128	6,834	7,282	8,284	7,733	6,747	5,030
South Hilo........ } North Hilo........ }	19,785	18,468	23,828	29,572	32,588	34,448	31,553
North Hilo........		4,077	5,644	5,028	4,468	3,505	2,493
Hamakua...........	6,919	9,037	9,122	8,864	8,244	6,056	5,221
North Kohala......	4,366	5,398	6,275	6,171	5,362	4,456	3,386
South Kohala......	600	922	1,304	1,250	1,352	1,505	1,538
North Kona........	3,819	3,377	3,709	4,728	3,924	3,607	4,451
South Kona........	2,372	3,191	3,703	4,677	4,024	3,723	4,292
Kau...............	3,854	4,078	4,028	4,751	5,581	4,303	3,368
Maui County.........	27,920	29,762	37,385	55,541	55,534	48,179	42,576
Hana..............	5,276	3,241	3,100	2,436	2,663	1,495	1,073
Makawao...........	7,236	8,855	10,900	17,021	14,915	12,800	10,409
Wailuku...........	7,953	11,742	14,941	21,363	21,051	19,835	19,391
Lahaina........... } Lanai............. }	4,951	4,787	7,142	7,938	8,291	5,973	4,844
Lanai.............		131	185	2,356	3,720	3,136	2,115
Molokai...........	2,504	1,006	1,117	4,427	4,894	4,940	4,744
Kalawao County......	...	785	667	605	446	340	279
Honolulu County.....	58,504	82,028	123,496	202,887	257,698	353,020	500,409
Honolulu..........	39,306	52,183	81,820	137,582	179,358	248,034	294,194
Koolaupoko........	2,844	3,251	4,035	6,385	9,006	20,779	60,238
Koolauloa.........	2,372	3,204	4,490	5,258	4,968	5,223	8,043
Waialua...........	3,285	6,083	7,641	8,129	8,397	7,906	8,221
Wahiawa...........	...	799	4,302	18,103	22,417	17,363	34,595
Waianae...........	1,008	1,846	1,802	1,923	2,948	7,024	16,452
Ewa...............	9,689	14,627	19,406	25,507	30,602	46,691	78,666
Kauai County........	20,734	23,952	29,438	35,942	35,818	29,905	28,176
Hanalei...........	2,630	2,457	2,549	2,186	2,065	1,619	1,312
Kawaihau..........	3,220	2,580	4,533	7,441	6,512	6,291	6,498
Lihue.............	4,434	4,951	6,223	7,515	7,896	6,760	6,297
Koloa.............	4,564	5,769	7,270	8,452	8,493	7,286	7,012
Waimea............	5,886	8,195	8,863	10,348	10,852	7,949	7,057

[a]Lanai organized from part of Lahaina in 1939. Kalawao reported with Molokai in 1900. Wahiawa organized from parts of Waialua and Waianae in 1913. For other boundary changes, see Robert D. King, "Districts in the Hawaiian Islands," in John Wesley Coulter, comp., _A Gazetteer of the Territory of Hawaii_, pp. 214-230.

Table 24.--POPULATION OF SELECTED URBAN PLACES: 1900 TO 1960

Island and place[a]	1900	1910	1920	1930	1940	1950	1960
Hawaii:							
Hilo[b]...........	...	6,745	10,431	19,468	23,353	27,198	25,966
Maui:							
Paia............	...	...	...	4,171	4,272	3,195	2,149
Puunene.........	...	...	...	...	4,456	6,306	3,054
Kahului.........	...	...	...	2,353	2,193		4,223
Wailuku.........	...	...	...	6,998	7,319	7,424	6,969
Lahaina.........	...	...	...	2,730	5,217	4,025	3,423
Oahu:							
Honolulu[c]........	39,306	52,183	81,820	137,582	179,358	248,034	294,194
Kailua-Lanikai...	...	...	...	...	1,540	7,740	25,622
Kaneohe.........	...	...	...	...	1,762	3,208	14,414
Wahiawa.........	...	...	...	3,370	5,420	8,369	15,512
Waipahu[d]........	...	...	...	5,874	6,906	7,169	...
Aiea............	...	...	...	3,021	3,553	3,714	11,826
Kauai:							
Lihue...........	...	...	...	2,399	4,254	3,870	3,908

[a]All places with a population of 10,000 or more in 1960 or 4,000 or more (5,000 on Oahu) in an earlier census.

[b]Boundaries greatly enlarged in 1941. The 1940 population of the annexed area was 893.

[c]The Honolulu Urbanized Area, first defined in 1960, included Aiea, Pearl City, and Waipahu, and had 351,336 inhabitants.

[d]Not separately reported in 1960.

Table 25.--AGE AND SEX: 1900 TO 1960

Age and sex	1900	1910	1920	1930	1940	1950	1960
Total, all ages.......	154,001	191,909	255,912	368,336	423,330	499,794	632,772
Under 5 years...........	15,084	24,065	38,550	48,180	40,085	63,991	80,962
5 to 14 years...........	19,587	32,592	52,255	85,161	90,925	92,146	136,796
15 to 24 years..........	31,914	33,726	45,408	76,257	99,415	94,264	105,427
25 to 44 years..........	70,220	75,645	78,653	105,152	126,715	158,847	183,092
45 to 64 years..........	13,956	22,587	36,138	45,845	53,121	70,127	97,333
65 years and over.......	2,677	3,238	4,795	7,638	12,914	20,419	29,162
Not reported...........	563	56	113	103	155	...	...
Median age (years)......	26.9	26.4	23.3	22.0	23.2	24.9	24.3
Percent, all ages.....	100.0	100.0	100.0	100.0	100.0	100.0	100.0
Under 5 years...........	9.8	12.5	15.1	13.1	9.5	12.8	12.8
5 to 14 years...........	12.8	17.0	20.4	23.1	21.5	18.4	21.6
15 to 24 years..........	20.8	17.6	17.8	20.7	23.5	18.9	16.7
25 to 44 years..........	45.8	39.4	30.7	28.6	29.9	31.8	28.9
45 to 64 years..........	9.1	11.8	14.1	12.4	12.6	14.0	15.4
65 years and over.......	1.7	1.7	1.9	2.1	3.0	4.1	4.6
Male, all ages........	106,369	123,099	151,146	222,640	245,135	273,895	338,173
Under 15 years..........	17,919	28,921	46,236	67,659	66,472	79,845	111,120
15 to 44 years..........	75,910	74,845	74,674	118,624	138,020	140,675	154,223
45 years and over.......	12,170	19,296	30,157	36,295	40,540	53,375	72,830
Not reported	370	37	79	62	103	...	...
Female, all ages......	47,632	68,810	104,766	145,696	178,195	225,899	294,599
Under 15 years..........	16,752	27,736	44,569	65,682	64,538	76,292	106,638
15 to 44 years..........	26,224	34,526	49,387	62,785	88,110	112,436	134,296
45 years and over.......	4,463	6,529	10,776	17,188	25,495	37,171	53,665
Not reported...........	193	19	34	41	52	...	...
Sex ratio, all ages...	223.3	178.9	144.3	152.8	137.6	121.2	114.8
Under 15 years..........	107.0	104.3	103.7	103.0	103.0	104.7	104.2
15 to 44 years..........	289.5	216.8	151.2	188.9	156.6	125.1	114.8
45 years and over.......	272.7	295.5	279.9	211.2	159.0	143.6	135.7

Table 26.--ETHNIC STOCK: 1900 TO 1960

Ethnic stock	1900[a]	1910	1920	1930	1940	1950	1960[b]
Total..........	154,001	191,909	255,912	368,336	423,330	499,769	632,772
Hawaiian...........	29,799	26,041	23,723	22,636	14,375	12,245	11,294
Part Hawaiian.......	7,857	12,506	18,027	28,224	49,935	73,845	91,109
Caucasian...........	28,819	44,048	54,742	80,373	112,087	124,344	202,230
Puerto Rican......	...	4,890	5,602	6,671	8,296	9,551	...
Spanish...........	...	1,990	2,430	1,219			
Portuguese........	...	22,301	27,002	27,588	103,791	114,793	...
Other Caucasian...	...	14,867	19,708	44,895			
Chinese............	25,767	21,674	23,507	27,179	28,774	32,376	38,197
Filipino...........	...	2,361	21,031	63,052	52,569	61,062	69,070
Korean.............	...	4,533	4,950	6,461	6,851	7,030	...
Japanese...........	61,111	79,675	109,274	139,631	157,905	184,598	203,455
Negro..............	233	695	348	563	255	2,651	4,943
Other groups........	415	376	310	217	579	1,618	12,474
Percent Distribution							
Total..........	100.0	100.0	100.0	100.0	100.0	100.0	100.0
Hawaiian...........	19.3	13.6	9.3	6.1	3.4	2.5	1.8
Part Hawaiian.......	5.1	6.5	7.0	7.7	11.8	14.8	14.4
Caucasian...........	18.7	23.0	21.4	21.8	26.5	24.9	32.0
Puerto Rican......	...	2.5	2.2	1.8	2.0	1.9	...
Spanish...........	...	1.0	0.9	0.3			
Portuguese........	...	11.6	10.6	7.5	24.5	23.0	...
Other Caucasian...	...	7.7	7.7	12.2			
Chinese............	16.7	11.3	9.2	7.4	6.8	6.5	6.0
Filipino...........	...	1.2	8.2	17.1	12.4	12.2	10.9
Korean.............	...	2.4	1.9	1.8	1.6	1.4	...
Japanese...........	39.7	41.5	42.7	37.9	37.3	36.9	32.2
Negro..............	0.2	0.4	0.1	0.2	0.1	0.5	0.8
Other races.........	0.3	0.2	0.1	0.1	0.1	0.3	2.0

[a]The 1900 Census apparently misclassified many part Hawaiians and used ethnic categories not entirely consistent with those of the 1910-1930 enumerations. Romanzo Adams made two separate efforts to adjust these data (see his The Peoples of Hawaii, p. 9 and Interracial Marriage in Hawaii, p. 8).

[b]A second tabulation of 1960 race statistics, using a different procedure for allocating nonresponse, resulted in significantly different totals for some groups, particularly the Hawaiians (see HDPED, SR 9 [Dec. 26, 1963]). The DPED report also discusses the composition of the large residual category (consisting of Koreans, Samoans, and other small groups) and the treatment of the Puerto Rican population.

Table 27.--PLACE OF BIRTH: 1900 TO 1960

Place of birth	1900	1910	1920	1930	1940	1950	1960
Total	154,001	191,909	255,912	368,336	423,330	499,794	632,772
Native	63,221	98,157	168,671	299,799	370,717	423,174	563,872
Hawaii	58,931	86,483	136,349	214,517	278,506	355,574	421,168
Other State	4,284	5,688	10,957	30,191	54,224	65,640	128,992
State not reported	...	...	...	...	...	...	8,750
Outlying area[a]	6	5,986	21,365	55,091	37,987	1,960	4,962
Foreign[b]	90,780	93,752	87,241	68,537	52,613	76,620	68,900
Portugal	6,512	7,585	5,794	3,713	2,397	1,508	764
Other Europe	3,570	5,622	4,894	4,539	4,309	3,560	4,629
China	21,741	14,486	11,164	7,477	4,868	3,625	3,541
Japan	56,234	59,800	60,690	48,425	37,362	30,808	24,658
Philippines[b]	...	...	...	...	...	33,832	28,649
Korea	...	4,172	3,498	2,977	2,454	1,772	1,124
All other and not rptd	2,723	2,087	1,201	1,406	1,223	1,515	5,545
Percent Distribution							
Total	100.0	100.0	100.0	100.0	100.0	100.0	100.0
Native	41.1	51.1	65.9	81.4	87.6	84.7	89.1
Hawaii	38.3	45.1	53.3	58.2	65.8	71.1	66.6
Other State	2.8	3.0	4.3	8.2	12.8	13.1	20.4
Other, not rptd[a]	...	3.1	8.3	15.0	9.0	0.4	2.2
Foreign[b]	58.9	48.9	34.1	18.6	12.4	15.3	10.9

[a]Includes persons born at sea or abroad of American parents. Prior to 1960, includes persons born in Alaska. Prior to 1950, includes persons born in the Philippines: 2,372 in 1910, 18,728 in 1920, 52,672 in 1930, and 35,778 in 1940.

[b]Philippines included with native population prior to 1950.

Table 28.--HAWAII-BORN PERSONS IN OTHER STATES: 1850 TO 1960

Year	Number	Year	Number	Year	Number
1850...	588	1890...	1,304	1930...	19,457
1860...	435	1900...	1,307	1940...	23,723
1870...	584	1910...	3,741	1950...	51,955
1880...	1,147	1920...	10,551	1960...	115,070

Table 29.--PLACE OF RESIDENCE FIVE YEARS PRIOR TO CENSUS DATE: 1950 AND 1960

Subject	1950	1960
Population 5 years old and over..........	435,135	551,781
Living in same house as 5 years earlier...	202,100	240,895
Percent................................	46.4	43.7
In-migrants from other States[a]...........	...	94,768
Out-migrants to other States[b]............	...	84,740

[a]Residents of Hawaii on census date who lived in another State 5 years earlier.

[b]Residents of other States on census date who lived in Hawaii 5 years earlier. Mainland residents, one year old and over, enumerated in 1950 and living in Hawaii one year earlier numbered 26,460.

Table 30.--MARITAL STATUS: 1900 TO 1960

Subject	Persons 15 years of age or over				Persons 14 years of age or over		
	1900	1910	1920	1930	1940	1950	1960
Males, total.......	88,450	94,178	104,910	154,981	183,448	197,874	232,805
Single..........	52,800	46,443	45,874	79,092	102,913	81,917	84,965
Married.........	32,464	42,491	52,977	68,187	71,715	103,475	134,421
Percent........	36.7	45.1	50.5	44.0	39.1	52.3	57.7
Widowed.........	2,493	4,278	5,011	6,030	6,211	7,352	7,075
Divorced........	247	912	956	1,622	2,609	5,130	6,344
Not reported.....	446	54	92	50	...	...	...
Females, total.....	30,880	41,074	60,197	80,014	118,238	153,515	193,684
Single..........	4,655	6,744	10,721	19,602	40,733	43,445	44,376
Married.........	24,048	31,380	45,550	53,948	66,569	94,520	128,528
Percent........	77.9	76.4	75.7	67.4	56.3	61.6	66.4
Widowed.........	1,998	2,559	3,479	5,523	8,819	11,736	15,099
Divorced........	120	364	416	934	2,117	3,814	5,681
Not reported.....	59	27	31	7	...	...	...
Single, widowed, or divorced: males per 100 females..	820.0	534.1	354.7	332.9	216.2	160.0	151.0

Table 31.--HOUSEHOLDS, FAMILIES, AND MARRIED COUPLES: 1900 TO 1960

Subject	1900	1910	1920	1930	1940	1950	1960
Households and group quarters[a]	36,922	52,219	65,670	77,070	...	...	...
Households[b]	29,763	...	...	...	86,855	111,858	153,064
Group quarters[c]	7,159	...	...	...	...	...	...
Population	154,001	191,909	255,912	368,336	423,330	499,794	632,772
Per household[d]	4.17	3.68	3.90	4.78	4.87	4.47	4.13
Pop. in households	110,306	...	...	...	...	463,230	592,807
Per household	3.71	...	...	...	...	4.14	3.87
Pop. in group quarters	43,695	...	...	...	...	36,564	39,965
Families	...	...	...	...	...	96,460	130,871
Unrelated individuals	...	...	...	...	...	57,230	67,996
Married couples	...	...	...	...	...	90,844	120,192

[a]"Families" before 1940.

[b]"Private families" before 1940.

[c]"Families not private" before 1940.

[d]Based on number of "families" (households and group quarters) before 1940.

Table 32.--SCHOOL ATTENDANCE, YEARS OF SCHOOL COMPLETED, ILLITERACY, AND ABILITY TO SPEAK ENGLISH: 1900 TO 1960

Subject	1900	1910	1920	1930	1940	1950	1960
School Attendance							
Persons 5 to 20 years old	33,774	49,875	77,662	127,354	150,596	146,815	204,150
Number attending school	15,284	28,695	48,825	82,428	109,009	113,140	170,890
Percent attending school	45.3	57.5	62.9	64.7	72.4	77.1	83.7
Years of School Completed[a]							
Median years completed	...	...	...	...	6.9	8.7	11.3
Illiteracy[b]							
Persons 15 years old and over[c]	119,330	135,252	165,107	234,995	...	...	426,489
Number illiterate	41,949	39,465	35,083	41,018	...	...	21,000
Percent illiterate	35.2	29.2	21.2	17.5	...	8.4	5.0
Ability to Speak English							
Persons 10 years old and over	127,768	148,789	187,167	273,037	...	...	...
Number unable to speak English	68,017	84,177	69,493	66,822	...	...	...
Percent unable to speak English	53.2	56.6	37.1	24.5	...	...	...

[a]For persons 25 years old and over.

[b]Not directly covered in censuses after 1930; data for 1950 and 1960 are estimates, reported in the USBC, Current Population Reports, Series P-23, No. 8 (Feb.12, 1963).

[c]Persons 14 years old and over for 1940 to 1960. Includes persons not reporting age for 1900 to 1930.

Table 33.--FERTILITY RATIO AND COMPLETED FERTILITY RATE: 1900 TO 1960

Subject	1900	1910	1920	1930	1940	1950	1960
Fertility Ratio							
Women 15 to 44 years old.........	26,224	34,526	49,387	62,785	88,110	112,436	134,296
Children under 5 years old.......	15,084	24,065	38,550	48,180	40,085	63,991	80,962
Per 1,000 women 15 to 44.......	575	697	781	767	455	569	603
Completed Fertility Rate							
Women 45 years old and over......	...	...	...	...	...	37,620	54,476
Ever married..................	...	...	...	...	...	36,045	51,848
Children ever born...............	...	...	...	...	...	164,370	213,616
Per 1,000 women...............	...	...	...	...	...	4,566	3,921
Per 1,000 women ever married...	...	...	...	...	...	4,775	4,120

Table 34.--GAINFULLY EMPLOYED, 1900 TO 1930, AND LABOR FORCE, 1940 TO 1960

Subject	1900[a]	1910	1920	1930	1940	1950	1960
Employment Status							
Both sexes, 14 and over......	121,044	137,727	169,164	241,782	301,686	351,375	426,495
Labor force[b]...............	90,172	100,900	111,613	154,086	188,232	207,952	265,707
Percent..................	74.5	73.3	66.0	63.7	62.4	59.2	62.3
Armed forces.............	245	1,608	4,366	16,291	27,000	22,856	47,267
Civilian employment[c]......	89,927	99,292	107,247	137,795	153,796	167,571	209,370
Unemployed[c]..............	...	...	...	...	7,436	17,525	9,070
Pct. of civ. lab. force..	...	...	...	...	4.6	9.5	4.2
Not in labor force.........	30,872	36,827	57,551	87,696	113,454	143,423	160,788
Males, 14 and over...........	89,369	95,477	107,026	158,381	183,448	197,864	231,707
Labor force[b]..............	84,047	89,719	97,439	136,400	151,648	157,088	188,071
Percent..................	94.0	94.0	91.0	86.1	82.7	79.4	81.2
Not in labor force.........	5,322	5,758	9,587	21,981	31,800	40,776	43,636
Females, 14 and over.........	31,675	42,250	62,138	83,401	118,238	153,511	194,788
Labor force[b]..............	6,125	11,181	14,174	17,686	36,584	50,864	77,636
Percent..................	19.3	26.5	22.8	21.2	30.9	33.1	39.9
Not in labor force.........	25,550	31,069	47,964	65,715	81,654	102,647	117,152
Industry							
Civilian employment[c].........	89,927	99,292	107,247	137,795	153,796	167,571	209,370
Agriculture[d]...............	57,125	56,122	56,087	63,478	54,629	31,806	15,982
Percent..................	63.5	56.5	52.3	46.1	35.5	19.0	7.6
Other industries...........	32,802	43,170	51,160	74,317	99,167	135,765	193,388
Occupation							
Civilian employment..........	...	...	...	...	153,796	167,571	209,370
Professional, technical....	...	...	...	...	11,289	16,408	25,299
Managers, officials, prop..	...	...	...	...	10,762	13,967	17,795
Other occupations..........	...	...	...	...	131,745	137,196	166,276
Percent..................	...	...	...	...	85.7	81.9	79.4
Class of Worker							
Civilian employment..........	...	...	...	...	153,796	167,571	209,370
Private wage, salary.......	...	...	...	...	113,551	111,036	144,602
Government.................	...	...	...	...	18,553	34,400	46,078
Self-employed..............	...	...	...	...	15,967	19,192	17,009
Unpaid family workers......	...	...	...	...	5,725	2,943	1,601

[a]Data on labor force and industry include a small number of gainful workers 10 to 13 years old.

[b]"Gainful workers" before 1940.

[c]Unemployed members of the experienced labor force included with civilian employment prior to 1940.

[d]Includes forestry and fisheries.

Table 35.--INCOME: 1940 TO 1960

Group	Median income (in dollars) during the preceding year		
	1940	1950	1960
Experienced labor force, both sexes[a]...	642	2,356	...
Male..............................	659	2,504	4,353
Female............................	520	1,772	2,407
Families and unrelated individuals.....	...	2,728	4,710
Families..........................	...	3,568	6,366
Unrelated individuals...............	...	1,583	1,998

[a]Persons 14 years old and over. Data for 1940 and 1950 refer to wage or salary income of all members of the experienced labor force (including armed forces) reporting wages or salary of $100 or more. Data for 1960 refer to earnings of members of the experienced civilian labor force (excluding armed forces) reporting any earnings.

Table 36.--HOUSING: 1900 TO 1960

Subject	1900	1910	1920	1930	1940	1950	1960
All Housing Units[a]							
All units	...	...	...	...	90,830	120,606	165,506
Vacant	...	...	...	...	3,975	8,316	12,442
Percent in 1-unit structures	...	...	...	...	78.9	71.9	74.2
Median number of rooms in unit	...	...	...	...	4.2	...	4.5
Percent needing major repairs	...	...	...	...	15.5	...	...
Percent dilapidated	...	...	...	...	...	13.0	8.7
Percent with flush toilet	...	...	...	...	63.2	80.4	93.8
Exclusive use	...	...	...	...	...	78.1	89.9
Percent with bathtub or shower	...	...	...	...	63.1	83.1	96.0
Exclusive use	...	...	...	...	...	80.6	91.3
Occupied Housing Units[a]							
All occupied units	29,763	52,219	65,670	77,070	86,855	112,290	153,064
Oahu	10,325	20,377	28,657	39,563	51,554	77,893	117,856
Other islands	19,438	31,842	37,013	37,507	35,301	34,397	35,208
Median number of occupants	...	...	...	...	4.0	3.8	3.7
Over 1.00 person per room	...	...	...	...	33,291	34,364	39,331
Percent	...	...	...	...	38.4	30.8	25.7
Owner occupied units	6,321	6,776	8,695	14,624	22,030	37,025	62,937
Percent of all occ. units	23.1	13.1	13.4	19.1	25.4	33.0	41.1
Median value ($)[b]	...	...	...	...	2,540	12,283	20,900
Renter occupied units	21,086	44,900	56,386	61,807	64,825	75,265	90,127
Median contract rent ($)	...	...	...	...	17	32	64
Tenure not reported	2,356	543	589	639	...	...	...

[a]"Private families" in 1900, "families" in 1910-1930, "dwelling units" in 1940 and 1950, and "housing units" in 1960. Data for 1910-1930 include group quarters.

[b]Data for 1950 exclude units on leased land.

V. POSTCENSAL ESTIMATES AND SURVEYS: 1960-1965

The five-year period following the 1960 U. S. Census was one of rapid growth for Hawaii, covered in considerable detail by official statistics. Although Oahu continued to account for most of the added population, several of the Neighbor Islands apparently halted their downward trend. There was a pronounced net in-migration. After more than sixty years as the largest ethnic group, the Japanese relinquished first place to the Caucasians. Aliens living in the Islands continued to decline. Both school attendance and the civilian labor force increased rapidly. Statistics on these postcensal trends were developed by a number of Federal, State, and County agencies, using official registration systems, sample surveys, symptomatic data, and other sources for their estimates.

Number and distribution of inhabitants

Postcensal population estimates, issued by the United States Bureau of the Census, United States Office of Business Economics, Hawaii State Department of Health, and Hawaii State Department of Planning and Economic Development, differ in coverage, methodology, and results.

Estimates of the resident population, total and civilian, are prepared annually by the Bureau of the Census. Definitions are similar to those used in the decennial population censuses taken by the same agency. The total population includes all civilians whose usual place of residence is in Hawaii, all members of the armed forces stationed ashore in Hawaii, and crews of ships in Hawaii ports on the estimate date. The civilian figure excludes armed forces but includes their dependents domiciled in the Islands. Estimates refer to July 1. Totals have been prepared separately for the Honolulu Standard Metropolitan Statistical Area (that is, Oahu); otherwise, no geographic breakdowns are shown.

The census bureau estimates are developed by averaging the results of the Component Method II and the Regression Method. The Component Method II involves (1) subtracting armed forces from the 1960 Census count to obtain the civilian population as of April 1, 1960, (2) adding to this civilian population the number of postcensal births, (3) subtracting postcensal civilian deaths, (4) adding an estimate of net civilian migration, (5) adding or subtracting the net movement of civilians into or out of the armed forces, and (6) adding an estimate of the number of persons in the armed forces stationed in the area on the estimate date. Net civilian migration is estimated in turn by averaging the figure based on passenger arrivals and departures ("smoothed" to minimize seasonality) with one derived by comparing postcensal school enrollment with the enrollment expected on the basis of 1960 Census data. The Regression Method (first described and tested by the present author) uses a multiple regression equation, computed from 1950-1960 data, relating postcensal population changes to corresponding changes in various symptomatic series. Both methodology and findings are presented in reports issued from time to time by the Bureau of the Census.[1]

Estimates of total resident population are prepared annually by the U. S. Office of Business Economics as a basis for computation of per capita personal income estimates for the State. These estimates include the mid-year civilian population estimated by the Bureau of the Census, plus a monthly or quarterly average of the number of military personnel stationed in Hawaii. The latter figure includes Naval personnel assigned to shore stations plus persons assigned to fleet units but temporarily stationed ashore for duty; it excludes crews of ships berthed in Hawaii ports if the crews are not stationed ashore. As noted earlier, the latter group is included in the census bureau estimates. The OBE population estimates were routinely reported in their publications some years ago but have been omitted in more recent studies. These estimates are available on request, however, and appear periodically in publications of the State Department of Planning and Economic Development.[2] Detailed statements of OBE methods and definitions have been quoted by the Honolulu Redevelopment Agency.[3]

De facto civilian population is estimated semi-annually, as of January 1 and July 1, by the Research, Planning and Statistics Office of the Hawaii State Department of Health. These estimates include visitors present but exclude residents temporarily absent; in this respect they differ significantly from those of the Census Bureau, OBE, and State Department of Planning and Economic Development estimates, all of which purport to show population by place of usual residence. The Health Department estimates are computed by adjusting 1960 census totals to a de facto basis (from data developed by the Hawaii Visitors Bureau and the Department of Planning and Economic Development), adding births, subtracting deaths, subtracting military inductions, adding separations, and adding or subtracting net civilian passenger movement. The latter figure is based on monthly passenger reports from each air and surface carrier, private and governmental, and records and reports of the State Department of Transportation and the Plant Quarantine Branch of the State Department of Agriculture. Semi-annual estimates are published for each county and island and for the cities of Hilo and Honolulu.[4] Estimates based on building permit data have been published for each of the 113 Oahu census tracts as of July 1, 1963, 1964, and 1965, and for census tracts and judicial districts in Hawaii County as of July 1, 1965.[5]

The Hawaii State Department of Planning and Economic Development prepares semi-annual estimates of resident population, total and civilian, for each county and island and for the cities of Hilo and Honolulu. For these estimates, DPED accepts the de facto civilian figures issued by the Department of Health, which it adjusts for the number of visitors present and residents temporarily absent. These adjustments are derived from results of a 20 percent sample survey, conducted by the Hawaii Visitors Bureau, of all passengers arriving aboard westbound civilian carriers. Finally, DPED adds the number of military personnel reported to the department semi-annually by local commanding officers. The latter count, it should be stressed, includes Navy and Coast Guard crews homeported in Hawaii, regardless of physical location on the estimate date, but excludes ships' crews from other areas temporarily in Hawaii waters. The DPED estimates are published annually as of January 1 and July 1.[6]

As might be expected, these series differ widely. The civilian population is treated on a de facto basis in one series but on a usual residence basis in the other three. Out of three agencies that include the armed forces, one classifies ships' crews by physical location, a second by home port, and the third omits them altogether. Even where two agencies attempt to measure the same phenomenon--the Census Bureau and DPED estimates of resident civilian population--important differences occur, largely because of different methods and sources.

Among Island statisticians, the Health Department estimates have won the widest acceptance by virtue of their conceptual clarity, straightforward methodology, accurate bases, and long establishment. Persons interested in population on a residence basis usually turn to the DPED series which, of course, is derived from the Health Department de facto figures. Sometimes the DPED data on armed forces are wedded to the Health Department civilian estimates. Although the OBE totals on armed forces are often quoted in local research studies, the Census Bureau civilian estimate used by OBE finds little favor in Island statistical work. Objections center on the lack of geographic detail, the indirect basis for estimating the migration component, failure to adjust adequately for the difference between de facto and resident population, and unreasonably low totals. The census treatment of ships' crews results in rapidly shifting armed forces figures, in contrast to the greater stability of the conceptually more meaningful OBE and DPED data.

The various series of postcensal estimates are compared in Table 37.[7] Differences were especially evident in 1962, when totals on armed forces ranged from 48,000 (according to OBE) through 59,702 (DPED) to 79,000 (U. S. Census). Additional detail appears in Tables 38 and 39.

Components of change

The components of population change include births, deaths, military inductions and separations, and net migration.

Postcensal estimates on components of change are published from time to time by the U. S. Bureau of the Census.[8] These estimates underlie the bureau's estimates of total and civilian resident population, described above; consequently, they share the same strengths and weaknesses.

More detailed information on components of change is available from the State Department of Health. These figures are on a de facto rather than residence basis. Unlike the census bureau data, they are prepared for semi-annual periods and small geographic areas. They have been published in a variety of reports and releases.

Further refinements are incorporated into estimates on components of change issued by the Department of Planning and Economic Development. The DPED estimates adjust the Health Department data to a residence basis and present separate figures for the armed forces, military dependents, and civilians other than military dependents. In-, out-, and net migration are estimated separately for the latter group. Data for 1960-1965 appear in Table 40.

Composition of the population

Postcensal data on age, sex, race and race mixture, citizenship, households, mobility, school enrollment, labor force status, place of work, family income, and religion are available.

Statistics on age are published by both the U. S. Bureau of the Census and the Hawaii State Department of Health. The census estimates are obtained by carrying forward 1960 census data for each age group and allowing for births, deaths, and net migration between April 1, 1960 and the estimate date. Net migration is inferred from school enrollment trends and nationwide sample data on interstate migration by age. Published results for five broad age groups are shown as of July 1.[9] The Health Department estimates, in contrast, are based on a probability sample (the Hawaii Health Surveillance Program survey, described below), are limited to Oahu, show data for six broad age groups, and refer to a span of months rather than a single point in time. The Bureau of the Census estimates are given in Table 41; those by the State Department of Health, in Table 42.

Population by sex is likewise estimated by the Health Department, based on findings of the Health Surveillance Program survey. These estimates, like the corresponding data on age, are affected by omission of persons in barracks and institutions. Consequently, they greatly understate the proportion of males in the population. Findings are cited in Table 42.

The Hawaii Health Surveillance Program survey, source of the Health Department estimates described above, is a three-year study designed to obtain information on health conditions and associated social, demographic, and economic variables. About 9,000 persons living in households and group quarters other than barracks and institutions are interviewed annually. Methodological notes and selected findings have appeared in various reports of the Department of Health.[10] In addition, special tabulations have been prepared by the department for the Honolulu Redevelopment Agency and State Department of Planning and Economic Development and have appeared in publications of those agencies.[11]

Postcensal data on race or ethnic stock have been published by the State Department of Health, the State Department of Planning and Economic Development, and the Honolulu Redevelopment Agency. The greatest detail is given by the Health Department series, which reports data for eight different groups (plus a residual "all other" category) and various combinations of these groups. These estimates, based on the Health Surveillance Program survey and hence limited to Oahu, are summarized in Table 43. The Department of Planning and Economic Development has published statewide estimates for seven groups (plus "all others"), total and civilian, based on the 1960 Census, postcensal births and deaths, and assumed migration levels.[12] The Honolulu Redevelopment Agency has published data on ethnic stock of Oahu household heads, tabulated from the "consumer analysis" sample survey of the Hawaii Newspaper Agency.[13]

Aliens living in each State are registered each January by the Immigration and Naturalization Service of the U. S. Department of Justice. Totals by nationality (and sometimes by county or other geographic unit) are issued as press releases or brief tabular summaries. These data, as well as previously unpublished counts by postal location, have been compiled periodically in reports of the Department of Planning and Economic Development.[14] Trends since 1940 are summarized in Table 44.

The Honolulu Redevelopment Agency has been responsible for numerous statistics on households and housing. The agency publishes annual estimates of the housing inventory, by control and by county, based on 1960 Census counts, building and demolition permits, and information supplied by government agencies operating housing.[15] These totals are sometimes used to derive estimates of the number of occupied units or households (see Table 45). Statistics on the characteristics of households and occupied housing units have been obtained from the "consumer analysis" conducted by the Hawaii Newspaper Agency and reported by HRA in considerable detail (see Table 46).

The "consumer analysis" is a sample survey primarily intended to obtain information on brand preferences. Many of the statistics from this survey have been analyzed and published by the Redevelopment Agency. Limited at first to Honolulu proper, the study was extended after 1957 to the entire island of Oahu, and on one occasion included the island of Hawaii. Data have been obtained on geographic distribution, military status, household size (usually overstated), family income, and a number of demographic and economic characteristics of the head of the household, such as age, race, place of birth, mobility, occupation, and place of work. Various characteristics of occupied housing units have similarly been covered. Temporarily suspended after October 1962, the survey was resumed, on a somewhat different basis, in July 1965.

Statistics on school enrollment, both public and private, are maintained and published annually by the State Department of Education. Trends since 1954-1955 are traced in Table 47.

Information on religious membership is hard to find. One source is the sample survey of drinking behavior made by the University of Hawaii Economic Research Center for the Honolulu Liquor Commission. In this survey, 2,106 Oahu adults were asked about their religion as well as their drinking habits.

Findings, disputed by several local authorities, are cited in Table 48.

Monthly labor force estimates are prepared and published by the Hawaii State Department of Labor and Industrial Relations. These estimates are derived from data on workers covered by the Hawaii Employment Security Law, unemployment compensation reports, 1960 census statistics, and other sources. Estimates of civilian employment by industry and total unemployment are shown for each county. These data are issued in the form of brief mimeographed releases. Trends since 1958, based on these estimates, are traced in Table 49. An annual report, largely limited to workers under the Employment Security Law, presents wage data by industrial classification.[16] In 1964 the department obtained information from employers on covered employment by census tract or judicial district.[17]

Family income statistics since 1960 have been compiled by several agencies. The U. S. Bureau of Labor Statistics conducted a survey of consumer expenditures and income in Honolulu and environs for the year 1961.[18] Family income statistics collected by the State Department of Health as part of its Health Surveillance Program have been published by the Hawaii Department of Planning and Economic Development.[19] The Hawaii Newspaper Agency has published household income data based on its "consumer analysis."[20] These sources differ significantly in coverage, methodology, and findings, and none, apparently, provides data directly comparable to 1960 census results.

Table 37.--ALTERNATIVE POPULATION ESTIMATES: JULY 1, 1960 TO 1965

Year (July 1)	U. S. Bureau of the Census[a]		U. S. Office of Business Economics: Total[b]	Hawaii Dept. of Health: Civilian[c]	Hawaii Dept. of Planning & Ec. Dev.[d]	
	Total	Civilian			Total	Civilian
1960....	641,000	582,000	624,000	595,024	634,703	581,231
1961....	658,000	597,000	643,000	612,673	655,332	598,984
1962....	695,000	616,000	662,000	635,888	682,682	622,980
1963....	685,000	625,000	671,000	655,546	697,651	640,558
1964....	712,000	639,000	689,000	674,951	720,741	660,901
1965....	710,000	657,000	705,000	702,030	744,756	688,643

[a]Resident basis. Total population includes crews of Navy and Coast Guard ships in Hawaii ports on the estimate date.

[b]Resident basis. Total population excludes crews of Navy and Coast Guard ships unless temporarily stationed ashore. The Office of Business Economics civilian population estimate is the same as that used by the Bureau of the Census.

[c]De facto basis. Includes visitors present but excludes residents absent.

[d]Resident basis. Total population includes crews of Navy and Coast Guard ships homeported in Hawaii. This report uses the Hawaii Department of Health estimates of de facto population.

Source: USBC, Current Population Reports, Series P-25, No. 348 (Sept. 16, 1966); U. S. Office of Business Economics, Survey of Current Business (Aug. 1966), pp. 12 and 13 (computed); HDH, mimeographed releases; HDPED, SR 44 (Oct. 21, 1966).

Table 38.--RESIDENCE AND MILITARY STATUS: 1964 AND 1965

Category	Jan. 1, 1964	July 1, 1964	Jan. 1, 1965	July 1, 1965[a]
Total resident population...	713,997	720,741	743,734	745,110
Civilian population............	654,371	660,901	680,898	688,997
Military dependents..........	65,976	69,090	72,812	65,816
Other civilians..............	588,395	591,811	608,086	623,181
Armed forces...................	59,626	59,840	62,836	56,113
Stationed ashore.............	48,242	47,959	48,227	42,960
Homeported Hawaii............	11,384	11,881	14,609	13,153
De facto civilian population....	670,959	674,951	695,458	702,030
Visitors present.............	22,597	25,153	22,167	26,271
Residents absent.............	6,009	11,103	7,607	13,238

[a]Preliminary. Revised total is 744,756 (see HDPED, SR 44 [Oct. 21, 1966], Table 2).

Table 39.--RESIDENT AND DE FACTO POPULATION, BY GEOGRAPHIC AREA:

APRIL 1, 1965

Geographic area	Resident population[a]	De facto civilian population[b]	Percent increase, 1960-65	
			Resident population[a]	De facto population[b]
Total	746,650	694,110	18.0	17.6
Hawaii County	58,385	58,479	-4.8	-4.4
City of Hilo	24,884	24,826	-4.2	-4.4
Remainder of county	33,501	33,653	-5.3	-4.5
Honolulu County[c]	617,774	564,223	23.5	23.1
City of Honolulu[c]	347,550	339,140	18.1	14.9
Remainder of county	270,224	225,083	31.0	38.0
Kalawao County	224	222	-19.7	-20.4
Kauai County	25,992	26,319	-7.8	-6.1
Island of Kauai	25,715	26,042	-7.9	-6.3
Island of Niihau	277	277	9.1	9.1
Maui County	44,275	44,867	4.0	5.5
Island of Kahoolawe[d]	75	...	...	...
Island of Lanai	2,713	2,712	28.3	28.2
Island of Maui	36,024	36,700	0.9	2.8
Island of Molokai (exc. Kalawao)	5,463	5,455	15.2	15.4

[a]Includes armed forces. For minor revisions, see HDPED, SR 44 (Oct. 21, 1966), Table 2.

[b]Excludes armed forces.

[c]Includes outlying islands legally part of the City of Honolulu (42 armed forces and no civilians).

[d]Uninhabited in 1960.

Table 40.--COMPONENTS OF CHANGE IN THE RESIDENT POPULATION: APRIL 1, 1960 TO 1965

Military status	Net change	Live births	Deaths	Net migration[a]
Total population....	109,819	87,837	18,003	39,985
Armed forces..........	3,455	...	312	3,767
Military dependents...	10,399	25,048	796	-13,853
Other civilians[b]......	95,965	62,789	16,895	50,071

[a]Includes net movement between military and civilian populations (separations less inductions).

[b]Migration estimate includes approximately 66,677 in-migrants (55,895 from North America, 10,782 from Asia, Australia, and the South Pacific) and 16,606 out-migrants.

Source of Tables 38-40: HDPED, SR 31 (June 21, 1965), Tables 1, 2, 8, 9, and SR 37 (Nov. 19, 1965), Tables 2, 3, 4, 5.

Table 41.--POPULATION BY AGE: APRIL 1, 1960 AND JULY 1, 1965

Age	Number		Percent distribution		Percent increase, 1960-65
	1965	1960	1965	1960	
All ages[a].......	710,000	632,772	100.0	100.0	12.2
Under 5 years.......	86,000	80,962	12.1	12.8	6.2
5 to 17 years.......	197,000	169,951	27.7	26.9	15.9
18 to 44 years......	274,000	255,364	38.6	40.4	7.3
45 to 64 years......	116,000	97,333	16.3	15.4	19.2
65 years and over...	36,000	29,162	5.1	4.6	23.4
14 years and over...	481,000	426,489	67.7	67.4	12.8
18 years and over...	427,000	381,859	60.1	60.3	11.8
21 years and over...	382,000	348,330	53.8	55.0	9.7

Total for 1965 estimated by State agencies was 744,756.

Source: USBC, "Estimates of the Population of States, by Age: July 1, 1965, With Provisional Estimates for July 1, 1966," Current Population Reports, Population Estimates, Series P-25, No. 354 (Dec. 8, 1966).

Table 42.--AGE AND SEX, BY MILITARY STATUS OF HOUSEHOLD, FOR OAHU: APRIL 1964 TO MARCH 1965

Kind of household[a] and sex of household members	Population	Age, in years (percent distribution)						
		All ages	Under 6	6 to 16	17 to 24	25 to 44	45 to 64	65 and over
All Households[b]								
Both sexes...	560,996	100.0	15.1	25.1	12.8	27.6	15.1	4.4
Male...............	277,422	100.0	15.0	25.3	12.4	26.7	16.4	4.2
Female.............	283,574	100.0	15.2	24.8	13.1	28.5	13.9	4.5
Military Households								
Both sexes...	94,406	100.0	24.4	23.0	15.3	34.6	2.4	0.3
Male...............	48,083	100.0	24.9	22.5	12.9	37.1	2.5	0.1
Female.............	46,323	100.0	23.9	23.6	17.8	32.0	2.3	0.4
Civilian Households								
Both sexes...	466,590	100.0	13.5	25.4	12.3	26.4	17.3	5.1
Male...............	229,339	100.0	13.2	25.8	12.3	24.8	18.9	5.0
Female.............	237,251	100.0	13.7	25.0	12.4	27.9	15.8	5.2

[a]By military status of household head. Excludes barracks and institutions but includes other group quarters.

[b]Age distribution computed from combined samples not weighted for different sampling intervals (60.4 for civilian households and 70.4 for military households).

Source: HDH, Health Surveillance Program sample survey of 9,066 persons (683 males and 658 females in military households, 3,797 males and 3,928 females in civilian households).

Table 43.--ETHNIC STOCK, BY MILITARY STATUS OF HOUSEHOLD HEAD, FOR OAHU: APRIL 1964 TO MARCH 1965

(Excludes persons in barracks and institutions. Household classification based on military status of head)

Ethnic stock	Percent distribution			Percent military
	All persons	In civilian households	In military households	
All races	100.0	100.0	100.0	14.8
Unmixed	73.7	71.5	86.7	17.4
Japanese	29.3	34.0	2.5	1.3
Portuguese	3.2	3.7	0.1	0.7
Other Caucasian	24.2	14.8	78.2	47.9
Hawaiian	1.1	1.2	0.2	3.0
Puerto Rican	0.6	0.7	...	0.0
Filipino	7.2	8.2	1.9	3.8
Chinese	6.5	7.5	0.4	1.0
Samoan	0.4	0.4	0.7	22.5
All other	1.2	1.0	2.5	31.5
Mixed, two strains[a]	13.1	13.9	8.8	9.9
Japanese	2.6	2.8	1.6	8.9
Portuguese	2.4	2.8	0.5	3.2
Other Caucasian	6.9	6.9	6.6	14.3
Hawaiian	6.5	7.3	2.4	5.4
Puerto Rican	0.6	0.7	0.2	5.2
Filipino	2.0	2.0	1.9	13.7
Chinese	3.8	4.2	1.6	6.0
Samoan	0.0	0.1	...	(b)
All other	1.3	1.0	2.8	33.0
Mixed, more than two strains	13.1	14.6	4.3	4.8
Part Hawaiian	11.5	12.9	3.2	4.1
Non-Hawaiian	1.6	1.7	1.0	9.7
Race not reported	0.1	0.1	0.3	(b)

[a]Adds to twice the indicated total because each race is represented twice.

[b]Base is too small to show a meaningful percentage.

Source: HDH, Health Surveillance Program sample survey of 9,065 persons.

Table 44.--ALIEN ADDRESS REPORTS RECEIVED: 1940 TO 1965

Year	Aliens	Year	Aliens
1940[a].........	91,447	1962.........	49,196
1951..........	66,181	1963.........	48,025
1960..........	51,316	1964.........	47,616
1961..........	50,101	1965.........	46,143

[a]Includes 38,340 from the Philippines and 3,385 from other U. S. possessions.

Source: HDPED, SR 29 (April 9, 1965), p. 14.

Table 45.--HOUSING UNITS AND HOUSEHOLDS, BY COUNTY: APRIL 1, 1964

County	Housing units	House-holds	Percent increase, 1960-64	
			Housing units	House-holds
Total.............	192,580	177,416	16.4	15.9
Hawaii.................	19,105	16,649	5.4	5.4
Honolulu..............	150,171	139,809	19.4	18.6
Kauai..................	9,306	8,356	3.4	3.4
Maui (incl. Kalawao)...	13,998	12,602	11.1	11.1

Source: HRA, Redevelopment and Housing Research, Supplement for Nov. 1964, p. 4.

Table 46.--HOUSEHOLD AND HOUSING CHARACTERISTICS, FOR OAHU: 1958 TO 1962

Subject	January 1958	December 1959	October 1962		
			Total	Military households	Civilian households
Households					
Number of households...........	104,000	116,000	129,200	23,900	105,300
Persons per household..........	4.50	4.35	4.25	3.99	4.30
Percent in same house as one year earlier[a]...............	75.7	72.9	72.9	42.8	79.8
Percent in armed forces[a].......	20.1	19.9	18.5	100.0	...
Percent employed downtown[a].....	15.4	16.5	13.8	0.4	16.8
Median family income ($).......	5,373	6,055	6,883	4,777	7,551
Occupied Housing Units					
Percent owner occupied.........	47.1	47.2	45.6	6.7	54.4
Median monthly rent ($)........	66	76	86	92	82
Median rent-income ratio (%)...	...	18.7	17.8	24.7	15.6
Percent over 1 person per room.	31.9	27.3	22.9	15.2	25.3
Percent with 5 rooms or more...	53.5	58.9	62.9	64.5	62.0
Percent in 1-unit structures...	66.6	63.5	68.4	41.6	71.4
Median year built..............	1946	1948	1950	1954	1950
Percent dilapidated............	...	11.3	13.9	17.7	13.0

[a]Refers to household head.

Source: HRA, "Honolulu Household and Housing Survey, October 1962," Redevelopment and Housing Research, No. 23 (July 1963), pp. 11, 12, 15-19.

Table 47.--SCHOOL MEMBERSHIP, PUBLIC AND PRIVATE: 1954-1955 TO 1964-1965

School year	Public and private schools			Public schools		Private schools	
	State	Oahu	Other islands	State	Oahu	State	Oahu
1954-1955...	139,162	98,797	40,365	113,544	77,759	25,618	21,038
1959-1960...	169,925	130,373	39,552	140,666	105,565	29,259	24,808
1964-1965...	193,047	153,579	39,468	160,681	125,610	32,366	27,969

Source: Hawaii Department of Education, Statistics on Public and Private School Pupil Membership, 1964-65 (April 19, 1965), pp. 3, 19.

Table 48.--RELIGION OF PERSONS 20 YEARS OLD AND OVER, FOR OAHU: 1960

Sex	Total	None	Roman Catholic	Mormon	Protestant	Buddhist	Other and not reported
Both sexes...	100.0	12.1	27.6	2.7	39.0	15.8	2.8
Male...........	100.0	16.0	27.9	2.5	34.2	17.6	1.8
Female.........	100.0	8.1	27.3	2.9	43.8	14.0	3.9

Source: Sample survey by University of Hawaii, Economic Research Center, as quoted in HDPR, Statistical Abstract of Hawaii, 1962, p. 16.

Table 49.--LABOR FORCE ESTIMATES, ANNUAL AVERAGES:

1958 TO 1965

Geographic area and year	Civilian labor force	Civilian employment	Labor disputes	Unemployed	
				Number	Percent
The State:					
1958..........	211,540	201,370	3,090	7,080	3.4
1959..........	222,980	216,140	...	6,840	3.1
1960..........	235,140	228,050	...	7,090	3.0
1961..........	242,850	232,910	...	9,940	4.1
1962..........	246,180	234,420	160	11,600	4.7
1963..........	250,880	238,630	230	12,020	4.8
1964..........	257,630	247,560	20	10,050	3.9
1965..........	269,020	259,680	90	9,250	3.4
Oahu:					
1960..........	184,660	179,350	...	5,310	2.9
1965..........	214,610	207,450	70	7,090	3.3
Other islands:					
1960..........	50,480	48,700	...	1,780	3.5
1965..........	54,410	52,230	20	2,160	4.0

Source: Hawaii Department of Labor and Industrial Relations, Labor Force Estimates, mimeographed series.

VI. BIRTH AND DEATH STATISTICS: 1848-1965

Official birth and death statistics for Hawaii go back to the 1840's. These data are often inaccurate and incomplete. Many of the figures lie buried in long-forgotten reports, disregarded by historians and demographers. Since 1915 or 1920, however, the quality of these statistics has been generally acceptable, and for the past quarter of a century has been superior. Taken as a whole, they mirror with some fidelity the changing demographic fortunes of Hawaii--the depressed fertility and catastrophic mortality of the 19th century, the rapid shifts in birth rates during the interwar and postwar periods, and the rapid lengthening in expectation of life over the past half-century.

The compilation of vital statistics

Knowledge of vital trends in Hawaii before the 1830's is either scanty or non-existent. The record is particularly hazy for the pre-contact period, from the earliest habitation of Hawaii more than 1,000 years ago to the arrival of Captain Cook. Information for the years following Cook's visit is somewhat more plentiful. An unpublished manuscript by Romanzo Adams, in fact, contains a valiant effort to reconstruct the statistical record back to 1778, in spite of formidable difficulties (see Table 10).

The rapid depopulation that followed the first contact did much to stimulate interest in vital statistics. Perhaps 300,000 Hawaiians lived in the Islands in 1778; by 1832, when the missionaries completed their first census, the number was less than 125,000. This decline became a cause of considerable concern.

The earliest contemporary figures on Island fertility and mortality are those compiled by the missionaries. In 1835 they passed a resolution specifying "that a register be kept at each station of all the births and deaths, as far as they come within our knowledge, to be embodied in the annual report of the stations."[1] Unfortunately, only a few of the stations heeded this resolution. There were also occasional efforts to estimate the infant mortality rate. These scattered reports suggested crude birth rates ranging from 10 to 26 per 1,000 population, death rates between 40 and 53, and infant mortality (based on deaths under 2 years of age) in excess of 500 per 1,000 live births.[2] Particularly severe epidemics drove these death rates even higher.

The official collection of vital statistics was first authorized a few years later. A law enacted on June 7, 1839 and approved on November 9, 1840 instructed the tax officers to "take a yearly account of the deaths and births, by which it may be ascertained whether the people of the kingdom are really diminishing in numbers or not ...."[3]

After it became apparent that the tax officials were not heeding this mandate, responsibility was transferred to the newly created Department of Public Instruction. An act approved on April 27, 1846 charged the Minister of Public

Instruction "with the stated enumeration of the inhabitants of this kingdom, of whom it shall be his duty to make a complete census ... including an annual bill of mortality, and of the natural increase." An amendment signed on August 7, 1850 provided for the appointment of local registrars "from among the school teachers, or other suitable persons," to be paid two cents for every event recorded "if deemed correct."[4] Legislation approved on May 17, 1859 required parents to notify the registrar of births within a period of three months, and the nearest relative to notify the registrar of deaths within a one-week period, under penalty of a $1.00 fine. An amendment dated January 10, 1865 assigned the functions of district registrar to school agents.[5]

Responsibility for birth and death registration was transferred to health officials in 1896. "An Act for Keeping Records of Births, Deaths and Marriages," passed by the 1896 Legislature, directed the Board of Health to appoint registrars for each district, listed items to be recorded, and set penalties for non-reporting.[6] Legislation approved on April 19, 1913 created the position of Registrar-General.[7] The Bureau of Vital Statistics, later named the Office of Health Statistics and now known as the Research, Planning and Statistics Office of the Department of Health, was established by the 1937 Territorial Legislature.[8] A model Public Health Statistics Act was approved on May 19, 1949.[9]

Statistics compiled by these agencies have typically been

published in annual or biennial reports (references are listed in Footnote 10). Birth and death totals for 1848, the first year with reasonably complete statistical coverage, appeared in conjunction with the 1849 census results. A similar tabulation was issued for 1849. From 1851 to 1863, annual totals appeared in reports of the Board of Education, often in considerable geographic detail. After a two-year hiatus, publication of annual data was assumed by the Board of Health, a practice it followed from 1866 to 1877. The Board of Education resumed publication of these data several years later, presenting biennial totals without any geographic breakdown for periods from 1868-1869 to 1888-1889. Then, in April 1876, the Board of Health initiated compilation of detailed statistics on deaths occurring in Honolulu, classified by age, sex, nationality, and cause of death. Birth data were added and the program was extended to the remainder of the Territory in January 1900. Statistics for succeeding years have regularly appeared in the annual reports of the Board (later Department) of Health.[10] Federal compilations first presented vital statistics for Hawaii in 1915.[11]

Findings

Trends revealed by these data are traced in the accompanying tables.

The first four present annual or decennial data on the number of registered births and deaths and the corresponding crude birth and death rates. Unfortunately, underregistration was quite common before 1910 or 1915, and in some years was especially noticeable. Any meaningful comparison between successive years, or even between successive decades, thus becomes exceedingly hazardous. Such comparisons are further complicated, even for the recent past, by the effects of shifting age and sex distributions.

The birth and death rates in Tables 51, 52, and 53--expressed as the number of vital events occurring annually per 1,000 mid-period civilian population--differ somewhat from rates published previously. Statistical reports prior to 1900 were usually limited to absolute totals. Although later tabulations included rates of one kind or another, these rates were usually computed either from outdated census totals, postcensal population estimates of dubious accuracy, or population data distorted by the inclusion of large numbers of military personnel. The recent revision of semi-annual civilian population estimates back to 1848 has made the present study possible (see Appendix).

Table 54 compares birth and death rates based on the number of registered events with corresponding rates adjusted for underregistration. In 1919-1920, for example, the crude birth rate, already high at 40.4, becomes 49.3 when corrected for underreporting. Less drastic changes are evident for later years. Unfortunately, accurate adjustments are possible only for the five years for which completeness of registration was surveyed.

Two alternate approaches to the measurement of fertility

are explored in Table 55. With the general fertility rate, annual births (both registered and adjusted) are related to the number of women 15 to 44 years of age rather than to total population, thus reducing the effect of shifting age and sex composition on fertility trends. The second measure, the fertility ratio, shows the number of children under 5 years old per 1,000 women 15 to 44 at each census. A rough adjustment has been made in the latter series to eliminate the effect of changes in infant mortality rates. Unfortunately, both the general fertility rate and the fertility ratio depend on data usually limited to census years. Inadequate information on completeness of registration and child mortality before 1915 or thereabouts further restricts the value of these measures for long-term trend analysis.

Gross and net reproduction rates for census years since 1930 are reported in Table 56. The gross reproduction rate is the average number of daughters that a hypothetical cohort of females starting life together would bear if they all survived from birth to the end of the childbearing period and if they experienced a given set of age-specific fertility rates. The net reproduction rate is the average number of daughters that a hypothetical cohort of females starting life together would bear if they experienced given sets of age-specific mortality and fertility rates.

Table 57 traces infant mortality rates from 1902 to 1965. These rates show the number of deaths among children under 1 year of age per 1,000 live births. Near-completeness in death registration was attained well in advance of that for births; consequently, infant mortality rates for the first quarter of the century tended to be seriously overstated.

Selected life-table values appear in Table 58. The earliest estimates available are rough approximations for Honolulu for 1884-1885. More accurate data, statewide in scope, are available at decennial intervals since 1920. Estimates for different islands or ethnic groups are as yet unpublished.

Tables 59 and 60 report data on age at death and cause of death for selected years since 1920.

The data in these tables help to chart--roughly at first, later with considerable accuracy--trends and fluctuations in fertility and mortality in the Islands. Full appreciation of their meaning, however, requires some knowledge of the underlying social, economic, and health conditions of the past. These can be mentioned only briefly here.

Causes of the high level of mortality during the nineteenth century were many and complex. Contemporary writers blamed alcohol, sexual promiscuity, and landlessness, among other reasons. More recent authorities have noted the limited state of medical knowledge, poor infant care, and economic disorganization. Taeuber stressed "increased mortality associated with intruded diseases and disturbed subsistence production."[12]

Epidemics occurred at frequent intervals. Measles and whooping cough struck in 1848, influenza in 1849, smallpox in

1853, scarlet fever in 1870, typhoid fever in 1880, smallpox again in 1881, measles again in 1890, Asiatic cholera in 1895, bubonic plague in 1899-1900, yellow fever in 1911, influenza in 1918-1920, epidemic meningitis in 1928, and measles again in 1936-1937. Venereal disease, tuberculosis, and Hansen's Disease were prominent causes of death well into the twentieth century. Major disasters affecting the death rate included the Pearl Harbor attack on December 7, 1941 and the tsunamis of April 1, 1946 and May 23, 1960.

Mortality would have been even greater if many older immigrant workers had not chosen to return to their homelands to die.

Reasons underlying changes in fertility are even more difficult to assign with any certainty. Regarding trends during the nineteenth century, Taeuber has suggested the likelihood of "a recurrent or localized low fertility associated with venereal disease, epidemics, or malnutrition ... Physiological sterility need not imply altered reproductive mores."[13] The role of syphilis has been mentioned frequently. In more recent times, birth rates in Hawaii have paralleled rates on the Mainland, dropping during economic recessions and rising in response to economic recovery or the threat of war. Other factors responsible for fluctuating fertility rates include the changing proportions of women of child-bearing age, shifts in ethnic composition, increasing knowledge of birth control techniques, and a growing acceptance of American family-size ideals.

Accuracy of the data

It should be emphasized that the foregoing discussion is based in large measure on data unadjusted for underregistration, and hence subject to considerable error for years marked by incomplete or inaccurate coverage. This possibility suggests the need for careful evaluation of the adequacy of the underlying data.

The population base used for computation of rates appears to be reasonably correct. Adams, who made a thorough study of the Hawaiian censuses, attested to their accuracy (at least as regards total numbers) for the years from 1850 forward.[14] The decennial enumerations conducted by the U. S. Bureau of the Census in Hawaii since 1900 likewise seem free of serious defects. The intercensal estimates used in this analysis are recent revisions based on the best available data and, with the possible exception of 1901-1909, appear to be adequate for most analytic purposes (see Appendix).

The birth and death data, unfortunately, inspire much less confidence. Numerous deficiencies mar these series well into the twentieth century. Because of these defects, Hawaii was not accepted into the U. S. Death Registration Area until 1917 and was excluded from the Birth Registration Area until 1929.

Officials were aware of these shortcomings from the beginning, and seldom hesitated to express their reservations:

The return of births and deaths for 1851, have been

> very imperfect, and from two districts on Hawaii, no returns at all have been received.[15]
>
> ... made by native agents, not all fully sensible to the importance of correctness in the matter, and cannot be relied upon as entirely accurate.[16]
>
> ... unusually imperfect this year [1855] ...[17]

This situation, bad as it appeared, soon worsened. Adams wrote: "The records of births and deaths, 1848 to 1860, kept by school teachers under the supervision of competent Ministers of Education, are valuable though incomplete as to district. After 1860 such reports became almost worthless ...."[18] Data were left untabulated or unpublished for 1864, 1865, and (except for Honolulu proper) throughout the 1890's.[19] Alternate sources sometimes showed variant values for certain years.[20] Although the official figures indicate a crude birth rate under 25 and a death rate below 30 for most of the years between 1882 and 1900, other evidence suggests rates twice as high: "The age ratios and the age structures of the populations of 1890 and 1896 suggest birth rates of 50 or more per 1,000 total population. If birth rates were at this level and [the Hawaiian] population was declining, death rates must have been above 50."[21] Official statistics on births, deaths, and migration failed to account for 30,500 of the 36,500 increase in population between 1900 and 1910 (see Appendix).

Registration was poor in Honolulu but was even worse elsewhere. The Executive Officer of the Board of Health complained in 1897 that "not half of the births in the city are registered."[22] Two years later he wrote that "The reports of births, marriages and deaths from most of the districts of the Islands outside of Honolulu are very unsatisfactory ...."[23] Mortality returns for rural areas were termed "merely nominal" and "of very little value from a statistical point of view."[24]

These considerations suggested the desirability of a separate tabulation of data limited to Honolulu proper. These statistics, shown in Table 52, cover the period from 1852, when Honolulu figures first became available, to 1910, when geographic differentials in completeness of registration began to lose their significance. It was hoped that computation of separate data for Honolulu would provide both a check on the admittedly defective all-island rates and a clue to mortality patterns for 1890 to 1899, when published tabulations omitted other areas. As it turned out, however, the Honolulu rates were sometimes lower than the all-island rates, particularly before 1864. During years when the Honolulu rates exceeded those for the entire kingdom by a sizeable margin (1867-1877), the former seemed so unreasonably high and the latter so close to expected values that one suspects that gross misallocation rather than differential completeness was at fault. As noted by the Board of Health:

> The death-rate of Honolulu ... is unfair; the number of non-residents dying in Honolulu is increasing continually ... The Chinese laborers particularly, find their way to Honolulu when sick, and many die within a few hours after landing.[25]

Non-resident deaths eventually dropped from 11 percent of the total in 1884-1885 to 2 percent in 1897.

Registration improved considerably after 1910. A test conducted by the U. S. Bureau of the Census in 1918 indicated that 98 percent of all deaths occurring in Hawaii were reported.[26] The same agency tested birth registration for the second half of 1919 and estimated it to have been 82 percent complete.[27] Their 1930 check found 93 percent of all births registered.[28] Reporting of births reached 97.7 percent completeness in 1940 and 99.9 percent in 1950, the last time a systematic test was conducted.[29]

The limitations of the nineteenth century data in the accompanying tables are evident. Underreporting and misallocation were frequent, and varied both from year to year and place to place. Statistics were particularly bad for rural areas during the last third of the century.

In spite of these shortcomings, the data offer much of value for social, demographic, and medical research. The crude birth and death rates and other vital indexes presented in the tables provide at least a rough quantitative measure of public health progress and demographic change in Hawaii over a 117-year period. Data covering the last half-century are quite adequate. Many possibilities remain for further exploitation of these statistical resources.

Table 50.--LIVE BIRTHS, DEATHS, AND CRUDE BIRTH AND DEATH RATES: ANNUAL AVERAGES FOR SELECTED PERIODS, 1848 TO 1965

(Place of occurrence basis. Not adjusted for underregistration, thought to be extensive in many of these years; see Table 54 for adjusted data for available years. Because of doubtful accuracy, the data before 1910 should be used with utmost caution)

Period	Live births	Deaths[a]	Birth rate[b]	Death rate[b]
1848-1859.........	1,635	3,641	21.3	45.8
1860-1869.........	1,751	2,638	27.1	40.8
1870-1879.........	2,320	2,922	41.0	51.4
1880-1889.........	1,799	1,923	23.6	25.3
1890-1899[c]........	...	...	...	26.4
1900-1909.........	2,796	2,763	16.6	16.6
1910-1919.........	6,872	3,530	31.3	16.3
1920-1929.........	11,590	4,181	39.5	14.4
1930-1939.........	9,680	3,548	26.2	9.6
1940-1949.........	12,042	3,062	26.6	6.8
1950-1959.........	15,883	3,043	31.8	6.1
1960-1965.........	17,476	3,543	27.3	5.5

[a]Includes armed forces to 1940 but excludes them thereafter.

[b]Annual events per 1,000 population computed as average of annual rates for period. Population base excludes armed forces after 1897. Residence basis to 1950; de facto basis thereafter.

[c]City of Honolulu only.

Source: Computed from Tables 51-53.

Table 51.--LIVE BIRTHS, DEATHS, AND CRUDE BIRTH AND DEATH RATES:

1848 TO 1910

(Place of occurrence basis. Not adjusted for underregistration, thought to be extensive in many of these years. Because of doubtful accuracy, these data should be used with utmost caution)

Year[a]	Live births	Deaths	Birth rate[b]	Death rate[b]	Year[a]	Live births	Deaths	Birth rate[c]	Death rate[c]
1848...	1,478	7,943	16.4	88.0	1872......	2,338	3,056	40.7	53.2
1849...	1,422	4,320	16.6	50.5	1873......	2,372	3,009	42.1	53.4
1850...	...	...	...	...	1874......	2,217	2,770	40.2	50.2
1851...	2,424	5,792	29.6	70.6	1875......	2,558	2,988	47.2	55.1
1852...	1,852	2,822	23.2	35.3	1876......	2,147	2,426	39.4	44.5
1853...	1,513	8,026	19.8	105.1	1877......	1,843	1,869	33.2	33.7
1854...	1,381	1,439	18.9	19.7	1878-79...	4,753	5,782	41.0	49.8
1855...	1,642	1,685	22.5	23.1	1880-81...	4,701	5,101	35.6	38.6
1856...	1,287	1,579	17.7	21.7	1882-83...	3,188	3,648	22.2	25.4
1857...	1,615	2,017	22.4	28.0	1884-85...	3,178	3,584	19.7	22.2
1858...	1,756	2,140	24.5	29.9	1886-87...	3,087	3,140	18.3	18.6
1859...	1,612	2,291	22.7	32.3	1888-89...	3,832	3,761	22.2	21.7
1860...	1,672	2,343	23.8	33.4	1890-99...	...	...	...	...
1861...	1,543	2,249	22.3	32.5	1900......	1,026	2,376	6.7	15.4
1862...	1,474	2,426	21.6	35.6	1901......	2,058	3,029	13.3	19.5
1863...	1,594	2,657	23.8	39.7	1902......	2,350	2,578	15.0	16.4
1864...	...	...	...	...	1903......	2,526	2,657	15.6	16.4
1865...	...	...	...	...	1904......	2,510	2,781	15.0	16.6
1866...	1,713	2,941	26.9	46.2	1905......	2,609	2,686	15.7	16.1
1867...	1,747	2,606	28.0	41.8	1906......	2,830	2,854	17.0	17.2
1868...	2,104	3,351	34.5	54.9	1907......	3,574	3,065	20.5	17.6
1869...	2,163	2,528	36.0	42.1	1908[c].....	2,138	1,376	23.7	15.2
1870...	2,413	3,819	40.8	64.6	1909......	4,941	2,851	26.8	15.4
1871...	2,559	3,502	44.0	60.2	1910......	4,302	2,941	22.8	15.6

[a]Calendar years ended December 31, 1848 to 1877 and 1900 to 1907; 24-month periods ended December 31, 1879 to 1889; six-month period ended June 30, 1908; twelve-month periods ended June 30, 1909 and 1910.

[b]Annual events per 1,000 mid-period population. Population base excludes armed forces after 1889.

[c]Six months.

Source: Births and deaths from official sources. Rates computed from population estimates in Appendix.

Table 52.--LIVE BIRTHS, DEATHS, AND CRUDE BIRTH AND DEATH RATES, FOR HONOLULU: 1852 TO 1910

(Place of occurrence basis. Not adjusted for underregistration, thought to be extensive in many of these years. Because of doubtful accuracy, these data should be used with utmost caution)

Year[a]	Live births	Deaths	Birth rate[b]	Death rate[b]	Year[a]	Live births	Deaths	Birth rate[b]	Death rate[b]
1852...	337	906	27.4	73.7	1882...	...	542	...	30.6
1853...	191	3,759	16.1	315.9	1883...	...	637	...	33.7
1854...	320	539	27.4	46.1	1884...	...	567	...	28.2
1855...	371	379	30.4	31.1	1885...	...	566	...	27.2
1856...	115	268	9.1	21.3	1886...	...	593	...	27.7
1857...	442	595	34.0	45.8	1887...	...	553	...	25.7
1858...	627	667	46.8	49.8	1888...	...	547	...	25.1
1859...	335	454	24.3	32.9	1889...	...	564	...	25.5
1860...	246	538	17.3	37.9	1890...	...	692	...	30.6
1861...	265	402	18.5	28.1	1891...	...	724	...	30.5
1862...	344	608	24.2	42.8	1892...	...	571	...	23.0
1863...	269	596	19.2	42.6	1893...	...	614	...	24.1
1864...	...	...	...	...	1894...	...	612	...	23.2
1865...	...	...	...	...	1895...	...	731	...	26.5
1866...	...	...	...	...	1896...	...	673	...	23.0
1867[c]..	661	1,052	48.6	77.4	1897...	...	659	...	21.5
1868[c]..	994	1,566	72.0	113.5	1898...	...	926	...	28.9
1869[c]..	1,016	1,549	72.1	109.9	1899...	...	1,153	...	32.3
1870[c]..	1,372	1,913	95.9	133.8	1900...	253	1,290	6.4	32.8
1871[c]..	1,561	2,000	107.7	137.9	1901...	562	1,125	14.1	28.2
1872[c]..	1,489	1,878	100.6	126.9	1902...	708	971	17.4	23.9
1873[c]..	1,353	1,639	92.7	112.3	1903...	596	864	14.1	20.4
1874[c]..	1,290	1,725	90.8	121.5	1904...	582	925	13.3	21.1
1875[c]..	1,553	1,703	112.5	123.4	1905...	606	792	13.8	18.0
1876[c]..	1,015	981	74.1	71.6	1906...	610	964	13.8	21.8
1877[c]..	764	624	55.8	45.5	1907...	798	988	17.2	21.2
1878...	...	545	...	39.2	1908[d]..	493	503	20.3	20.7
1879...	...	777	...	52.5	1909...	1,096	925	22.0	18.6
1880...	...	607	...	38.2	1910...	1,116	1,030	21.8	20.2
1881...	...	818	...	48.7					

[a]Calendar years, 1852 to 1907; six-month period ended June 30, 1908; twelve-month periods ended June 30, 1909 and 1910.

[b]Annual events per 1,000 mid-period population.

[c]Values for 1867-1877 appear to be seriously overstated.

[d]Six months.

Source: Births and deaths from official sources. Rates computed from population estimates in Hawaii Historical Review, I (6), Jan. 1964, pp. 123-124.

Table 53.--LIVE BIRTHS, DEATHS, AND CRUDE BIRTH AND DEATH RATES: 1911 TO 1965

(For 12-month periods ended June 30. Place of occurrence basis, except where otherwise specified. Not adjusted for underregistration; see Table 24 for adjusted data)

Year	Live births	Deaths[a]	Birth rate[b]	Death rate[b]	Year	Live births	Deaths[a]	Birth rate[b]	Death rate[b]
1911...	4,494	3,296	23.3	17.1	1939...	9,038	3,216	23.1	8.2
1912...	5,147	3,071	26.1	15.6	1940...	9,524	3,025	24.1	7.6
1913...	5,568	3,232	27.0	15.7	1941[c]..	9,607	3,047	23.8	7.6
1914...	6,756	3,707	31.4	17.2	1942...	10,385	3,301	24.3	7.7
1915...	7,278	3,556	33.1	16.2	1943...	10,979	2,989	24.5	6.7
1916...	7,899	3,940	35.1	17.5	1944[c]..	12,211	2,984	26.7	6.5
1917...	8,707	3,498	37.4	15.0	1945...	12,597	2,861	27.3	6.2
1918...	9,404	4,010	39.3	16.8	1946...	11,945	3,095	25.7	6.7
1919...	9,164	4,051	37.4	16.5	1947...	14,050	3,155	29.7	6.7
1920...	10,165	4,564	40.4	18.1	1948...	14,523	3,002	30.0	6.2
1921...	10,156	3,789	39.6	14.8	1949...	14,604	3,160	29.8	6.4
1922...	11,249	4,113	42.5	15.5	1950...	14,124	2,897	29.5	6.1
1923...	11,335	4,654	40.8	16.8	1951...	13,845	2,909	29.2	6.1
1924...	12,128	4,218	41.9	14.6	1952...	15,024	2,947	32.0	6.3
1925...	13,109	4,017	43.3	13.3	1953...	16,150	2,808	34.7	6.0
1926...	12,417	4,056	39.6	13.0	1954...	15,928	2,964	33.6	6.3
1927...	12,296	3,929	38.4	12.3	1955...	16,146	3,140	33.4	6.5
1928...	11,543	3,992	35.0	12.1	1956...	17,112	3,112	33.8	6.1
1929...	11,498	4,481	33.7	13.1	1957...	16,852	3,228	32.0	6.1
1930...	10,873	3,976	31.1	11.4	1958...	16,944	3,295	30.5	5.9
1931...	10,831	3,805	30.2	10.6	1959...	16,701	3,134	29.4	5.5
1932...	10,652	3,688	29.1	10.1	1960...	17,236	3,519	29.2	6.0
1933...	10,014	3,646	27.2	9.9	1961...	17,338	3,368	28.6	5.6
1934...	9,431	3,679	25.7	10.0	1962...	17,988	3,376	28.5	5.3
1935...	9,252	3,236	25.1	8.8	1963...	17,679	3,655	27.2	5.6
1936...	8,960	3,335	24.0	8.9	1964...	17,508	3,690	26.1	5.5
1937...	8,763	3,684	23.1	9.7	1965...	17,107	3,652	24.6	5.3
1938...	8,986	3,219	23.4	8.4					

[a]Includes armed forces to 1940; excludes them thereafter.

[b]Annual events per 1,000 mid-period (January 1) population. Population base excludes armed forces. Residence basis to 1950; de facto basis thereafter.

[c]Mortality data on place of residence basis.

Source: Births and deaths from official sources. Rates computed from population estimates in Appendix.

Table 54.--LIVE BIRTHS, DEATHS, AND CRUDE BIRTH AND DEATH RATES, ADJUSTED AND UNADJUSTED FOR UNDERREGISTRATION: SPECIFIED YEARS, 1918 TO 1950

Years ending June 30	Percent complete	Number		Rate[a]	
		Unadjusted	Adjusted	Unadjusted	Adjusted
Live births:					
1920[b].....	82	10,165	12,396	40.4	49.3
1930......	93	10,873	11,691	31.1	33.4
1940......	97.7	9,524	9,748	24.1	24.6
1950......	99.9	14,124	14,138	29.5	29.6
Deaths:					
1918......	98	4,010	4,092	16.8	17.1

[a]Annual events per 1,000 mid-period civilian population.

[b]Percent complete based on data for July-November 1919.

Source: Percent complete from tests conducted by U. S. Bureau of the Census. Unadjusted data from Table 53. Adjusted data computed. Rates computed from Appendix.

Table 55.--GENERAL FERTILITY RATES AND FERTILITY RATIOS:

1872 TO 1960

Year	Women 15 to 44[a]	Live births[b]			Children under 5[c]		
		Number registered	Per 1,000 women 15-44		Number reported	Per 1,000 women 15-44	
			Unadjusted	Adjusted[d]		Unadjusted	Adjusted[e]
1872...	12,617	2,355	187	...	5,724	454	750
1878...	11,642	2,376	204	...	6,340	545	850
1884...	14,899	1,589	107	...	8,492	570	850
1890...	15,534	...	...	...	9,512	612	900
1896...	18,199	...	...	...	13,234	727	1,000
1900...	26,224	...	...	...	15,084	575	780
1910...	34,526	4,398	127	180	24,065	697	900
1920...	49,387	9,792	198	240	38,550	781	900
1930...	62,785	11,019	176	190	48,180	767	850
1940...	88,110	9,460	107,	110	40,085	455	485
1950...	112,436	14,141	126	126	63,991	569	585
1960...	134,296	17,122	127	127	80,962	603	620

[a]Estimated before 1890.

[b]Annual averages for two-year periods centered approximately on census dates. Not available for 1890, 1896, and 1900.

[c]Estimated before 1900. Not adjusted for underenumeration.

[d]For underregistration. Registration was assumed around 70 percent complete in 1910, as given in Table 54 for 1920-1950, and complete in 1960. No basis exists for postulating adjustments before 1910, although the 1872 and 1878 ratios appear reasonably accurate and the 1884 ratio is obviously understated, perhaps by as much as 50 percent.

[e]For effects of infant mortality, assumed to have declined from 400 per 1,000 live births in 1868-1872 to about 260 in 1896-1900. Adjustments for 1906-1910 to 1956-1960 were computed from Table 57.

Table 56.--GROSS AND NET REPRODUCTION RATES: 1930 TO 1960

Year	Gross reproduction rate	Net reproduction rate
1930..........	2.48	1.99
1940..........	1.48	1.34
1950..........	1.64	1.57
1960..........	1.85	1.82

Source: HDH, records.

Table 57.--INFANT MORTALITY: 1902 TO 1965

Year[a]	Number[b]	Rate[c]	Year[a]	Number[b]	Rate[c]	Year[a]	Number[b]	Rate[c]
Urban:[d]			1921...	1,275	119.7	1944...	389	30.6
1902...	323	360.5	1922...	1,500	134.3	1945...	340	27.6
1903...	307	389.1	1923...	1,587	135.4	1946...	389	30.7
1904...	244	286.0	1924...	1,296	100.3	1947...	449	30.8
1905...	308	319.5	1925...	1,414	112.2	1948...	415	28.7
1906...	323	355.7	1926...	1,157	94.2	1949...	358	25.2
			1927...	1,150	97.3	1950...	335	23.8
Total:			1928...	973	83.4	1951...	341	23.6
1906...	757	283.3	1929...	1,135	101.0	1952...	331	21.2
1907...	863	303.0	1930...	889	82.3	1953...	338	21.0
1908...	714	155.5	1931...	799	76.3	1954...	363	22.4
1909...	765	154.8	1932...	799	76.1	1955...	336	20.6
1910...	884	205.5	1933...	695	72.1	1956...	384	22.4
1911...	1,042	231.9	1934...	699	75.1	1957...	407	23.9
1912...	1,033	190.6	1935...	620	67.4	1958...	385	23.0
1913...	1,111	181.3	1936...	627	73.0	1959...	409	24.0
1914...	1,244	178.5	1937...	617	68.7	1960...	399	23.2
1915...	1,210	156.8	1938...	530	58.5	1961...	381	21.7
1916...	1,259	157.6	1939...	489	52.7	1962...	369	20.6
1917...	1,250	137.4	1940...	422	43.7	1963...	399	22.5
1918...	1,280	138.8	1941...	408	40.3	1964...	342	19.8
1919...	1,019	105.8	1942...	406	39.0	1965...	349	21.5
1920...	1,083	108.8	1943...	444	38.2			

[a]Years ended June 30, 1902 to 1911; calendar years 1912 to 1965.

[b]Deaths under 1 year of age occurring in Hawaii.

[c]Deaths under 1 year of age per 1,000 live births. Rates before 1908 are probably overstated because of underregistration of births.

[d]City of Honolulu and Hilo Judicial District.

Source: Report of the President of the Board of Health, Territory of Hawaii for 1902-1911; Annual Report, Department of Health, State of Hawaii, Statistical Supplement for 1960-1965.

Table 58.--AVERAGE REMAINING LIFETIME IN YEARS AT SELECTED AGES, BY SEX: 1884-1885 TO 1959-1961

Sex and period	Birth	1	15	25	45	65
Both sexes:[a]						
1884-1885...	36.5	41.2	33.9	27.8	18.4	5.1
Male:						
1919-1920...	47.79	...	...	...	...	...
1929-1931...	52.63	57.24	46.43	38.03	22.01	8.71
1939-1941...	59.46	61.79	49.38	40.31	23.37	9.10
1949-1951...	67.76	68.77	55.54	46.20	28.01	13.70
1959-1961...	69.10	69.84	56.32	46.95	28.35	13.10
Female:						
1919-1920...	47.27	...	...	...	...	...
1929-1931...	55.31	58.55	47.38	39.10	23.63	9.16
1939-1941...	62.60	64.32	51.67	42.51	25.26	9.85
1949-1951...	71.29	71.86	58.51	48.93	30.50	15.11
1959-1961...	73.23	73.63	60.10	50.38	31.44	15.17

[a]City of Honolulu only. Preliminary.

Source: HDH, unpublished data for two year period ended March 31, 1885 (computed especially for the present study); USBC, _United States Abridged Life Tables, 1919-1920_, (1923), pp. 24 and 26; _Annual Report, Department of Health, State of Hawaii, Statistical Supplement, 1963_, p. 4.

Table 59.--DEATHS, BY AGE: 1920 TO 1960

Age	Percent distribution[a]					Rate per 1,000 population[a]				
	1920	1930	1940	1950	1960	1920	1930	1940	1950	1960
All ages........	100.0	100.0	100.0	100.0	100.0	18.0	10.5	7.3	5.8	5.7
Under 1 year........	23.6	23.0	13.6	11.5	11.1	126.2	93.0	50.6	26.7	23.7
1 to 4 years........	10.5	8.9	3.2	2.8	1.4	16.1	8.9	3.1	1.6	0.8
5 to 14 years.......	4.8	4.3	3.5	1.5	1.8	4.2	2.0	1.2	0.5	0.5
15 to 24 years......	9.9	7.1	6.3	3.5	3.1	10.0	3.6	1.9	1.1	1.0
25 to 44 years......	24.8	17.4	17.7	11.0	9.1	14.6	6.4	4.1	2.1	1.8
45 to 64 years......	17.9	23.3	26.9	30.4	26.8	22.9	19.8	19.8	12.6	9.9
65 to 74 years......	5.0	9.3	16.4	19.8	20.5	61.9	61.1	50.2	40.1	37.6
75 years and over...	3.5	6.7	12.4	19.5	26.2	141.4	146.6	135.6	94.7	98.9

[a]Absolute totals were 4,600 in 1920, 3,865 in 1930, 3,089 in 1940, 2,919 in 1950, and 3,596 in 1960. All data include armed forces.

Source: Annual Report, Department of Health, State of Hawaii, Statistical Supplement, 1960, p. 32.

Table 60.--LEADING CAUSES OF DEATH: 1920 TO 1960

Cause of death	Percent distribution[a]					Rate per 100,000 population[a]				
	1920	1930	1940	1950	1960	1920	1930	1940	1950	1960
All causes[b]	100.0	100.0	100.0	100.0	100.0	1,767	1,043	724	583	568
Influenza and pneumonia	32.3	12.6	7.2	4.6	3.6	572	132	52	27	21
Tuberculosis (all forms)	11.5	9.8	8.3	3.9	0.4	204	102	60	23	2
Diarrhea and enteritis	9.6	8.6	1.0	0.7	0.4	169	89	7	4	3
Diseases of early infancy	5.4	6.6	6.7	6.7	7.5	96	69	48	39	43
Heart diseases	4.8	11.7	18.1	29.6	33.0	86	122	131	173	188
Accidents (all forms)	4.8	7.0	7.6	6.0	7.6	84	73	55	35	43
Nephritis and nephrosis	3.8	6.2	9.2	2.0	1.3	68	65	67	12	8
Cancer and other malignant neoplasm	3.3	5.8	9.8	15.4	17.2	59	61	71	90	98
Cerebral hemorrhage	3.0	4.7	6.0	8.9	8.8	53	49	43	52	50
Deliveries and complications of pregnancy	1.9	1.7	0.7	0.4	0.1	33	18	5	2	1
Suicide	1.2	1.7	2.6	1.9	1.3	20	18	19	11	7
Beriberi	1.2	1.6	0.5	0.1	0	20	17	4	1	0
Congenital malformations	0.8	1.1	1.8	2.8	2.2	13	11	13	16	12
Diabetes mellitus	0.4	1.1	2.0	3.0	2.6	7	11	14	18	15

[a]All data include armed forces.

[b]Including causes not shown separately.

Source: Annual Report, Department of Health, State of Hawaii, Statistical Supplement, 1960, p. 34.

VII. MIGRATION STATISTICS: 1823-1965

Hawaiian migration statistics go back about one and a half centuries, or approximately one-tenth of the time spanned by the movement of people to and from the Islands. Hawaii's earliest inhabitants (and first in-migrants) arrived more than 1,000 years ago, according to most authorities. Movement between Hawaii and the rest of the world was resumed soon after Captain Cook's visits. Statistical estimates on migration have been extended back to 1823, when foreigners were first arriving in quantity and whalers were starting to recruit Island seamen in appreciable numbers. Regular series on migration are available from 1850, two years before the first organized importation of foreign labor. Many Chinese, Portuguese, Japanese, Filipino, and other workers were brought to Hawaii between 1852 and 1946. Recent history, marked by rapid turnover in a large population of military personnel and dependents, the in-migration of people from the Mainland, and a growing body of Hawaii-born persons out-migrating to California and elsewhere, has been documented in considerable depth by a diversity of statistical studies.

The demographer can turn to a number of sources for Hawaiian migration data, with expectations of varying success. Much has been written about the arrivals, for example, but relatively little regarding departures. Statistics especially on the latter are often lacking, at least in the desired form or detail; where available, they exist only in scattered, little known sources or in unpublished form.

This chapter summarizes some of the major series. Emphasis has been placed on statistical totals of in-, out-, and net migration available on an annual or decennial basis over a period of years. Passenger movement as such, which includes business and vacation travel as well as changes in residence, has been disregarded. Some attention has been given to inter-island migration (moving, say, from Maui to Oahu), but none at all to purely local shifts (for example, from Kakaako to Kapahulu or from Hookena to Hilo). Limitations of time and space have unfortunately precluded analysis of migrant characteristics--their origin or destination, age, sex, race, marital status, education, or occupation--despite the availability and obvious importance of such data.

Estimates on place of birth are available back to 1823. Romanzo Adams published a series on the number of non-Hawaiians living in Hawaii and developed (but left unpublished) a comparable series on Hawaiians and part Hawaiians absent from the Islands.[1] Adams's estimates pertain to race rather than place of birth, but prior to 1878 (when 947 Hawaii-born persons of foreign parentage were enumerated in the Islands) the two concepts were virtually synonymous. These series are shown in Table 61.

Census counts on place of birth by place of residence date back to 1849. In that year, official census statistics on the foreign-born (as well as native-born) population of Hawaii were first compiled. A year later, the decennial census of the United States first offered data on the number of Hawaii-born persons living on the Mainland. These subjects have been included in every census since that time, whether conducted by the Hawaiian Government or the U. S. Bureau of the Census.[2] Unfortunately, the data on Hawaii-born persons living elsewhere are limited to the continental United States for most census years, and thus exclude Islanders at sea, in U. S. territories or possessions, or in foreign countries. Hawaiians serving aboard fur traders or whalers (included, incidentally, in Adams's estimates) were a sizeable group in the 1840's and 1850's. So were those who had moved to places other than the United States.[3] Reports for recent censuses include data on the age, color, and sex of migrants, in addition to geographic totals.[4] Trend data appear in Tables 62 and 63.

Quarterly and annual series on net passenger movement were initiated in July 1859 (references are listed in Footnote 5). These data were published in the Polynesian through the third quarter of 1863, disappeared for twenty-seven months, then were resumed in broadside form. From 1872 to 1900 they were published in the annual reports of the Collector General of Customs. Data for the first ten years of the present century appeared in a publication of the U. S. Department of Commerce and Labor. The annual reports of the Governor of Hawaii to the Secretary of the Interior extended this series to 1934; similar information, somewhat broader in coverage, appeared in Thrum's

Hawaiian Annual for most of these years. After mid-1928, records were kept by the Territorial (later State) Department of Health.[5] Separate totals were published for arrivals and departures, and until 1934 both series were presented by nationality or point of origin, often with separate totals for men, women, and children. Coverage was not complete, however: from 1900 to 1905, data were limited to Orientals; from 1911 to 1934, to steerage passengers; and after mid-1940, to civilian passengers. Although not stated, figures prior to 1940 probably excluded movements aboard military transports. Data for most of these series were confined to arrivals and departures at the Port of Honolulu, a restriction that was unlikely to exclude many overseas passengers. Purely inter-island travel was omitted in any case.

Passenger statistics must be used with considerable caution. As noted earlier, they include tourists and businessmen as well as migrants. Even the net passenger total (the difference between arrivals and departures) provides only a rough measure of migration, as such data may reflect growth in the number of visitors present (or residents absent) rather than a true migration. The data may also reflect a turnover in a large body of high-fertility military couples (29.5 percent of all live births in Hawaii in 1960 occurred in military families); the babies are born and promptly move on, thereby increasing both the birth and out-migration rates.

Pertinent statistics on net passenger movement are

summarized in Tables 64-67.

An alternate approach to migration analysis involves comparison of census totals on net change with data on natural increase or decrease based on birth and death statistics. Net migration is computed as a residual, the difference between overall increase (or decrease) and natural increase (or decrease). The U. S. Bureau of the Census has published State and county migration estimates prepared by this technique for the intercensal decade from 1950 to 1960.[6] Decennial rates were carried by the present author back to 1900, at which point incompleteness of birth and death registration precluded further analysis.[7] These estimates are presented in Tables 68 and 69.

Immigration statistics were initiated in 1852. High mortality and reduced fertility had cut the Hawaiian population to less than one-third of its pre-contact level by the middle of the nineteenth century. The resulting shortage of plantation workers brought about passage in 1850 of a law providing for indenture. On January 3, 1852, the first shipload of indentured Chinese coolies arrived. Annual totals on immigrant arrivals were eventually compiled and published by the Bureau of Immigration.[8] The series was continued in reports of the Committee on Immigration and Naturalization,[9] the Commissioner of Labor, and the Governor of Hawaii. Arrivals and departures were tabulated by nationality, often separately for men, women, and children. The value of these statistics declined in later years, as emigration began to overtake immigration and as increasing proportions of the totals represented persons making temporary visits to their homelands or returning to Hawaii on a second or third contract. Annual totals for the last half of the nineteenth century are recapitulated in Table 70.

A monthly series on "intended residents" was begun in October 1950. Passengers arriving aboard westbound civilian ships and airplanes are asked to complete a baggage declaration form for the State Department of Agriculture (previously the Board of Agriculture and Forestry). Additional questions regarding visitor status and characteristics were added at the request of the Hawaii Visitors Bureau, which publishes monthly, quarterly, or annual tabulations in its research reports. Data on "intended residents," initially limited to monthly totals in the HVB reports, are now analyzed in considerable detail by the State Department of Planning and Economic Development.[10] Annual counts since 1951 appear in Table 71.

A variety of new migration statistics has appeared in recent years (references are listed in Footnote 11). The 1950 U. S. Census contained a question regarding place of residence on V-J Day (for Hawaii residents) or April 1, 1949 (for persons enumerated on the Mainland); the 1960 Census asked about place of residence in April 1955 (see Table 72). A follow-up survey of 1952 high school graduates from Hawaii was made in 1956. The American Association of Collegiate Registrars and Admissions

Officers and the U. S. Office of Education have published college enrollment statistics cross-tabulated by state of residence and state of attendance. From 1957 to 1962, the Honolulu Star-Bulletin "consumer analysis," an annual sample survey of Oahu households, included a question on residence one year earlier. The State Department of Labor and Industrial Relations has issued data on labor mobility between Hawaii and the Mainland. Totals on aged Social Security beneficiaries moving to or from Hawaii were first compiled in 1961-1962. Taeuber published net migration rates classified by age, sex, race, and county for the 1950-1960 period.[11]

Table 61.--NON-HAWAIIANS PRESENT AND HAWAIIANS AND PART HAWAIIANS ABSENT: 1823 TO 1878

Year	Non-Hawaiians present in Hawaii[a]	Hawaiians absent from Hawaii	Year	Non-Hawaiians present in Hawaii[a]	Hawaiians absent from Hawaii
1823...	175	200	1853...	2,119	4,000
1832...	400	400	1860...	2,816	3,500
1836...	600	600	1866...	4,194	1,500
1848...	(NA)	3,500	1872...	5,366	800
1850...	1,572	4,000	1878...	10,477	400

NA Not available.

[a]Includes Hawaii-born children of foreign parents (291 in 1853, 849 in 1872, and 947 in 1878).

Source: Romanzo Adams, Interracial Marriage in Hawaii, p. 8, and unpublished manuscript; present study, Table 16.

Table 62.--HAWAII POPULATION BORN ELSEWHERE: 1853 TO 1960

Year	Number	Percent	Year	Number	Percent
1853.....	1,828	2.5	1910.....	105,426	54.9
1872.....	4,517	7.9	1920.....	119,563	46.7
1878.....	9,530	16.4	1930.....	153,819	41.8
1884.....	34,306	42.6	1940.....	144,824	34.2
1890.....	41,873	46.5	1950.....	144,220	28.9
1896.....	55,783	51.2	1960[a]....	211,604	33.4
1900.....	95,070	61.7			

[a]Includes 8,750 persons not reporting State of birth.

Table 63.--POPULATION EXCHANGE BETWEEN HAWAII AND MAINLAND: 1853 TO 1960

Year	Hawaii-born population of Hawaii and Mainland				Mainland-born, living in Hawaii	Net cumulative migration gain
	Total	Living in Hawaii	Living on Mainland			
			Number[a]	Percent		
1853...	71,843	71,310	533	0.7	692	159
1872...	53,109	52,380	729	1.4	889	160
1878...	49,522	48,455	1,067	2.2	1,276	209
1884...	47,491	46,272	1,219	2.6	2,066	847
1890...	49,421	48,117	1,304	2.6	1,928	624
1896...	54,543	53,237	1,306	2.4	2,266	960
1900...	60,238	58,931	1,307	2.2	4,284	2,977
1910...	90,224	86,483	3,741	4.1	5,688	1,947
1920...	146,900	136,349	10,551	7.2	10,957	406
1930...	233,974	214,517	19,457	8.3	30,191	10,734
1940...	302,229	278,506	23,723	7.8	54,224	30,501
1950...	407,529	355,574	51,955	12.7	65,640	13,685
1960[b]..	536,238	421,168	115,070	21.5	128,992	13,922

[a]Data estimated by interpolation for 1853-1884 and 1896. The actual number enumerated in the decennial U. S. census was 588 in 1850, 435 in 1860, 584 in 1870, and 1,147 in 1880.

[b]Includes Alaska with Mainland U. S. Excludes 8,750 Hawaii residents not reporting State of birth.

Table 64.--NET PASSENGER MOVEMENT TO (+) OR FROM (-) HONOLULU: 1860 TO 1900

(Excludes inter-island passengers)

Calendar year	Net movement	Calendar year	Net movement	Calendar year	Net movement	Calendar year	Net movement
1860...	+22	1870...	+401	1880...	+3,665	1890...	+3,164
1861...	+46	1871...	+873	1881...	+4,302	1891...	+4,965
1862...	+36	1872...	+43	1882...	+2,877	1892...	+1,166
1863[a]..	-123	1873...	-42	1883...	+7,452	1893...	+1,915
1864...	(NA)	1874...	-25	1884...	+2,809	1894...	+2,637
1865...	(NA)	1875...	+196	1885...	+3,552	1895...	+3,454
1866...	+224	1876...	+2,054	1886...	+1,627	1896...	+7,127
1867...	+76	1877...	+1,218	1887...	+903	1897...	+4,875
1868...	+163	1878...	+3,212	1888...	+2,143	1898...	+9,916
1869...	+279	1879...	+6,245	1889...	+1,305	1899...	+23,662
						1900[b]..	+4,642

NA Not available.

[a]First nine months.

[b]January 1 to June 14.

Source: Custom House statistics.

Table 65.--NET PASSENGER MOVEMENT OF SPECIFIED IMMIGRANT GROUPS TO (+) OR FROM (-) HAWAII, 1900 TO 1905, AND HONOLULU, 1905 TO 1910

(Excludes inter-island passengers)

Group, area, and period	Net movement
Chinese, Japanese, and Koreans (Hawaii):	
June 14, 1900 to June 30, 1902[a]	-1,424
July 1, 1902 to June 30, 1904	+4,530
July 1, 1904 to June 30, 1905	-4,145
July 1 to December 31, 1905	-2,664
All immigrant groups (calendar years, Honolulu only):	
1905	-6,487
1906	+1,404
1907	+7,269
1908	-55
1909	-1,133
1910, first six months	+1,055

[a]Excludes arrivals before July 1, 1900.

Source: U. S. Department of Commerce and Labor, Fourth Report of the Commissioner of Labor on Hawaii, Bulletin of the Bureau of Labor, No. 94 (May 1911), pp. 724-725.

Table 66.--NET MOVEMENT OF STEERAGE PASSENGERS TO (+) OR FROM (-) HAWAII: 1910 TO 1934

Year ending June 30	Net movement	Year ending June 30	Net movement	Year[a]	Net movement[a]
1911...	-21	1919...	+34	1927[b]...	-1,446
1912...	+3,481	1920...	-582	1927[c]...	+3,939
1913...	+7,303	1921...	-3,742	1928[c]...	+3,959
1914...	+1,292	1922...	+5,302	1929[c]...	-555
1915...	-937	1923...	+4,351	1930[c]...	+1,410
1916...	+1,230	1924...	+2,378	1932[b]...	-2,764
1917...	+1,141	1925...	+5,546	1933[b]...	-9,319
1918...	-1,564	1926...	-3,679	1934[b]...	-6,094

[a]Port of Honolulu only, 1930-1934. Excludes inter-island passengers.

[b]Year ending June 30.

[c]Calendar year.

Source: Annual reports of the Governor of Hawaii to the Secretary of the Interior.

Table 67.--NET PASSENGER MOVEMENT, 1928 TO 1940, AND NET CIVILIAN MOVEMENT, 1940 TO 1965, TO (+) AND FROM (-) HAWAII

(For years ending June 30. Data on civilian movement include military inductions and separations)

Year	Amount	Year	Amount	Year	Amount
1929...	+867	1942...	+30,119	1955...	+4,443
1930...	+1,080	1943...	-2,913	1956...	+6,215
1931...	+1,560	1944...	+3,814	1957...	+12,424
1932...	-1,133	1945...	-15,923	1958...	+8,473
1933...	-8,240	1946...	+3,192	1959...	+6,489
1934...	-6,578	1947...	-4,947	1960...	+821
1935...	-1,990	1948...	+3,423	1961...	+3,549
1936...	-176	1949...	-21,499	1962...	+8,631
1937...	-1,336	1950...	-23,765	1963...	+5,649
1938...	+2,238	1951...	-11,895	1964...	+5,626
1939...	-1,421	1952...	-21,495	1965...	+13,646
1940...	-2,618	1953...	-7,560		
1941...	+4,699	1954...	-6,868		

Source: HDH, Civilian Population, Births, Deaths, and Migration Data of Hawaii by Geographic Area, 1950-1964 (March 1964), Table 4, and records.

Table 68.--NET MIGRATION TO (+) OR FROM (-) HAWAII:

1900 TO 1963

Period	Net migration	Percent of population at beginning of period
1900-1910....	+33,325	+21.6
1910-1920....	+26,346	+13.7
1920-1930....	+37,045	+14.5
1930-1940....	-5,924	-1.6
1940-1950....	-15,695	-3.7
1950-1960....	+2,765	+0.6
1960-1963....	+16,000	+2.3

Source: Robert C. Schmitt, "Hawaii on the Move," Paradise of the Pacific, 65 (Aug. 1953), p. 25; USBC, "Components of Population Change, 1950 to 1960, for Counties, Standard Metropolitan Statistical Areas, State Economic Areas, and Economic Subregions," Current Population Reports, Series P-23, No. 7, (Nov. 1962), p. 22, and "Estimates of the Population of States: July 1, 1964," Current Population Reports, Series P-25, No. 324 (Jan. 20, 1966), p. 10.

Table 69.--NET MIGRATION, TOTAL AND CIVILIAN, BY COUNTIES: 1950 TO 1960

County	Net total migration		Net civilian migration	
	Number	Rate[a]	Number	Rate[a]
All counties.............	+2,765	+0.6	-23,637	-5.0
City and County of Honolulu...	+40,873	+11.6	+13,450	+4.1
Other counties...............	-38,108	-26.0	-37,087	-25.3
Hawaii......................	-17,813	-26.1	-17,384	-25.4
Maui and Kalawao...........	-13,457	-27.7	-13,004	-26.8
Kauai......................	-6,838	-22.9	-6,699	-22.4

[a]Net migration as percent of population at beginning of period.

Source: USBC, "Components of Population Change, 1950 to 1960, for Counties, Standard Metropolitan Statistical Areas, State Economic Areas, and Economic Subregions," _Current Population Reports_, Series P-23, No. 7 (Nov. 1962), p. 22.

Table 70.--IMMIGRANT ARRIVALS: 1852 TO 1899

(Data for Europeans limited to those "who came here under the auspices of the Board, and as a part of some organized scheme of immigration")

Year	Arrivals[a]	Year	Arrivals[a]	Year	Arrivals[a]	Year	Arrivals[a]
1852...	293	1864...	9	1876...	1,283	1888...	4,554
1853...	64	1865...	654	1877...	557	1889...	2,035
1854...	12	1866...	117	1878...	2,858	1890...	3,764
1855...	61	1867...	214	1879...	4,549	1891...	6,271
1856...	23	1868...	199	1880...	3,547	1892...	3,129
1857...	14	1869...	204	1881...	5,723	1893...	4,158
1858...	13	1870...	327	1882...	3,927	1894...	5,428
1859...	171	1871...	248	1883...	9,892	1895...	3,270
1860...	21	1872...	61	1884...	4,363	1896...	8,656
1861...	2	1873...	48	1885...	5,194	1897...	3,122
1862...	13	1874...	69	1886...	1,784	1898...	10,274
1863...	8	1875...	151	1887...	1,429	1899...	19,932

Source: _Report of the President of the Bureau of Immigration to the Legislative Assembly of 1886_, pp. 266, 278; _Labor Problems in Hawaii. Hearings Before the Committee on Immigration and Naturalization, House of Representatives_ (1921), p. 542.

Table 71.--INTENDED RESIDENTS ARRIVING BY WESTBOUND CIVILIAN CARRIER: 1951 TO 1965

Year	Including armed forces	Excluding armed forces	Year	Including armed forces	Excluding armed forces
1951...	5,860	5,789	1958...	16,472	13,972
1952...	6,685	6,640	1959...	18,374	15,868
1953...	6,472	6,452	1960...	15,030	12,942
1954...	5,788	5,808	1961...	16,720	13,745
1955...	8,332	7,704	1962...	21,070	18,125
1956...	11,268	9,428	1963...	20,200	17,425
1957...	16,544	14,008	1964...	24,030	19,155
			1965...	24,855	16,720

Year	Total	Armed forces	Military dependents	Other civilians	Not reported
1960 (9 mo.).	11,460	1,185	1,445	8,325	505
1961.........	16,720	2,975	2,950	9,875	920
1962.........	21,070	2,945	6,025	11,165	935
1963.........	20,200	2,775	5,230	11,370	825
1964.........	24,030	4,875	5,835	12,490	830
1965.........	24,855	8,135	4,840	11,330	550

Source: HDPED, SR 39 (June 10,1966), p. 4.

Table 72.--RESIDENCE IN 1955, BY COUNTY: 1960

Residence in 1955	Hawaii	Honolulu County	Other counties
Population 5 and over, 1960......	551,781	434,269	117,512
Same county in 1955 as 1960..........	416,866	307,332	109,534
Different county in Hawaii...........	15,281	11,550	3,731
Honolulu County....................	3,170	...	3,170
Other county.......................	12,111	11,550	561
Different State......................	94,768	92,119	2,649
Abroad...............................	19,402	18,301	1,101
Moved, 1955 residence not reported...	5,464	4,967	497
Out-migrants.........................	84,740	78,283	21,177
Intra-State........................	...	3,170	11,550
To other states....................	84,740	75,113	9,627
Net migration........................	+10,028	+25,386	-15,358
Intra-State........................	...	+8,380	-8,380
Inter-State........................	+10,028	+17,006	-6,978

Source: 1960 U. S. census data, as analyzed in HDPED, SR 13 (Feb. 15, 1964), p. 6.

VIII. MARRIAGE AND DIVORCE STATISTICS: 1829-1965

Annual statistics on marriages and divorces in Hawaii go back to the second quarter of the nineteenth century. The American missionaries began compiling marriage totals before 1830, about the same time that the first laws regarding marriage and divorce were proclaimed. Legislation governing the granting and reporting of marriage licenses was first enacted in 1840. The first official statistics on marriage were compiled in 1845; on divorce, in 1848. Except for a 37½-year break in the marriage record, these series were faithfully maintained. In later years tabulation programs were expanded to include data by geographic area, age, race, previous marital status, and many other characteristics of persons entering into or dissolving a marriage. Statistics on interracial marriage received special attention.

Legislation[1]

Legislation has affected both the availability and levels of statistics on marriage and divorce. Periodic reporting by official agencies on these events owes its existence to statutory requirements. Changes in the law are presumably a major factor in trends in the marriage and divorce rates.

Marriage was treated quite casually by early nineteenth century Hawaiians. Couples would begin to live together or separate with little or no ceremony. A man might have more than one wife, and a woman might have more than one husband.

American missionaries introduced the Christian form of

marriage soon after their arrival, with the first taking place in 1822. Christian marriages were at first relatively rare but became widespread toward the end of the decade. Church authorities drew up rules regarding monogamy, blood relationship, marriages to foreigners, and divorce.

The first laws regarding marriage and divorce were proclaimed during the late 1820's. Marriage under the old customs was forbidden on Maui in 1826 and in Kona in 1827. The "Law Against Licentiousness," published in 1829, forbade polygamy, legalized existing marriages, provided for divorce on grounds of adultery, and regulated the remarriage of divorced persons. A law enacted later that year specifically endorsed Christian marriage. Enforcement was unexpectedly easy. Penalties for marital and sexual offenses were severe.

The major legal limitations on marriage were those relating to monogamy, consanguinity, age, and literacy. The ability to read became a prerequisite for a marriage license on Maui in 1835 and throughout the kingdom six years later. (This law was repealed in 1850.) The minimum age for marriage was initially set at fourteen years for boys and twelve for girls; in 1845-1846 it was raised to seventeen for males and fourteen for females; in 1913, to eighteen and fifteen, respectively; and in 1937, to eighteen and sixteen.[2]

Grounds for divorce, at first quite restricted, were gradually extended and liberalized. The 1834 penal code provided for divorce for "frequent adultery and bad conduct." Six years later, desertion and other grounds were added, but an 1846 law recognized only adultery as permissible grounds. In divorce case rulings, however, the governors continued to follow the 1840 statute. In 1853 the Legislature approved divorce for desertion and imprisonment as well as for adultery, and transferred jurisdiction from the governors to the courts. The law was further liberalized in 1859 and 1870, when extreme cruelty, habitual intemperance, and non-support were added as legal grounds. Numerous minor changes were enacted in later years, including the addition of incurable insanity (1919) and grievous mental suffering (1949) as further grounds.[3] The rules regarding remarriage of divorced persons, at first quite stringent, were relaxed in 1859 and abolished in 1866.[4]

All marriages had to be recorded (references to laws on marriage statistics are cited in Footnote 5). On September 21, 1829, Kauikeaouli decreed: "... let their names be both written in the marriage certificate, so they will be observing the laws of the present time." An 1840 law required that "whoever solemnizes marriages shall keep a book where he shall record the names of the persons whom he marries. On [December 31] every year ... [he] shall give notice of the number of marriages which he has solemnized during the year." These provisions were extended and reinforced by "An Act to Facilitate the Proof of Marriage" passed in 1864.

Official registrars were first provided for in 1850, when an "Act Relating to the Registry of Births, Deaths and Marriages" required the school inspectors to appoint "registers [sic] ... for each okana, or township" to record vital events and report on a quarterly basis to the Minister of Public Instruction. The registrars were paid two cents per event, if deemed correct. A companion act, passed in 1851, transferred the registration of births, deaths, and marriages from the office of the Minister of the Interior to that of the Minister of Public Instruction. Minor changes were enacted in 1859 and 1865. Responsibility for appointing district registrars was transferred to the Director of the Board of Health in 1896. Seventeen years later, the position of Registrar-General was created within the Board of Health, with primary responsibility for the registration and statistical analysis of all births, deaths, and marriages occurring in the Territory. This work was further institutionalized by legislation enacted in 1937 and 1949.[5]

Divorce statistics, in contrast, did not receive an explicit legislative mandate until 1951. The governors of the Islands were required to report their official actions (presumably including all divorces) on a quarterly basis but seldom did so. Jurisdiction over divorces passed to the courts in 1853; from that year forward, the Chief Justice routinely maintained records and published statistical totals, although apparently not compelled to do so by any specific law.[6] Beginning in 1951, the clerk of the court was required to submit data regarding each divorce and annulment granted to the Bureau of

Vital Statistics for inclusion in their statistical analyses.[7]

Sources and reliability of data

Statistics on marriage and divorce in Hawaii have been compiled or published at one time or another by the American missionaries, the Minister of the Interior, the Minister of Public Instruction or President of the Board of Education, the Chief Justice of the Supreme Court, the Board (later Department) of Health, and a number of United States Government agencies. The accuracy and completeness of the statistical record has been quite satisfactory since the early 1900's. A number of special studies of Hawaiian marriage and divorce data, particularly with reference to interracial marriage, have been published by sociologists and demographers in recent years.

The earliest statistics on marriage in Hawaii were those compiled by the Sandwich Islands Mission. William Richards wrote on April 14, 1828 that "the whole number of marriages in Lahaina during the past year, is 611, making the whole number of persons married 1,222."[8] Four of the six mission stations in the kingdom reported data for 1829, giving a combined total of 1,317 marriages performed that year.[9] Later data usually referred to annual periods ending on the eve of the general meeting of the Mission, most frequently around June 1. Published totals by station appeared in the Extracts from the Minutes of the General Meeting of the Sandwich Islands Mission, the Missionary Herald (a monthly published in Boston by the American Board of Commissioners for Foreign Missions), and the

Missionary Register (a similar monthly issued in London).[10]

Unfortunately, the totals reported by the missionaries were invariably incomplete, even for marriages performed in their own churches. In 1831, for example, only five of the seven stations submitted data, accounting for 1,678 of the estimated 1,937 marriages solemnized by the missionaries.[11] In 1847, ten out of twenty-four failed to report; in 1849, three out of twenty-one; and in 1852, seven out of twenty-two. Except for in 1831, no effort has been made to adjust for the incomplete response.

Moreover, an unknown number of marriages occurred outside the auspices of the Protestant missionaries. In spite of claims that the Christian form of marriage was generally accepted by 1830, reason exists for suspecting that more casual unions, of varying degrees of permanence, continued to take place in the more remote sections of the kingdom well after that date. (Even today, needless to say, joint living arrangements are sometimes initiated without first securing the proper papers.) Arrival of the Roman Catholic missionaries on July 7, 1827 further complicated the statistical picture. Although, thanks to their head start and to repressive measures by the government, the Protestants continued to dominate Island religious life, the Catholics accounted for a rapidly increasing proportion of marriages from 1839 onward.[12] The value of the missionary statistics is further reduced by the inclusion of couples already married under the old custom who renewed their vows in the

Christian manner.

Some notion of the incompleteness of the missionary data may be obtained by comparing them with corresponding official figures. In a two-year period ending in May 1848, for example, 1,882 marriages were reported by the Sandwich Islands Mission, far fewer than the 3,198 shown by the government (see Tables 73 and 74). Similar discrepancies are evident in other years.

The first official statistics on marriages were compiled in 1845. Totals by island for that year were published by the Minister of the Interior, who warned that they "may not be perfectly correct" and added that "the number of divorces has not been mentioned."[13] A similar tabulation for the following year was accompanied by a remark that "the number of marriages actually solemnized is supposed to exceed these returns, but it is uncertain."[14] Data for 1847 were published without comment. The next year to be reported was 1849. An explanatory paragraph noted that "the reports of Marriages have not been made according to law. How many were celebrated during the year 1848, is not known, owing to the delinquency on the part of those who are authorized to celebrate them."[15] Subsequent reports by the Minister of the Interior made no mention of the subject.

The series was resumed in 1851 and continued until 1863 by the office of the Minister of Public Instruction. Annual totals were published, sometimes by district or religion.[16] No explanation was given for the wide, erratic fluctuations in the year-to-year figures. It seems likely, however, that marriages were seriously underreported in some years, particularly after 1860. The 1863 total was the last issued before a 37½-year break in the marriage record. Except for census statistics on marital status, no further information on the subject was published by the Board of Education, in spite of its legislative mandate.

Divorce statistics fared far better. Data on the number of divorce cases tried in Superior Court each year since 1848 appeared in the First Annual Report of the Chief Justice of the Supreme Court, issued in 1853. These totals failed to account for divorces granted by the governors, presumably a sizeable number; after 1853, however, the courts had full jurisdiction, and their statistics offered complete coverage of divorce actions. Subsequent annual and biennial reports of the Chief Justice extended the yearly series initiated in the first report, continuing without interruption until 1940.[17] Tabulations for 1851 to 1873 and 1898 to 1940 gave separate totals for divorces granted and the number denied, but from 1874 to 1897 the all-island totals were limited to the number of cases, without any indication of their disposition. For this twenty-four-year period it is necessary to resort to estimates based on more detailed data shown for several of the circuit courts.

No serious flaws can be found in the published statistics on divorce. The chief exceptions to this statement, other than the incomplete coverage before 1853 and the failure to report denials separately during the last quarter of the century, occurred in 1907 and 1910. The figure for the former was later labeled "improbable" and "probably erroneous"; the total for the latter was found to be wrong and was subsequently corrected.[18]

Statistics on marriage became available again soon after annexation. The Board of Health, given custody of such data in 1896, made an abortive effort to re-establish the series but had to admit temporary defeat: "The reports of births, marriages and deaths ... are very unsatisfactory ...."[19] Beginning with data for the year ended June 30, 1902, however, the figures issued by the board can apparently be treated with some confidence.[20] Annual totals, often reported in considerable geographic and subject detail, appear in succeeding annual reports of the Board (or Department) of Health. Annual totals from 1912 forward, adjusted to a calendar year basis, were recapitulated in the 1960 report.[21] Beginning in 1937, marriages were tabulated according to various social and demographic characteristics of the partners.[22]

Responsibility for the tabulation, analysis, and publication of statistics on divorce was assumed by the Department of Health in mid-1951. Although the Chief Justice of the Supreme Court had terminated his 93-year-old series on divorce after 1940, the Health Department statisticians were able to reconstruct the figures for the missing years and continue the series without a break. Much analytic detail appeared in subsequent reports.[23] The totals published by the Department of Health have explicitly included the small number of annulments granted annually. (It is not clear whether annulments were included or omitted in the reports of the Chief Justice.)

Marriage and divorce statistics for Hawaii have been published in U. S. Government reports since 1946. This information, much like that issued by the Department of Health in its regular statistical reports, appears annually in Vital Statistics of the United States.[24] The program was greatly expanded in recent years by the organization of both a Marriage-Registration Area (in January 1957) and Divorce-Registration Area (in 1958).[25] Hawaii was a charter member of both areas.

Census statistics on marital status have been compiled since 1853. Such figures differ from those described in the preceding part of this chapter by referring to status as of a given moment in time rather than to events occurring within a period of time. The 1853 and 1860 censuses reported the number of married persons in the population, but the lack of satisfactory age detail precluded the extraction of much meaning from the figures (see Chapter III). This handicap was largely overcome in 1866, when it became possible to relate the married population to the number of marriageable age. Information on persons widowed or divorced as well as those married was first collected in 1890. Data on persons married but separated were first compiled in 1950. Marital status has been cross-tabulated with numerous other characteristics, such as age, race, labor force status, and family composition, in recent census reports (see Chapter IV).

Many special tabulations of registration data on marriage and divorce have been undertaken for or by sociologists and demographers. Most of this work has concerned interracial marriage rates. Books or articles on this subject have been written by Adams, Lind, Yamamoto, Cheng and Yamamura, Taeuber, Schmitt, Schmitt and Souza, and others.[26] A smaller number of articles have dealt with other aspects of marriage and divorce in the Islands.[27] All of these works have been strongly statistical in their orientation, often presenting previously unpublished data.

Statistical trends

Statistical trends revealed by the series described in this chapter are shown in the accompanying tables.

Several different kinds of annual rates are given:

1. Marriages or divorces per 1,000 civilian population. Such rates are readily computed because of the availability of semi-annual population estimates going back to 1848. Unfortunately, a civilian population base includes many persons not part of the "risk" population, such as persons who are already married (and hence ineligible for a second marriage), single, widowed, or divorced (and thus without a current partner to divorce), or below the legal age for marriage. In omitting members of the armed forces, it excludes a group that accounted for almost one out of four grooms during a recent two-year

period.

2. Divorces per 100 marriages. This kind of rate can be easily computed on an annual basis. Most marriages dissolved in a given year were contracted in an earlier period and are accordingly not represented in the base; given wide year-to-year fluctuations in marriage or divorce totals, such a rate can be highly misleading. At best, it is often misinterpreted by careless readers.

3. Marriages or divorces per 1,000 "risk" population. The base for this kind of rate is usually the number of single, widowed, or divorced women of marriageable age (for marriages) or the number of married women (for divorces). Unfortunately, base figures are available only for census years. A comparison of rates based on the "risk" population with corresponding rates per 1,000 civilian population reveals some strikingly divergent trends (see Table 78).

None of these rates makes allowance for non-resident or out-of-State events. During 1961 and 1962, for example, 659 (out of 10,782) marriages performed in the State involved at least one non-resident partner, and in 200 of them both partners were non-residents.[28]

Table 73 lists annual totals on the number of marriages reported by Protestant church officials, from 1829 to 1853. Lack of intercensal population estimates for most of this period precludes the computation of annual rates. In any event, serious deficiencies in the data would render such rates virtually meaningless.

Official statistics on the number of marriages performed in Hawaii are shown in Table 74. Annual totals are given for the period from 1845 to 1863 and from 1902 forward; rates per 1,000 civilian population begin in 1849. Some of the annual fluctuations evident in this table, particularly during the nineteenth century, are obviously attributable to underreporting. It seems unlikely, for example, that the marriage rate should have fallen from 29.2 per 1,000 population in 1854 to 12.8 in 1855 and 1856, and then risen to 22.5 in 1857. Data on marriages are unavailable from 1864 to 1901.

Interracial marriage rates are traced in Table 75.

Table 76 presents annual data on the number of divorces granted by Island courts from 1848 to the present time. Besides absolute totals, two kinds of divorce rate are shown: divorces per 1,000 population and divorces per 100 marriages. (The latter measure depends, of course, on accurate marriage statistics, which were unavailable for a number of years.) Data used in estimating divorce totals from 1874 to 1897 are reproduced in Table 77.

Marriages and divorces per 1,000 "risk" population are reported in Table 78. Corresponding rates per 1,000 civilian population are shown for comparative purposes. Accurate base data for computing rates on a risk basis are available only for census years; this table, accordingly, presents rates for two-year periods centering on census dates.

Table 79 traces trends in the proportion of males and females who were married, widowed, or divorced as of each census date, beginning in 1866.

The reasons behind the trends revealed by these tables are sometimes obscure.

The age and sex composition of the population is obviously an important factor. In 1900, unattached males outnumbered unattached women by an alarming margin, but by 1960 the male surplus was down to 51 percent. Rates are inevitably affected by such changes.

War and the prospect of war exercise a strong and sometimes complex influence. The approach of hostilities may stimulate some men to marry to avoid military conscription, others to complete arrangements before shipping off. Accelerated economic activity resulting from war preparations gives many workers enough income to undertake responsibilities they could not previously afford. Later, the absence of sweethearts may reduce marriage rates. A second increase normally follows the end of hostilities, as men return after a long absence. If the prewar and postwar marriage booms resulted in many hasty unions, each was followed a year or so later by a corresponding spurt in divorces.

Economic depressions likewise affect marriage and divorce rates. Workers with reduced incomes may be reluctant to assume the expensive obligations of marriage. Divorce, too, becomes infeasible under such conditions.

Legal factors further complicate interpretation of trends. The nineteenth century prohibition on the marriage of illiterates, increases in the minimum age for marriage, and changes in the legal grounds for divorce may reasonably be expected to have affected the rates. A sudden liberalization of the divorce law may have less effect than an expected tightening of the regulations; both timing and overall levels will probably be influenced in either case.

The reasoning cited above is generally borne out by the historical record. World War I, World War II, and the Korean War were all preceded, accompanied, and followed by sharp shifts in both marriage and divorce rates. Economic slumps and depressions have been marked by corresponding dips in marriage and divorce data, with notable examples occurring in 1932 to 1933 and in 1949.

Changes in divorce laws have had a less perceptible effect. Legal grounds were extended in 1853, 1870, 1919, and 1949, but the statistical consequences were inconclusive. Even the judges have been unable to agree in some instances. The sharp increase noted between 1876-1877 and the following biennium, for example, was attributed in one report to excessive liberalization of the divorce law and in another to clearing the docket of many long-standing cases of desertion.[29]

Divorce statistics, no matter how accurate and complete, are at best only a rough index of trends in marital dissolution. For one thing, they omit legal separations. Even more importantly, they take no account of desertion until--and unless--it eventuates in a legal divorce. This problem is particularly serious in reference to data for the nineteenth century, when restless husbands found it easy to escape to sea and never return. Confronted by the legal complexities and the costs of a court divorce, the deserted partners may in many cases have dispensed with such a formality. It thus appears likely that the low divorce rates in evidence before 1900 masked a high rate of marital break-up.

Table 73.--MARRIAGES PERFORMED IN PROTESTANT CHURCHES: 1829 TO 1853

(Not adjusted for churches failing to report. The number of non-responding churches exceeded 30 percent of the total in some years)

Year[a]	Marriages	Year[a]	Marriages	Year[a]	Marriages	Year[a]	Marriages
1829...	1,317	1835...	1,546	1841......	1,314	1849...	1,104
1830...	...	1836...	1,358	1842......	924	1850...	1,374
1831[b]..	1,678	1837...	1,082	1843......	994	1851...	1,074
1832...	1,610	1838...	1,259	1844......	1,314	1852...	1,068
1833...	1,290	1839...	1,143	1845-46...	2,171	1853...	924
1834...	1,125	1840...	1,221	1847-48...	1,882		

[a]Calendar year 1829; 12-month periods ending in May, June, or July, 1831 to 1844 and 1849 to 1853; 24-month periods ending in May or June, 1846 and 1848.

[b]Including churches not reported, estimated total was 1,937.

Source: Missionary Herald, Oct. 1830, March 1832, July 1847, Oct. 1849, March 1851, Dec. 1851, Nov. 1852, and Dec. 1853; Missionary Register, Oct. 1832; Extracts from the Minutes of the General Meeting of the Sandwich Islands Mission for 1832 to 1844 and 1848.

Table 74.--MARRIAGES AND MARRIAGE RATES: 1845 TO 1863 AND 1902 TO 1965

Year	Number	Rate[a]	Year	Number	Rate[a]	Year	Number	Rate[a]
1845...	1,831	...	1911[b]..	2,266	11.8	1937...	3,556	9.3
1846...	1,763	...	1912[b]..	2,882	14.6	1938...	3,868	9.9
1847...	1,435	...	1913[b]..	3,231	15.7	1939...	3,963	10.1
1848...	...	...				1940...	5,355	13.5
1849...	1,810	21.1	1912...	3,223	16.0	1941...	6,066	14.8
1850...	...	...	1913...	3,184	15.0	1942...	7,093	15.9
1851...	1,771	21.6	1914...	2,769	12.7	1943...	4,984	11.0
1852...	1,493	18.7	1915...	2,705	12.2	1944...	4,882	10.5
1853...	1,954	25.6	1916...	2,778	12.2	1945...	4,978	10.9
1854...	2,128	29.2	1917...	2,635	11.1	1946...	5,945	12.6
1855...	933	12.8	1918...	2,398	9.9	1947...	5,846	12.3
1856...	930	12.8	1919...	2,013	8.1	1948...	5,671	11.5
1857...	1,623	22.5	1920...	2,127	8.4	1949...	5,316	11.0
1858...	1,060	14.8	1921...	2,338	9.1	1950...	5,575	11.8
1859...	1,130	15.9	1922...	2,493	9.2	1951...	5,860	12.4
1860...	1,075	15.3	1923...	2,795	9.9	1952...	5,743	12.4
1861...	906	13.1	1924...	3,354	11.4	1953...	5,633	12.0
1862...	596	8.7	1925...	2,736	8.8	1954...	5,362	11.3
1863...	726	10.9	1926...	2,617	8.3	1955...	5,431	10.9
			1927...	2,626	8.1	1956...	5,158	10.1
1902[b]..	1,314	8.4	1928...	2,737	8.1	1957...	4,897	9.1
1903[b]..	996	6.2	1929...	2,565	7.4	1958...	4,727	8.4
1904[b]..	1,182	7.2	1930...	2,443	6.9	1959...	4,958	8.5
1905[b]..	1,180	7.0	1931...	2,629	7.2	1960...	5,237	8.8
1906[b]..	1,238	7.5	1932...	2,726	7.4	1961...	5,298	8.6
1907[b]..	1,680	10.0	1933...	2,621	7.1	1962...	5,484	8.6
1908[b]..	2,214	12.3	1934...	2,838	7.7	1963...	5,750	8.8
1909[b]..	1,648	8.9	1935...	2,985	8.0	1964...	5,790	8.6
1910[b]..	1,959	10.4	1936...	3,292	8.7	1965...	6,071	8.6

[a]Marriages per 1,000 civilian population.

[b]Year ending June 30.

Source: Reports of the Minister of the Interior, 1846-1850; reports of the Minister of Public Instruction, 1852-1855; reports of the Board of Education, 1856-1864; Report of the Governor of the Territory of Hawaii to the Secretary of the Interior, 1903, p. 78; Thos. G. Thrum, comp., Hawaiian Almanac and Annual for 1906 and 1909 (p. 21); reports of the Board of Health, 1909-1913; Annual Report, Department of Health, State of Hawaii, Statistical Supplement for 1960-1965. Rates were computed from population estimates in the Appendix.

Table 75.--INTERRACIAL MARRIAGES: 1912 TO 1965

Year[a]	Percent inter-racial[b]	Year[a]	Percent inter-racial[b]	Year[a]	Percent inter-racial[b]
1912-16...	11.5	1942...	25.7	1953...	30.5
1916-20...	...	1943...	29.1	1954...	31.2
1920-24...	18.0	1944...	31.9	1955...	31.3
1924-28...	21.9	1945...	32.2	1956...	35.1
1928-30...	21.3	1946...	27.1	1957...	34.4
1930-34...	21.6	1947...	28.8	1958...	37.6
1935......	20.0	1948[c]..	29.0	1959...	37.3
1936......	22.1			1960...	37.3
1937......	24.6	1948[d]..	29.5	1961...	36.1
1938......	24.2	1949...	29.9	1962...	37.7
1939......	22.6	1950...	29.7	1963...	38.6
1940......	25.0	1951...	30.6	1964...	38.3
1941......	23.9	1952...	31.5	1965...	38.1

[a]Four-year periods ending June 30, 1916, 1920, 1924, 1928, and 1934; two-year period ending June 30, 1930; one-year periods ending June 30, 1935 to 1948; calendar years beginning in 1948.

[b]Data for 1963-1965 based on eleven groups, including "all other"; earlier years based on nine groups, including "all other."

[c]Year ending June 30.

[d]Calendar year.

Source: Robert C. Schmitt, "Demographic Correlates of Interracial Marriage in Hawaii," Demography, 2 (1965), Table 1, p. 466; HDH, annual reports.

Table 76.--DIVORCES AND DIVORCE RATES: 1848 TO 1965

Year[a]	Number[b]	Per 1,000 civ. pop.[c]	Per 100 marriages	Year[a]	Number[b]	Per 1,000 civ. pop.[c]	Per 100 marriages
1848......	0	0.0	...	1916...	379	1.7	14
1849......	1	0.0	0	1917...	383	1.6	15
1850......	7	0.1	...	1918...	557	2.3	23
1851-52...	81	0.5	2	1919...	525	2.1	26
1853......	31	0.4	2	1920...	570	2.2	27
1854......	87	1.2	4	1921...	562	2.2	24
1855......	78	1.1	8	1922...	555	2.0	22
1856......	85	1.2	9	1923...	560	2.0	20
1857......	106	1.5	7	1924...	557	1.9	17
1858......	58	0.8	5	1925...	627	2.0	23
1859......	54	0.8	5	1926...	618	2.0	24
1860-61...	173	1.2	9	1927...	676	2.1	26
1862-63...	127	0.9	10	1928...	595	1.8	22
1864-65...	52	0.4	...	1929...	563	1.6	22
1866-67...	101	0.8	...	1930...	529	1.5	22
1868-69...	152	1.3	...	1931...	598	1.6	23
1870-71...	76	0.7	...	1932...	527	1.4	19
1872-73...	18	0.2	...	1933...	541	1.5	21
1874-75...	7	0.1	...	1934...	595	1.6	21
1876-77...	39	0.4	...	1935...	690	1.9	23
1878-79...	228	2.0	...	1936...	730	1.9	22
1880-81...	158	1.2	...	1937...	815	2.1	23
1882-83...	174	1.2	...	1938...	862	2.2	22
1884-85...	107	0.7	...	1939...	866	2.2	22
1886-87...	108	0.6	...	1940...	946	2.4	18
1888-89...	96	0.6	...	1941...	1,147	2.8	19
1890-91...	97	0.5	...	1942...	1,517	3.4	21
1892-93...	101	0.5	...	1943...	1,610	3.6	32
1894......	71	0.7	...	1944...	1,671	3.4	32
1895......	68	0.7	...	1945...	1,530	3.3	31
1896......	77	0.7	...	1946...	1,453	3.1	24
1897......	66	0.6	...	1947...	1,178	2.5	20
1898......	53	0.4	...	1948...	1,388	2.8	24
1899......	38	0.3	...	1949...	1,052	2.2	20
1900......	48	0.3	...	1950...	1,173	2.5	21
1901......	85	0.5	...	1951...	1,185	2.5	20
1902......	56	0.4	4	1952...	1,300	2.8	23
1903......	62	0.4	6	1953...	1,287	2.7	23
1904......	89	0.5	8	1954...	1,270	2.7	24
1905......	109	0.7	9	1955...	1,343	2.7	25
1906......	87	0.5	7	1956...	1,305	2.5	25
1907......	271	1.6	16	1957...	1,182	2.2	24
1908......	131	0.7	6	1958...	1,228	2.2	26
1909......	223	1.2	14	1959...	1,378	2.4	28
1910......	197	1.0	10	1960...	1,270	2.1	24
1911......	284	1.5	13	1961...	1,556	2.5	29
1912......	352	1.8	11	1962...	1,471	2.3	27
1913......	337	1.6	11	1963...	1,515	2.3	26
1914......	324	1.5	12	1964...	1,690	2.5	29
1915......	389	1.8	14	1965[d]..	1,111	1.6	18

[a] One- and two-year periods ending December 31, except 1860-1861 (two-year period ending March 31, 1862).

[b] Divorce cases tried in Superior Court, 1848 to 1850; divorces granted, 1851 to 1964. Data for 1874-1897 estimated from incomplete reports.

[c] Annual basis.

[d] Data exclude interlocutory decrees of one year required under Act 52, SLH 1965 (enacted May 8, 1965) for divorces involving minor children.

Source: Estimates for 1874-1897 from Table 77; other years from annual and biennial reports of the Chief Justice, 1853-1940, and annual reports of the Department of Health, 1960-1965. Rates computed from Tables 74 and 83.

Table 77.--DIVORCE CASES AND DIVORCES GRANTED, TOTAL AND REPORTED: 1870 TO 1897

Calendar years	All courts		Courts reporting disposition of cases			
			Divorce cases		Divorces granted	
	Divorce cases[a]	Divorces granted	Number	Percent[b]	Number	Percent[c]
1870-1873...	108	94	108	100.0	94	87.0
1874-1875...	8	7	...	...	...	87.6
1876-1877...	44	39	...	...	...	88.1
1878-1879...	258	228	...	...	...	88.5
1880-1881...	178	158	90	50.6	80	88.9
1882-1883...	176	174	70	39.8	69	98.6
1884-1885...	144	107	144	100.0	107	74.3
1886-1887...	121	108	86	71.1	77	89.5
1888-1889...	108	96	108	100.0	96	88.9
1890-1891...	97	97	39	40.2	39	100.0
1892-1893...	105	101	29	27.6	28	96.6
1894........	84	71	59	70.2	50	84.7
1895........	87	68	50	57.5	39	78.0
1896........	102	77	97	95.1	73	75.3
1897........	93	66	86	92.5	61	70.9

[a]Data for 1890-1897 include separation cases. Data for 1886-1887, 1890-1891, and 1894-1897 differ slightly from all-court summary totals published in the original reports.

[b]Cases in reporting courts as percent of cases in all courts.

[c]Divorces granted as percent of divorce cases.

Source: Divorce cases for all courts and reporting courts and divorces granted by reporting courts from biennial reports of the Supreme Court. Number granted in all courts based on percent granted in reporting courts. Percent granted computed for 1870-1873 and 1880-1897, interpolated for 1874-1879.

Table 78.--ALTERNATE MARRIAGE AND DIVORCE RATES: 1866 TO 1961

Event analyzed and year	Civilian population[a]	Risk population[b]	Marriages or divorces[c]	Rates	
				Per 1,000 civ. pop.	Per 1,000 risk pop.
Marriages:[d]					
1910........	190,266	9,667	2,112	11.1	218
1920........	251,515	14,616	2,070	8.2	142
1930........	352,009	26,059	2,504	7.1	96
1940........	396,537	51,669	4,659	11.7	90
1950........	476,938	58,995	5,446	11.4	92
1960........	585,505	65,156	5,098	8.7	78
Divorces:					
1866........	62,959	15,470	50	0.8	3
1872........	56,897	12,682	9	0.2	1
1878........	57,985	11,789	114	2.0	10
1884........	80,578	12,835	54	0.7	4
1890........	89,990	14,497	48	0.5	3
1896........	109,020	15,634	72	0.7	5
1900........	153,756	24,048	43	0.3	2
1910........	190,266	31,380	210	1.1	7
1920........	251,515	45,550	548	2.2	12
1930........	352,009	53,948	546	1.6	10
1940........	396,537	66,569	906	2.3	14
1950........	476,938	94,520	1,112	2.3	12
1960........	585,505	128,528	1,324	2.3	10

[a]Based on census data rather than intercensal estimates used in Tables 73 and 75.

[b]For marriages, unmarried females 15 and over (1910-1930) or 14 and over (1940-1960); for divorces, married females 15 and over (1866-1930) or 14 and over (1940-1960). Excludes not reported.

[c]Annual averages for 2-year periods centering on the census date.

[d]Not available for census dates before 1910.

Source: Computed from official census data and Tables 74 and 76.

Table 79.--MARRIED, WIDOWED, AND DIVORCED PERSONS, BY SEX: 1866 TO 1960

Year	Married (percent)[a]		Widowed (percent)[a]		Divorced (percent)[a]	
	Male	Female	Male	Female	Male	Female
1866...	61.6	75.1	...	...	...	...
1872...	56.2	71.2	...	...	...	...
1878...	48.0	72.8	...	...	...	...
1884...	36.3	70.4	...	...	...	...
1890...	36.9	72.9	5.0	9.9	0.4	0.6
1896...	34.4	71.0	3.5	9.6	0.4	1.0
1900...	36.7	77.9	2.8	6.5	0.3	0.4
1910...	45.1	76.4	4.5	6.2	1.0	0.9
1920...	50.5	75.7	4.8	5.8	0.9	0.7
1930...	44.0	67.4	3.9	6.9	1.0	1.2
1940...	39.1	56.3	3.4	7.5	1.4	1.8
1950...	52.3	61.6	3.7	7.6	2.6	2.5
1960...	57.7	66.4	3.0	7.8	2.7	2.9

[a]Based on population over 15 before 1900, 15 and over from 1900 to 1930, and 14 and over after 1930. Data for married persons include those separated (1.0 percent of males and 0.7 percent of females in 1950, 0.7 percent of males and 0.6 percent of females in 1960; not reported separately before 1950).

Appendix

INTERCENSAL POPULATION ESTIMATES: 1848-1965

This appendix presents semi-annual population estimates for Hawaii, from 1848 to the present time. They were prepared both for the light they throw on the history of population decline and growth in the Islands and for their usefulness in computing a large number of social and economic rates.

Intercensal population estimates, strictly defined, have been available for Hawaii only since 1940. Although the U. S. Bureau of the Census and various agencies of the Kingdom, Republic, and Territory of Hawaii have prepared postcensal estimates in past years, no effort was ever made to revise these figures in the light of subsequent census findings. It was not until publication of final 1950 census counts that revisions of this type, extending back to 1940, were developed. Such intercensal estimates were prepared by both the U. S. Bureau of the Census and the Hawaii Department of Health, but neither agency has so far extended its revisions prior to 1940. Persons requiring annual population totals for earlier years have accordingly had to fall back on the old unrevised postcensal series, notwithstanding the deficiencies of these data.

The present report recapitulates both of the official intercensal series for the 1940's and 1950's, and in addition presents a new set of semi-annual estimates for the years before 1940. These earlier estimates are based on official census reports, available in accurate form since 1850, and on official records of births and deaths, compiled since 1848, and passenger movement, first issued for 1852.

Coverage of the estimates varies somewhat over the 117-year span. Beginning with annexation (1898), totals are limited to the civilian population. Prior to that time, few military personnel were stationed in Hawaii. During the middle third of the twentieth century, however, the military constituted a significant proportion of the population, and at the height of World War II they almost outnumbered the civilian residents of Hawaii. A second conceptual change begins in 1950, when the estimates switch from a place-of-usual-residence basis to a de facto basis. Data since 1950 include visitors present in the Islands but exclude residents temporarily absent, in contrast to the practice for earlier dates.

Many of these estimates should be viewed as rough approximations. Birth and death statistics were missing for 1864, 1865, and throughout the 1890's, and were obviously incomplete or inaccurate (particularly in the case of births) well into the twentieth century. Death totals include military personnel until 1940. Migration statistics were unavailable before 1852, limited to immigrant arrivals until 1859, and restricted to Oriental passengers for a 4½-year period following annexation. "Error of closure"--the amount necessary to make the components of change add to the net change between censuses--was often an important factor in the estimates, proving particularly significant between 1900 and 1910.

The semi-annual estimates were derived from census totals and records of births, deaths, and net passenger movement, using interpolative procedures where necessary. Error of closure was distributed equally for each six-month period within an intercensal period. Since birth, death, and migration data were readily available only for twelve-month periods, semi-annual figures were necessarily computed by linear interpolation.

For 1900 to 1910, alternative estimates based on symptomatic data (chiefly on school enrollment) were tried but rejected.

Complete information appears in the accompanying tables. Table 80 presents official census totals from 1850 forward. Table 81 cites official statistics on natural increase (or decrease) and net passenger movement from 1848 forward. Table 82 lists intercensal totals for net population change, natural increase or decrease, net migration, and error of closure. Table 83 reports the final semi-annual population estimates recommended by this study. An alternative series for the period since 1940, developed by the U. S. Bureau of the Census, appears in Table 84.

Table 80.--ENUMERATED POPULATION: 1850 TO 1960

Census date	Total population	Census date	Total population	Civilian population[a]
January 1850....	84,165	Sept. 27, 1896...	109,020	...
Dec. 20, 1853...	73,138	June 1, 1900.....	154,001	153,756
Dec. 24, 1860...	69,800	Apr. 15, 1910....	191,874	190,266
Dec. 7, 1866....	62,959	Jan. 1, 1920.....	255,881	251,515
Dec. 27, 1872...	56,897	Apr. 1, 1930.....	368,300	352,009
Dec. 27, 1878...	57,985	Apr. 1, 1940.....	422,770	396,537
Dec. 27, 1884...	80,578	Apr. 1, 1950.....	499,794	476,938
Dec. 28, 1890...	89,990	Apr. 1, 1960.....	632,772	585,505

[a]Includes Coast Guard personnel, 1900-1930, and commissioned officers, 1900-1940.

Table 81.--NATURAL INCREASE AND NET MIGRATION: 1848 TO 1964

Year	Period[a]	Natural increase[b]	Net migration[c]
1848...	C	-6,465	...
1849...	C	-2,898	...
1850...	C	...	...
1851...	C	-3,368	...
1852...	C	-970	293
1853...	C	-6,513	64
1854...	C	-58	12
1855...	C	-43	61
1856...	C	-292	23
1857...	C	-402	14
1858...	C	-384	13
1859...	C	-679	171
1860...	C	-671	22
1861...	C	-706	46
1862...	C	-952	36
1863...	C	-1,063	-123
1864...	C	...	9
1865...	C	...	654
1866...	C	-1,228	224
1867...	C	-859	76
1868...	C	-1,247	163
1869	C	-365	279
1870...	C	-1,406	401
1871...	C	-943	873
1872...	C	-718	43
1873...	C	-637	-42
1874...	C	-553	-25
1875...	C	-430	196
1876...	C	-279	2,054
1877...	C	-26	1,218
1878...	C	-1,029 (1878-1879)	3,212
1879...	C		6,245
1880...	C	400 (1880-1881)	3,665
1881...	C		4,302
1882...	C	-460 (1882-1883)	2,877
1883...	C		7,452
1884...	C	-406 (1884-1885)	2,809
1885...	C		3,552
1886...	C	-53 (1886-1887)	1,627
1887...	C		903
1888...	C	71 (1888-1889)	2,143
1889...	C		1,305
1890...	C	...	3,164
1891...	C	...	4,965
1892...	C	...	1,166
1893...	C	...	1,915
1894...	C	...	2,637
1895...	C	...	3,454
1896...	C	...	7,127
1897...	C	...	4,875
1898...	C	...	9,916
1899...	C	...	23,662
1900...	C5½	-1,350	4,642
1901...	CF	-971	-1,424 (1901-1902)
1902...	CF	-228	
1903...	CF	-131	4,530 (1903-1904)
1904...	CF	-271	
1905...	C	-77	(d)
1906...	C	-24	1,404
1907...	C	509	7,269
1908...	6C	762	-55
1909...	FC	2,090	-1,133
1910...	F6	1,361	1,055
1911...	F	1,198	-21
1912...	F	2,076	3,481
1913...	F	2,336	7,303
1914...	F	3,049	1,292
1915...	F	3,722	-937
1916...	F	3,959	1,230
1917...	F	5,209	1,141
1918...	F	5,394	-1,564
1919...	F	5,113	34
1920...	F	5,601	-582
1921...	F	6,367	-3,742
1922...	F	7,136	5,302
1923...	F	6,681	4,351
1924...	F	7,910	2,378
1925...	F	9,092	5,546
1926...	F	8,361	-3,679
1927...	F	8,367	(e)
1928...	FC	7,551	3,959
1929...	F	7,017	867
1930...	F	6,897	1,080
1931...	F	7,026	1,560
1932...	F	6,964	-1,133
1933...	F	6,368	-8,240
1934...	F	5,752	-6,578
1935...	F	6,016	-1,990
1936...	F	5,625	-176
1937...	F	5,079	-1,336
1938...	F	5,767	2,238
1939...	F	5,822	-1,421
1940...	F	6,499	-2,618
1941...	F	6,560	4,699
1942...	F	7,084	30,119
1943...	F	7,990	-2,913
1944...	F	9,227	3,814
1945...	F	9,736	-15,923
1946...	F	8,850	3,192
1947...	F	10,895	-1,947
1948...	F	11,521	3,423
1949...	F	11,444	-21,499
1950...	F	11,227	-23,765
1951...	F	10,936	-11,895
1952...	F	12,077	-21,495
1953...	F	13,342	-7,560
1954...	F	12,964	-6,868
1955...	F	13,006	4,443
1956...	F	14,000	6,215
1957...	F	13,624	12,424
1958...	F	13,649	8,473
1959...	F	13,567	6,489
1960...	F	13,717	821
1961...	F	13,970	3,549
1962...	F	14,612	8,631
1963...	F	14,024	5,649
1964...	F	13,818	5,626

[a]C: calendar year ending December 31; F: fiscal year ending June 30; 5½: 5½-month period ending June 14; 6: six-month period ending June 30. Where two symbols appear, the first refers to natural increase and the second to net migration.

[b]Not adjusted for underregistration. Excludes military deaths after July 1, 1940. Minus sign (-) indicates natural decrease.

[c]Immigration, 1852 to 1859, 1864, and 1865; net passenger movement for other years. Excludes non-Orientals, June 14, 1900 to June 30, 1905. Excludes military personnel and includes difference between military separations and inductions, 1941 to 1962; data for earlier years presumably limited to civilian movements. Minus sign (-) indicates net out-migration.

[d]For fiscal 1905, -4,145; for calendar 1905, -6,487.

[e]For fiscal 1927, -1,446; for calendar 1927, -3,939.

Table 82.--COMPONENTS OF INTERCENSAL CIVILIAN POPULATION CHANGE: 1850 TO 1960

Period	Net change[a]	Natural increase[b]	Net migration	Error of closure
1850 to 1853...	-11,000	-10,900	400	-500
1853 to 1860...	-3,300	-2,500	300	-1,100
1860 to 1866...	-6,800	-3,900	800	-3,700
1866 to 1872...	-6,100	-5,500	1,800	-2,400
1872 to 1878...	1,100	-2,400	6,600	-3,100
1878 to 1884...	22,600	-1,600	27,400	-3,200
1884 to 1890...	9,400	-200	12,700	-3,100
1890 to 1896...	19,000	...	19,500	-500
1896 to 1900...	44,700	...	44,900	-200
1900 to 1910...	36,500	1,900	3,700	30,500
1910 to 1920...	61,200	35,100	12,100	14,000
1920 to 1930...	100,500	76,500	14,000	10,000
1930 to 1940...	44,500	61,000	-18,800	2,300
1940 to 1950...	80,400	93,400	-18,500	5,500
1950 to 1960...	108,600	130,300	-15,100	-6,600

[a]Excludes military personnel after 1900.

[b]Not adjusted for underregistration or missing years.

Minus sign indicates natural decrease.

Table 83.--ESTIMATED CIVILIAN POPULATION: JANUARY 1 AND JULY 1, 1848 TO 1965

(By place of usual residence prior to July 1950; de facto basis, including visitors present but excluding residents absent, July 1950 and thereafter. Military personnel, present in small numbers in earlier years, omitted from totals beginning in 1898)

Year	Jan. 1	July 1	Year	Jan. 1	July 1	Year	Jan. 1	July 1
1848...	93,500	90,300	1888...	84,900	85,700	1928...	330,200	336,400
1849...	87,100	85,600	1889...	86,500	86,900	1929...	340,900	345,300
1850...	84,200	83,900	1890...	87,300	88,700	1930...	349,700	354,100
1851...	83,700	82,000	1891...	90,000	92,400	1931...	358,500	362,900
1852...	80,300	80,000	1892...	94,900	95,400	1932...	365,900	368,900
1853...	79,600	76,400	1893...	96,000	96,900	1933...	368,100	367,300
1854...	73,100	73,000	1894...	97,800	99,100	1934...	367,000	366,700
1855...	72,900	72,900	1895...	100,400	102,000	1935...	368,800	370,900
1856...	72,800	72,600	1896...	103,700	107,300	1936...	373,800	376,600
1857...	72,400	72,100	1897...	110,800	113,200	1937...	378,600	380,600
1858...	71,800	71,600	1898...	115,600	120,600	1938...	384,700	388,800
1859...	71,300	71,000	1899...	125,500	137,300	1939...	391,100	393,500
1860...	70,600	70,200	1900...	149,100	153,900	1940...	395,500	397,405
1861...	69,800	69,300	1901...	154,500	155,200	1941...	403,033	408,660
1862...	68,800	68,200	1902...	156,000	157,100	1942...	427,390	446,119
1863...	67,600	66,900	1903...	159,700	162,300	1943...	448,664	451,209
1864...	66,100	65,500	1904...	165,000	167,600	1944...	457,730	464,250
1865...	64,900	64,600	1905...	167,500	166,400	1945...	461,167	458,084
1866...	64,300	63,600	1906...	164,100	166,400	1946...	464,119	470,153
1867...	62,900	62,400	1907...	168,700	174,200	1947...	473,140	476,127
1868...	61,800	61,000	1908...	179,600	182,000	1948...	483,772	491,146
1869...	60,300	60,000	1909...	184,600	186,600	1949...	490,767	481,537
1870...	59,800	59,100	1910...	188,300	191,300	1950...	478,119	472,780
1871...	58,400	58,200	1911...	192,600	193,900	1951...	474,624	471,853
1872...	57,900	57,400	1912...	197,400	200,900	1952...	468,957	462,494
1873...	56,900	56,300	1913...	206,400	212,000	1953...	464,966	468,301
1874...	55,700	55,200	1914...	214,900	217,800	1954...	473,743	474,391
1875...	54,600	54,200	1915...	219,900	222,000	1955...	483,720	491,899
1876...	53,900	54,500	1916...	225,300	228,600	1956...	506,760	512,200
1877...	55,100	55,500	1917...	232,500	236,400	1957...	527,109	538,296
1878...	55,800	56,900	1918...	239,100	241,700	1958...	555,222	560,448
1879...	58,000	60,600	1919...	245,000	248,300	1959...	568,661	580,505
1880...	63,200	64,600	1920...	251,500	254,500	1960...	590,650	595,024
1881...	66,100	67,900	1921...	256,300	258,100	1961...	605,336	612,673
1882...	69,700	70,700	1922...	264,800	271,500	1962...	631,927	635,888
1883...	71,800	75,100	1923...	277,500	283,500	1963...	649,590	655,546
1884...	78,500	79,500	1924...	289,200	294,800	1964...	670,959	674,951
1885...	80,600	82,000	1925...	302,600	310,400	1965...	695,458	702,030
1886...	83,400	84,000	1926...	313,200	316,100			
1887...	84,500	84,700	1927...	320,000	324,000			

Source: Estimates for January 1940 and earlier dates from present study; July 1940 and later dates from HDH, *Civilian Population, Births, Deaths, and Migration Data of Hawaii by Geographic Area, 1950-1964* (March 1964), mimeographed releases, and records.

Table 84.--ESTIMATED RESIDENT POPULATION, TOTAL AND CIVILIAN: JULY 1, 1940 TO 1965

(In thousands)

Year (July 1)	Total resident popu-lation	Civilian resident popu-lation	Year (July 1)	Total resident popu-lation	Civilian resident popu-lation	Year (July 1)	Total resident popu-lation	Civilian resident popu-lation
1940...	428	398	1949...	511	480	1958...	605	550
1941...	459	411	1950...	498	478	1959...	622	565
1942...	582	446	1951...	514	470	1960...	641	582
1943...	650	450	1952...	517	460	1961...	658	597
1944...	859	452	1953...	510	463	1962...	695	616
1945...	815	460	1954...	505	468	1963...	685	625
1946...	545	480	1955...	539	482	1964...	712	639
1947...	526	488	1956...	559	501	1965...	710	657
1948...	517	484	1957...	584	525			

Source: USBC, Current Population Reports, Population Estimates, Series P-25: "Revised Estimates of the Population of Alaska, Hawaii, Puerto Rico, the Canal Zone, and the Virgin Islands of the United States: 1940 to 1950," No. 80 (Oct. 7, 1953); "Revised Estimates of the Population of States and Components of Population Change: 1950 to 1960," No. 304 (April 8, 1965); and "Estimates of the Population of States: July 1, 1965," No. 348 (Sept. 16, 1966).

NOTES

Abbreviations

HDH: Hawaii Department of Health

HDPED: Hawaii Department of Planning and Economic Development

HDPR: Hawaii Department of Planning and Research

HRA: Honolulu Redevelopment Agency

USBC: U. S. Bureau of the Census

USCO: U. S. Census Office

LHM: Laws of His Majesty

RR: Research Report

SLH: Session Laws of Hawaii

SR: Statistical Report

Chapter II

1. Albert S. Baker, "Ahua a Umi," Hawaiian Almanac and Annual for 1917, p. 63. See also Clarice B. Taylor, "The Origin of Aha-a-Umi," Honolulu Star-Bulletin, March 14, 1960.

2. For the work of Romanzo Adams, see his two untitled, undated, and unpublished manuscripts in custody of the Department of Sociology, University of Hawaii. The first, which consists of four chapters from a work in progress, runs from p. 86 to p. 151. The second, apparently prepared as a substitute for the first, consists of an appendix running from p. 439 to p. 463. Parts of both are quoted in Bernhard Lothar Hormann, Extinction and Survival: A Study of the Reaction of Aboriginal Populations to European Expansion (unpublished Ph. D. dissertation, Department of Sociology, University of Chicago, 1949).

3. Adams, MS, pp. 105-106 (Hormann, op. cit., p. 221).

4. Extracts from the Minutes of the General Meeting of the Sand-

wich Islands' Mission, Held at Honolulu, June and July, 1835 (Oahu, 1835), p. 17.

5. Missionary Herald, July 1837, p. 277.

6. Hawaiian Spectator, Oct. 1838, pp. 426-427; Sandwich Island Gazette, Oct. 6, 1838.

7. Polynesian, Aug. 15, 1840 and Oct. 17, 1840; George Simpson, Narrative of a Journey Round the World During the Years 1841 and 1842 (London, 1847), II, 11.

8. "Laws of the Hawaiian Islands," Polynesian, Sept. 18, 1841.

9. Statute LHM Kamehameha III (1846), Part IV, Sect. III, p. 222.

10. "Report of the Minister of Public Instruction," Polynesian, May 22, 1847.

11. Report of the Minister of the Interior ... April 28th, 1848, p. 3.

12. "Census of the Hawaiian Islands ... January, 1849," Polynesian, Nov. 10, 1849.

13. Friend, Nov. 15, 1849; "Report of the Minister of Pub. Instruction ... April 22, 1850," Polynesian, May 4, 1850; Ralph S. Kuykendall, The Hawaiian Kingdom, 1778-1854 (Honolulu, 1938), p. 336.

14. Robert C. Schmitt, "A Census Comparison of Hawaii's Citizens," Paradise of the Pacific, June 1953, pp. 28-29 (revised as HDPR, RR 25, July 11, 1962).

15. "Report ... April 22, 1850," Polynesian, May 4, 1850; Adams, MS, p. 106 (Hormann, op. cit., p. 221).

16. Kenneth P. Emory, Changing Hidden Worlds of Polynesia (paper presented to the Social Science Association, Dec. 3, 1962), p. 5; discussion with Dr. Emory, Feb. 7, 1964.

17. Adams, MS, p. 88.

18. Ibid., pp. 87-88 (Hormann, op. cit., p. 220); Kenneth P.

Emory, The Island of Lanai: A Survey of Native Culture, Bishop Museum Bulletin 12 (1924), p. 122; Samuel M. Kamakau, Ruling Chiefs of Hawaii (Honolulu, 1961), p. 235.

19. Andrew W. Lind, An Island Community (Chicago, 1938), p. 93.

20. Footnote by W. F. Wilson, editor, in Archibald Menzies, Hawaii Nei 128 Years Ago (Honolulu, 1920), p. 136.

21. James Cook, The Three Voyages of Captain James Cook Round the World (London, 1821), VII (by James King), 118-119.

22. Rupert T. Gould, "Bligh's Notes on Cook's Last Voyage," Mariner's Mirror, Oct. 1928, p. 385.

23. George Dixon, A Voyage Round the World, (2nd ed.; London, 1789), p. 267.

24. V. M. Golovnin, Tour Around the World (1822). MS translation by Ella M. Embree (in Sinclair Library, University of Hawaii), pp. 74, 75, 80, 81.

25. "An Inquiry into the Causes of Decrease in the Population of the Sandwich Islands," Hawaiian Spectator, Jan. 1838, p. 53; S. E. Bishop, Why Are the Hawaiians Dying Out? (paper read to the Honolulu Social Science Association, Nov. 1888), p. 2.

26. Editorial, Nov. 6, 1862.

27. A. O. Forbes, "The Decrease of the Hawaiian People and the Causes Assigned for It," Hawaiian Gazette, Jan. 10, 1883.

28. A. Mouritz, Our Western Outpost Hawaii (Honolulu, 1935), p. 26. I have been unable to find Mouritz's source for Malo's estimates.

29. Henry T. Cheever, The Island World of the Pacific (New York, 1851), p. 84; W. B. Elkin, "An Inquiry Into the Causes of the Decrease of the Hawaiian People," American Journal of Sociology, VIII (Nov. 1902), 399.

30. S. E. Bishop, loc. cit.

31. Simpson, op. cit., II, 10; Manley Hopkins, Hawaii: the Past, Present, and Future of Its Island Kingdom (2nd ed.; New York, 1869), p. 368; Joseph King Goodrich, The Coming Hawaii (Chicago, 1914), p. 84.

32. C. E. Dutton, The Hawaiian Islands and People (Washington, 1884), p. 27.

33. A. Marques, "The Population of Hawaiian Islands: Is the Hawaiian A Doomed Race? Present and Future Prospects," Journal of the Polynesian Society, II (Sept. 1893), 257; Goodrich, loc. cit.

34. Editorial, "What Was Hawaii's Native Population?" Honolulu Star-Bulletin, July 16 and 17, 1951.

35. Jack A. Myerson, Depopulation Among the Native Hawaiians (unpublished M.A. thesis, University of California, Los Angeles, June 1953), p. 39.

36. Menzies, op. cit., p. 42.

37. Log and MS journal, both cited in Kuykendall's notes in custody of Sinclair Library, University of Hawaii.

38. George Vancouver, A Voyage of Discovery to the North Pacific Ocean and Round the World ... (London, 1801), III, 391-393; Menzies, op. cit., pp. 135-136.

39. Emory, Lanai, p. 122.

40. James Montgomery, comp., Journal of Voyages and Travels by the Rev. Daniel Tyerman and George Bennet, Esq. ... (Boston, 1832), II, 15-16.

41. James Jackson Jarves, History of the Hawaiian or Sandwich Islands (London, 1843), pp. 366-377.

42. Romanzo Adams, Interracial Marriage in Hawaii (New York, 1937), p. 2, and Adams, MS, p. 112; Hormann, op. cit., p. 223; Andrew W. Lind, Hawaii's People (Honolulu, 1955), pp. 4, 15; lecture

notes cited by Mrs. Marion Kelly, Bishop Museum, in letter to present author, March 15, 1963.

43. HDPR, Statistical Abstract of Hawaii, 1962 (May 1962), p. 7; HDPR, Historical Statistics of Hawaii, 1778-1962 (Sept. 1962), p. 5.

44. Louis de Freycinet, Voyage Autour du Monde (Paris, 1839), II, 585. Translation by Dr. Lewis Schipper.

45. In custody of Sinclair Library, University of Hawaii.

46. Adams, MS, p. 117.

47. Ibid., p. 457 (Hormann, op. cit., p. 233).

48. A. Mouritz, Booklet II. History of the Pacific Navigators and Explorers (Honolulu, 1942), p. 27. I have been unable to find any other references to Malo's 1798 estimate, and no source is given.

49. Pacific Commercial Advertiser, Nov. 6, 1862.

50. MS, pp. 112, 457 (the latter quoted by Hormann, op. cit., p. 223).

51. Montgomery, op. cit., II, 35.

52. Gilbert Farquhar Mathison, Narrative of a Visit to Brazil, Chile, Peru, and the Sandwich Islands (London, 1825), p. 439.

53. Missionary Herald, June 1824, p. 185.

54. C. S. Stewart, Journal of a Residence in the Sandwich Islands During the Years 1823, 1824, and 1825 ... (London, 1828), pp. 141, 25-27.

55. William Ellis, A Narrative of a Tour Through Hawaii (Honolulu, 1917), pp. 20-32.

56. Jarves, op. cit., p. 373.

57. Interracial Marriage in Hawaii, p. 8.

58. Extracts from the Minutes of the General Meeting of the Sandwich Islands' Mission, Held at Honolulu, June and July, 1836 (Oahu, 1836), p. 18; W. C. Woodbridge, He Hoikehonua (Geography)

(Oahu, 1836), back cover.

59. Hormann, op. cit., p. 222.

60. Andrew W. Lind, personal discussion.

61. Interracial Marriage in Hawaii, p. 4, as corrected to include the non-Hawaiian population indicated on p. 8.

62. Report of the American Board of Commissioners for Foreign Missions, Read at the Twenty-Sixth Annual Meeting ... 1835 (Boston, 1835), Table 1, p. 78; Extracts from the Minutes of the General Meeting of the Sandwich Islands Mission Held at Honolulu, June and July 1834 (Oahu, 1834), p. 32.

63. Extracts ... General Meeting ... 1836, p. 18.

64. Woodbridge, loc. cit.

65. Interracial Marriage in Hawaii, p. 8.

66. Simpson, loc. cit.

67. Hawaiian Kingdom, 1778-1854, p. 336.

68. "Migrations in the Pacific Ocean," Polynesian, July 24, 1847.

69. Polynesian, Aug. 2, 1862.

70. Polynesian, Nov. 10, 1849.

71. "Report of the Minister of Pub. Instruction ... April 22, 1850," Polynesian, May 4, 1850.

72. Cook, op. cit., VI, 212.

73. John Ledyard's Journal of Captain Cook's Last Voyage, James Kenneth Munford, ed. (Corvallis, 1963), p. 129.

74. Extracts ... General Meeting ... 1836, p. 18. Slightly different totals for 1835-1836 are shown in Woodbridge, loc. cit. A third set of data, somewhat different from other two, appears in Ke Kumu Hawaii for Dec. 9, 1835, Jan. 20, 1836, March 2, 1836, March 16, 1836, and April 13, 1836. Table 5 uses data from Extracts.

75. 1798: Ebenezer Townsend, Jr., Extract from the Diary of

Ebenezer Townsend, Jr., Hawaiian Historical Society Reprints, No. 4 (Honolulu, 1921), pp. 24-25. 1821: *Missionary Herald*, July 1822, p. 209. 1822: James Montgomery, *op. cit.*, II, 30. 1822: Mathison, *loc. cit.* Others: cited in Daniel James Kittelson, *A Population Table for Hawaii* (May 24, 1960), copy of typescript in Sinclair Library, University of Hawaii.

76. John F. G. Stokes, "Honolulu and Some Speculative Phases of Hawaiian History," *Forty-Second Annual Report of the Hawaiian Historical Society for the Year 1933*, pp. 41-42.

77. "Extracts from the Journal of Mr. Bingham at Honolulu," *Missionary Herald*, Nov. 1832, pp. 353-354.

78. *Report to the American Board of Commissioners for Foreign Missions ... 1835* (Boston, 1835), Table 2, pp. 78-79; *Answers by the Sandwich Islands Missionaries to the Questions in the Circular of March 15, 1833 ...*, typescript dated April 30, 1936 in Hawaiian Historical Society Library.

79. Woodbridge, *loc. cit.*; Edwin O. Hall, "Notes of a Tour Around Oahu," *Hawaiian Spectator*, Jan. 1839, p. 112.

80. 1822: Montgomery, *op. cit.*, II, 29. 1822: Mathison, *op. cit.*, p. 448. 1822 or 1823: *Missionary Herald*, Oct. 1823, p. 315. 1823: Ellis, *op. cit.*, p. 27. 1828: A. Duhaut-Cilly, *Voyage Autour du Monde ...* (Paris, 1835), II, 301. Mid-1830's: Alonzo Chapin, "Remarks on the Sandwich Islands ...," *Hawaiian Spectator*, July 1838, p. 265. 1838: John Diell, "Sketch of Honolulu, Oahu," *Hawaiian Spectator*, April 1838, p. 84. 1840: Gustavas Hines, *Wild Life in Oregon* (New York, 1887), p. 79. Early 1840's: Alexander Simpson, *The Sandwich Islands: Progress of Events ...* (London, 1843), p. 108. 1845: *Friend*, Oct. 1, 1845, p. 145.

81. Ellis, *op. cit.*, p. 311; *Answers by the Sandwich Islands Missionaries ...*, p. 22.

82. Missionary Herald, April 1821, p. 121.

83. Report to the ABCFM ... 1835, pp. 78-79; Woodbridge, loc. cit.; George Simpson, op. cit., II, 169.

84. Woodbridge, loc. cit.

85. Cook, op. cit., VI, 212; Vancouver, op. cit., I, 406.

86. Ibid., I, 405-406; Answers by the Sandwich Islands Missionaries ..., p. 38.

87. Missionary letter (III, 914) cited in the notes of Ralph S. Kuykendall, in custody of Sinclair Library, University of Hawaii.

88. Polynesian, Nov. 10, 1849; Robert C. Schmitt, "The Population of Northern Kauai in 1847," Hawaii Historical Review, II (April 1966), 300-304.

89. John Turnbull, Voyages in the Pacific Ocean (London, 1805?), p. 229.

90. Ellis, op. cit., p. 329.

91. Missionary Herald, July 1829, pp. 211-212.

92. Missionary Herald, July 1822, p. 209; Montgomery, op. cit., II, 15-16; Ellis, op. cit., p. 91; Emory, Lanai, p. 122.

93. Missionary Herald, Oct. 1823, p. 315.

94. Mary Charlotte Alexander, comp., William Patterson Alexander In Kentucky The Marquesas Hawaii (Honolulu, 1934), p. 195.

95. Alonzo Chapin, op. cit., p. 265. See also Robert Crichton Wyllie, "Notes ...," Friend, July 1, 1844, p. 61. The all-island population base used by Alexander was evidently about 129,540, only slightly less than the 1831-1832 missionary count and well over the 1835-1836 total.

96. Polynesian, Nov. 10, 1849.

97. Polynesian, May 4, 1850. These 1848 and 1849 rates were computed from end-of-year population totals. For rates based on

estimated mid-year population, see Chapter VI.

98. Irene B. Taeuber, "Hawaii," Population Index, 28 (April 1962), 100. For a different view on life expectancy before 1778, see Kamakau, op. cit., p. 235.

99. Lind, Hawaii's People, p. 17.

100. Adams, MS, pp. 108-109, 111, 455 (Hormann, op. cit., p. 225).

101. Adams, MS, p. 455.

102. David Malo (translated by L. Andrews), "On the Decrease of Population on the Hawaiian Islands," Hawaiian Spectator, April 1839, p. 125. See also the editorial in Pacific Commercial Advertiser, Nov. 6, 1862.

103. Missionary Herald, Dec. 1829, p. 371.

104. Kuykendall, op. cit., p. 49.

105. Adams, MS, p. 117.

106. Forbes, op. cit. See also Adams, MS, p. 129.

107. Friend, Nov. 15, 1849; "Hawaiian Epidemics," Hawaiian Almanac and Annual for 1897, p. 97; Kamakau, op. cit., pp. 236-237, 410-411.

108. "An Inquiry into the Causes of Decrease in the Population of the Sandwich Islands," Hawaiian Spectator, Jan. 1838, p. 54.

109. Adams, MS, pp. 98-104, 108-109.

110. Taeuber, op. cit., pp. 98-99.

111. Emory, Changing ... Polynesia, pp. 1-2. See also Kenneth P. Emory, "East Polynesian Relationships. Settlement Pattern and Time Involved as Indicated by Vocabulary Agreements," Journal of the Polynesian Society, 72 (June 1963), 78-100.

112. Adams, MS, p. 88.

113. David Kittelson, "Hawaiians and Fur Traders," Hawaii Historical Review, I (Jan. 1963), 16.

114. Ibid., p. 19.

115. Marques, _op. cit_., pp. 263-264.

116. Adams, MS, p. 112.

117. _The Hawaiian Kingdom, 1778-1854_, p. 312.

118. _Ibid_., p. 328. See also, _Missionary Herald_, Oct. 1849, p. 362.

119. Quoted in _Polynesian_, Oct. 2, 1847.

120. Robert C. Schmitt, "A Century of Hawaiian Out-Migration," _Social Process in Hawaii_, 20 (1956), 40.

121. _Ibid_., p. 39.

Chapter III

1. _Polynesian_, Sept. 18, 1841, p. 58.

2. _Statute LHM Kamehameha III ..._ (1846), p. 222.

3. _LHM Kamehameha III ... 1851_, p. 87.

4. _The Civil Code of the Hawaiian Islands: Passed in Year of Our Lord 1859_, Sec. 759, 760, 761.

5. _LHM, Kamehameha V ... 1864-65_, Sec. 41, 42, 43.

6. Archives of Hawaii, Accounts A166 and file on "Census--1843."

7. _Privy Council Records_ (typescript translation), II, 46.

8. _Report of the Minister of Public Instruction ... April twenty-ninth, 1847_, p. 7. Also published in _Polynesian_, May 22, 1847.

9. Untitled circular in Archives 1846 [sic] census file.

10. _Report ... 1847_, p. 7.

11. Archives 1847-1866 census file. These data have been summarized and evaluated in Robert C. Schmitt, "The Population of Northern Kauai," _Hawaii Historical Review_, II (April 1966), 300-304.

12. _Report of the Minister of the Interior ... April 28th, 1848_, p. 3. Also published in _Polynesian_, May 13, 1848.

13. _Polynesian_, Dec. 30, 1848.

14. "Papa Helu i Na Kanaka o Hawaii Nei No Ka Makahiki 1849," filed in Archives 1847-1866 census file.

15. "Census of the Hawaiian Islands--From Official Documents--Taken January, 1849," _Polynesian_, Nov. 10, 1849; _Friend_, Nov. 15, 1849. The census results had been presented to the Privy Council on Oct. 31, 1849; see _Privy Council Records_ (typescript translation), III A, 395.

16. "General Instructions," handwritten statement dated March 7, 1849, in Archives 1849 census file.

17. _Privy Council Records_, III A, 233.

18. "Census of the Islands," _Friend_, Nov. 15, 1849, p. 79.

19. "Report of the Minister of Pub. Instruction ... April 22, 1850," _Polynesian_, May 4, 1850, p. 202.

20. Romanzo Adams, "The Hawaiian Censuses, 1831-1896," unpublished MS formerly filed in the Romanzo Adams Social Research Laboratory of the University of Hawaii. Ralph S. Kuykendall, _The Hawaiian Kingdom 1778-1854_ (Honolulu, 1938), p. 336.

21. "Report ... 1850."

22. Archives 1850 census file. All census schedules, when extant, are in the Archives census file for the year of the relevant census.

23. "Report ... 1850."

24. Romanzo Adams, untitled and undated MS in files of Department of Sociology, University of Hawaii, pp. 106, 451.

25. Kuykendall, _loc. cit_.

26. _Privy Council Records_ (typescript translation), VI A, 66.

27. A copy of these instructions is kept in a folder, "Statistics of Population," in the Hawaiian Mission Children's Society Library, Honolulu.

28. Report of the Minister of Public Instruction ... April 8, 1854, p. 13. The same report also appeared in the Polynesian, April 15, 1854, where it gave the census date as "the 20th of Dec. last ...." According to the Friend, March 1, 1854, p. 21, the census was taken during the last week of December.

29. "Census Table of the Hawaiian Islands for 1853. The Polynesian Race only is included" and "Foreign Census of the Hawaiian Islands for the Year 1853"; Report ... 1854, pp. 13-14 and unpaged table at end of the report; Polynesian, April 15 and April 22, 1854.

30. The census was scheduled for December 24, 1860; see Polynesian, Dec. 22, 1860.

31. "Census," Polynesian, Dec. 22, 1860.

32. "Census of the Hawaiian Islands, Taken December 7th, 1866," broadside table, footnote.

33. "Census of the Hawaiian Islands for 1860"; "The Census" and table, "Census Tables of the Hawaiian Islands for 1860," Polynesian, Feb. 2, 1861; Biennial Report of the President of the Board of Education ... 1862, pp. 23-36 and Table III.

34. LHM Kamehameha IV ... 1860, p. 39.

35. "Table 1/Papa 1" in Archives 1866 census file.

36. "Census of the Hawaiian Islands, Taken December 7th, 1866" and "Census of the Kona (Honolulu) District, Island of Oahu, Taken Dec. 7th, 1866"; Hawaiian Gazette, Jan. 30 and April 3, 1867; Biennial Report of the President of the Board of Education ... 1868, p. 7 and table after p. 10.

37. LHM Kamehameha V ... 1866-67, p. 24.

38. "Census of the Hawaiian Islands, Taken December 27th, 1872," broadside table published in both English and English-Hawaiian versions; "The Census of 1872. Report of the Inspector-General of

Schools" and half-page insert, "Census of the Hawaiian Islands, Taken December 27th, 1872," Hawaiian Gazette, April 9, 1873; Biennial Report of the President of the Board of Education ... 1874, pp. 16-17 and table at end.

39. LHM Kamehameha V ... 1872, Chap. XXXV, p. 38.

40. Hawaiian Gazette, April 9, 1873.

41. Office of the Board of Education, "Prospectus or Plan to be Followed for Taking the Census of the Kingdom in 1878" (1878), in folder "Statistics of Population," in the Hawaiian Mission Children's Society Library.

42. "Census Table, 1878. Papa Helu i Na Kanaka, 1878," in Archives 1878 census file.

43. "Census of the Hawaiian Islands, taken December 27th, 1878, under the Direction of the Board of Education," Pacific Commercial Advertiser, March 22, 1879; Biennial Report of the President of the Board of Education ... 1880, following p. 35. I have been unable to locate a broadside version, although one was probably issued. Brief narratives accompanied the table in both the Advertiser ("The Census") and the Biennial Report, p. 31. Another account, without table, appeared in the Hawaiian Gazette, March 5, 1879.

44. LHM Kalakaua ... 1878, Chap. XXXII, p. 58.

45. Census of the Hawaiian Islands Taken December 27th, 1884, Under the Direction of the Board of Education. Helu Kanaka o Ko Hawaii Paeaina ....

46. Bureau of Public Instruction, Report of the General Superintendent of the Census, 1890, p. 6.

47. Report of Committee on Census of 1888, on Bill Relating to the Subject.

48. LHM Kalakaua I ... 1884, Chap. LIV, p. 119; Biennial Re-

port of the President of the Board of Education ... 1886, p. 40.

49. Department of Public Instruction, Report of the General Superintendent of the Census, 1896, p. 11. Personnel expenses for 1890 and 1896 are also given.

50. Report ... 1888 ..., pp. 3-10.

51. Report ... 1890, p. 7.

52. LHM Kalakaua I ... 1890, Chap. LI, p. 98.

53. Report ... 1890, pp. 36-39.

54. Irene B. Taeuber, "Hawaii," Population Index, 28 (April 1962), 99-100.

55. Report ... 1896, p. 117.

56. Romanzo Adams, "The Hawaiian Census Classifications of Population Before 1900," undated typescript in files of Department of Sociology, University of Hawaii, p. 2.

57. Report ... 1896.

58. Laws of the Republic of Hawaii ... 1896, Act 56, p. 174.

59. For changes in judicial district boundaries, see Robert D. King, "Districts in the Hawaiian Islands," in John Wesley Coulter, comp., A Gazetteer of the Territory of Hawaii (Honolulu, 1935), pp. 214-230.

60. Romanzo Adams, The Peoples of Hawaii (Honolulu, 1933), pp. 7-9, and Interracial Marriage in Hawaii (New York, 1937), p. 8.

61. Andrew W. Lind, Hawaii's People (Honolulu, 1955), p. 27.

Chapter IV

1. Mary Louise Mark, Statistics in the Making, Bureau of Business Research Publication No. 92 (Columbus, 1958), p. 28.

2. Robert C. Schmitt, "From Umi to Univac: Data Processing in Hawaii, 1500-1965," Seventy-Fourth Annual Report of the Hawaiian

Historical Society for the Year 1965 (1966), pp. 17-28.

3. USCO, Census Reports, Vol. II, Twelfth Census of the United States, Taken in the Year 1900, Population, Part II (1902), p. ccxvii.

4. For comment, see Robert C. Schmitt, "Statehood and National Statistics," American Statistician, 15 (Feb. 1961), 27, 28, 30.

5. Census Reports, Vol. II, Twelfth Census ..., Population, Part II, p. ccxvi. See also, ibid., Vol. I, Twelfth Census ..., Population, Part I (1901), pp. xv, xvii-xviii.

6. See Robert D. King, "Districts in the Hawaiian Islands," in John Wesley Coulter, comp., A Gazetter of the Territory of Hawaii (Honolulu, 1935), pp. 214-230.

7. Letter to the author from Henry S. Shryock, Jr., Acting Chief, Population Division, USBC, Nov. 6, 1964. Information on the costs of all censuses through 1960 is from this letter.

8. Census Reports, Vol. I, Twelfth Census ..., Population, Part I; ibid., Vol. II, Twelfth Census ..., Population, Part II.

9. USBC, Thirteenth Census of the United States Taken in the Year 1910, Vol. III, Population 1910, Nebraska-Wyoming, Alaska, Hawaii, and Puerto Rico (1913), p. 1155.

9a. Paradise of the Pacific, Vol. XXIV, No. 12 (Dec. 1911), p. 64.

10. Ibid., pp. 1155-1178; ibid., Abstract of the Census ... with Supplement for Hawaii, pp. 565-619; ibid., Vol. IV, Population 1910, Occupation Statistics (1914).

11. USBC, Fourteenth Census of the United States Taken in the Year 1920, Vol. I, Population 1920, Number and Distribution of Inhabitants (1921), p. 682; ibid., Vol. III, Population 1920, Composition and Characteristics of the Population by States (1922), pp. 1171-1193;

ibid., Vol. IV, Population 1920, Occupations (1923).

12. USBC, Fifteenth Census of the United States: 1930, Outlying Territories and Possessions (1932).

13. For a complete history of the development of the census tract system in Hawaii, see Honolulu Census Tract Committee, Census Tracts in Hawaii, 1937-1964, Report CTC-7 (Nov. 20, 1964).

14. Information supplied by John F. Child, Jr., Jan. 25, 1965.

15. USBC, 16th Census of the United States: 1940, Population, First Series, Number of Inhabitants, Hawaii (1942), and Population, Second Series, Characteristics of the Population, Hawaii (1943); 16th Census ..., Housing, General Characteristics, Hawaii (1943); 16th Census ..., Population, Vol. I, Number of Inhabitants (1942), pp. 1207-1214.

16. USBC, Enumerator's Reference Manual, 1950 Census of Hawaii, 17 Fld-100 Hawaii (n.d.); USBC, The 1950 Censuses--How They Were Taken, Procedural Studies of the 1950 Census, No. 2 (1955).

17. Information supplied by Lloyd Lee, formerly of the Territories and Possessions Section, USBC, in a discussion sometime before 1958.

18. USBC, U. S. Census of Population: 1950, Report P-B52 (1952), p. vi.

19. For additional discussion, see HRA, Redevelopment and Housing Research, No. 5 (July 1956), pp. 31-39 and No. 14 (Dec. 1958), pp. 22-24, 27.

20. USBC, Bulletin P-C52, p. vii.

21. Letter from H. S. Shryock, Jr., 1964.

22. U. S. Census of Population: 1950, Reports P-A52, P-B52, P-C52; USBC, U. S. Census of Housing: 1950, General Characteristics, Hawaii, Report H-A52 (1952); U. S. Census of Population: 1950, Vol. III, Census Tract Statistics, Chap. 62, Honolulu, Territory of Hawaii and Adjacent

Area (1952).

23. U. S. Census of the Population: 1950, Vol. I, Number of Inhabitants (1952), pp. 52:1-52:8; ibid., Vol. II, Characteristics of the Population, Parts 51-54, Territories and Possessions (1953), pp. 52:1-52:154; U. S. Census of Housing: 1950, Vol. I, General Characteristics, Part 7: Alaska, Hawaii, Puerto Rico, Virgin Islands of the U. S. (1953), pp. 52:1-52:22.

24. USBC, Enumerator's Reference Manual, 1960 Census of Population and Housing, F-210 (1960); USBC, United States Censuses of Population and Housing, 1960: Principal Data-Collection Forms and Procedures (1961), and Procedural Report of the 1960 Censuses of Population and Housing, Working Paper No. 16 (1963).

25. USBC, U. S. Census of Population: 1960, Vol. I, Characteristics of the Population, Part 13, Hawaii (1963), p. xxvi.

26. U. S. Census of Population: 1960, Subject Reports, Nonwhite Population by Race, Final Report PC(2)-1C (1963), Table 61.

27. For a summary of data in these reports and a detailed discussion of the treatment of race in 1960, see HDPED, SR 9 (Dec. 26, 1963).

28. HDPED, SR 3 (Aug. 27, 1963).

29. Procedural Report of the 1960 Censuses of Population and Housing, Working Paper No. 16 (1963).

30. Honolulu Star-Bulletin, May 24, 1960; U. S. Department of Commerce, "Preliminary County Totals for Hawaii, 1960 Census of Population," transmitted June 9, 1960; USBC, 1960 Census of Population, Preliminary Reports, Population Counts for Standard Metropolitan Statistical Areas, Honolulu, PC(P2)-69 (June 1960); ibid., Preliminary Reports, Population Counts for States, Hawaii, PC(P1)-13 (July 1960) (see also Honolulu Advertiser and Honolulu Star-Bulletin for July 25,

1960); 1960 Census of Population, Advance Reports, Final Population Counts, Hawaii PC(A1)-13 (Nov. 10, 1960); ibid., Advance Reports, General Population Characteristics, Hawaii, PC(A2)-13 (March 30, 1961).

31. Final Report PC(1)-13A (1961), later bound in U. S. Census of Population: 1960, Vol. I, Characteristics of the Population, Part A, Number of Inhabitants (1961), pp. 13:1-13:11; Final Report PC(1)-13B (1961); Final Report PC(1)-13C (1962); Final Report PC(1)-13D (1962); U. S. Census of Population: 1960, Vol. I, Characteristics of the Population, Part 13, Hawaii (1963).

32. U. S. Census of Population and Housing: 1960, Census Tracts, Final Report PHC(1)-62, Honolulu, Hawaii, Standard Metropolitan Statistical Area (1962).

33. USBC, U. S. Census of Housing: 1960, Vol. I, States and Small Areas, Hawaii, Final Report HC(1)-13 (1961), also bound as Vol. I, States and Small Areas, Part 3: Delaware-Indiana (1963), pp. 13:1-13:44; U. S. Census of Housing: 1960, Metropolitan Housing, Final Report HC(2)-80 (1962), also bound as Metropolitan Housing, Part 3: Dallas-Kalamazoo Standard Metropolitan Statistical Areas (1963), pp. 80:1-80:30; U. S. Census of Housing: 1960, Vol. III, City Blocks, Series HC(3), No. 125, Hilo (1961); ibid., No. 126, Honolulu (1961); ibid., No. 127, Lahaina (1961); ibid., No. 128, Wailuku (1961).

34. For example, the following: U. S. Census of Population: 1960, Subject Reports, State of Birth, Final Report PC(2)-2A (1963); ibid., Mobility for States and State Economic Areas, Final Report PC(2)-2B (1963).

35. HDPED, SR33 (July 26, 1965) and SR 34 (Aug. 2, 1965).

36. The Honolulu consumer price index (March 1943 = 100) was 77.1 in March 1940, 126.0 in March 1950, and 163.0 in March 1960.

See HDPR, Statistical Abstract of Hawaii, 1962, p. 73.

37. USBC, unpublished data for enumeration districts.

38. Detailed discussion of the 1960 treatment of race appears in HDPED, SR 9 (Dec. 26, 1963).

39. Hawaii Department of Transportation, records.

40. USBC, 16th Census of the United States: 1940, Population, Second Series, Characteristics of the Population, Hawaii (1943), p. 2.

41. Hawaii Department of Labor and Industrial Relations, Research and Statistics Office, Comparison and Analysis of Employment Data Reported in the U. S. Census of 1960 with Revised Employment Estimates Published by the Hawaii State Department of Labor and Industrial Relations, April 1960 (Jan. 1965), and Comparison and Analysis of Unemployment Data Reported in the U. S. Census of 1960 with Revised Estimates Published by the Hawaii State Department of Labor and Industrial Relations, State of Hawaii, April 1960 (Jan. 1965).

42. HDPED, SR 33 and SR 34.

43. USBC, "Estimates of the Population of States: July 1, 1963," Current Population Reports, Population Estimates, Series P-25, No. 289 (Aug. 31, 1964).

44. Office of Secretary of Defense, Directorate for Statistical Services, records.

45. Hawaii State Planning Office, Military Personnel and Dependents in Hawaii, 1960, Staff Research Memorandum 29 (June 27, 1960).

46. Interracial Marriage in Hawaii, pp. 14-15.

47. Among the most important works are the following: State Department of Health, Office of Health Statistics, The Race Item in Vital Statistics Records (n.d.); Andrew W. Lind, Hawaii's People (Honolulu, 1955), pp. 19-25; Bernhard L. Hormann, "'Racial' Statistics

in Hawaii," Social Process in Hawaii, XII (1948), as reprinted in Hormann, ed., Community Forces in Hawaii (Honolulu, 1956), pp. 268-273; Newton E. Morton, Chin S. Chung, and Ming-Pi Mi, Genetics of Interracial Crosses in Hawaii (Basel, 1967); Norma McArthur, "Essays in Multiplication: European Seafarers in Polynesia," Journal of Pacific History, I (1966), 91-105.

Chapter V

1. See, for example, USBC, "Estimates of the Population of States: July 1, 1965," Current Population Reports, Population Estimates, Series P-25, No. 348 (Sept. 16, 1966), and "Provisional Estimates of the Population of the Largest Metropolitan Areas: July 1, 1965," Current Population Reports, Population Estimates, Series P-25, No. 347 (Aug. 31, 1966).

2. Annual estimates from 1940 to 1964 are reported in HDPED, SR 31 (June 21, 1965), Table 6, p. 10. Revised OBE estimates, 1960 to 1965, appear in HDPED, SR 43 (Sept. 30, 1966), Table 3.

3. Letters from USBC and Office of Business Economics officials, cited in HRA, Redevelopment and Housing Research, No. 5 (July 1956), pp. 31-32, and No. 14 (Dec. 1958), pp. 22-23.

4. HDH, Civilian Population, Births, Deaths, and Migration Data of Hawaii by Geographic Area, 1950-1964 (March 1964) and semi-annual mimeographed releases.

5. HDH, Estimated Civilian Population and Dwelling Units of Oahu Census Tracts, July 1, 1965 (April 1966), and Estimated Population and Dwelling Units of Hawaii County Census Tracts, April 1, 1960 and July 1, 1965 (Nov. 1965).

6. Under the series title The Population of Hawaii, see, for example, SR 29 (April 9, 1965), SR 31 (June 21, 1965), and SR 37

(Nov. 19, 1965). The April date, not normally used, was chosen for SR 31 because it fell midway between the 1960 and 1970 census dates. Statistics on armed forces and dependents are issued in a separate series under the title Military Personnel and Dependents in Hawaii; see, for example, HDPED, SR 36 (Sept. 24, 1965).

7. For comparisons back to 1940, see HDPED, SR 31, Table 6. Detailed comparisons of data on the armed forces, 1960 to 1965, appear in HDPED, SR 43 (Sept. 30, 1966), Table 3.

8. See, for example, USBC, "Estimates of the Population of States: July 1, 1963," Current Population Reports, Population Estimates, Series P-25, No. 289 (Aug. 31, 1964), pp. 10-11.

9. See, for example, USBC, "Estimates of the Population of States, by Age: 1960 to 1965," Current Population Reports, Population Estimates, Series P-25, No. 354 (Dec. 8, 1966).

10. See, for example, The Health Surveillance Program. April-September 1964, Report No. 1, and Demographic and Health Characteristics of Military Households (Dec. 1, 1965). See also Interviewer's Manual, Health Surveillance Program, 1964. These publications were issued jointly by the Research, Planning and Statistics Office and the Public Health Nursing Branch.

11. HRA, Redevelopment and Housing Research, Supplemental Research Notes for March 1965, pp. 3-4 (family income data), April 1965, pp. 1, 3 (income of the aged), and Nov. 1965, pp. 1, 3 (vacancy rates); HDPED, SR 37, Tables 12, 13 (age, sex, military status, and ethnic stock).

12. SR 31, Tables 12, 13, pp. 15-16.

13. "Honolulu Household and Housing Survey, October 1962," Redevelopment and Housing Research, No. 23 (July 1963), pp. 1-24.

14. See, for example, SR 23 (Oct. 30, 1964), Table 18, p. 20;

SR 29, Tables 13, 14, pp. 14-16.

15. See, for example, "Changes in Hawaii's Housing Supply, 1964-1965," Redevelopment and Housing Research, No. 25 (July 1965), pp. 1-10.

16. Hawaii State Department of Labor and Industrial Relations, Employment and Payrolls in Hawaii, 1965 (Dec. 1966).

17. Hawaii State Department of Labor and Industrial Relations, Where Do People Work in Hawaii? (in press).

18. U. S. Department of Labor, Bureau of Labor Statistics, Survey of Consumer Expenditures: 1960-61. Consumer Expenditures and Income: Honolulu, Hawaii, 1961, BLS Report 237-78 (Advance Report) and Supplement 1 (Nov. 1963).

19. See, for example, HDPED, SR 38 (April 15, 1966).

20. Hawaii Newspaper Agency, 1963 Consumer Analysis of Metropolitan Honolulu (1963), p. 8.

Chapter VI

1. Extracts from the Minutes of the General Meeting of the Sandwich Islands' Mission, Held at Honolulu, June and July, 1835 (Oahu, 1835), p. 17.

2. See, for example, Mary Charlotte Alexander, comp., William Patterson Alexander In Kentucky The Marquesas Hawaii (Honolulu, 1934), p. 195, and Alonzo Chapin, "Remarks on the Sandwich Islands ...," Hawaiian Spectator, July 1838, p. 265, regarding W. P. Alexander's work at Halelea; and Extracts from the Minutes of the General Meeting of the Sandwich Islands Mission, Held at Honolulu, May and June, 1848 (Oahu, 1848) regarding data for Koloa. Alexander used his findings to make estimates for the entire kingdom (see Table 9). With respect to

infant mortality, see for example, Artemas Bishop, "An Inquiry into the Causes of Decrease in the Population of the Sandwich Islands," *Hawaiian Spectator*, Jan. 1838, p. 54, and a letter written by Dr. Seth Lathrop Andrews on January 8, 1844 and published in "Island Mission Letters Found," *Sunday Star-Bulletin & Advertiser*, April 11, 1965.

3. "Laws of the Hawaiian Islands," *Polynesian*, Sept. 18, 1841.

4. *Statute LHM Kamehameha III*, An Act to Organize the Executive Departments of the Hawaiian Islands, Part IV, Department of Public Instruction, General Provisions, Section III, p. 222. Amendment in *Penal Code of the Hawaiian Islands Passed by the House of Nobles and Representatives on the 21st of June, A. D. 1850; to which are appended the other acts passed ... 1850*, pp. 200-201.

5. *The Civil Code of the Hawaiian Islands ... 1859*, Title 2, Art. XXIX, Sec. 762-765. Amendment in *LHM Kamehameha V ... 1864-65*, Sec. 44.

6. *Laws of the Republic of Hawaii ... 1896*, Act 50.

7. *Laws of the Territory of Hawaii ... 1913*, Act 86.

8. *Laws of the Territory of Hawaii ... 1937*, Act 86. Approved April 28, 1937.

9. *Laws of the Territory of Hawaii ... Regular Session 1949*, Act 327.

10. 1848: *Polynesian*, Nov. 10, 1849. 1849: *Polynesian*, May 4, 1850. 1851-1863: *Report of the Minister of Public Instruction* for years 1852-1855; *Report of the President of the Board of Education* for 1856 and 1858; *Biennial Report of the President of the Board of Education* for 1860, 1862, and 1864. These reports present data for each year from 1851 to 1863. Data for 1850, 1864, and 1865 were apparently never published. 1866-1877: *Report of the Board of Health* for 1868, 1870, 1872, 1874, 1876, and 1878. Education: *Biennial Report of the*

President of the Board of Education for 1882, 1884, 1886, 1888, and 1890. Health (deaths): Biennial Report of the Board of Health ... 1878; Report of the President of the Board of Health for 1880, 1884, 1886, 1888, 1890, 1892, 1894, 1895, and 1899; Board of Health Report ... 1882; Report of the Board of Health ... 1897. Health (births added): Annual data for the period from 1900 to 1909 were recapitulated in Report of the President of the Board of Health ... 1909, pp. 33-46. Health: Report of the President of the Board of Health for years 1909-1930; Annual Report of the Governor of Hawaii to the Secretary of the Interior for 1931 and 1932; Board of Health of the Territory of Hawaii, Its Major Activities, 1933; Annual Report, Board of Health for years 1934-1939; Board of Health, Territory of Hawaii, Report for Fiscal Year 1940. Because of changing coverage and reporting periods, 1941-1965 data used in the present study were obtained directly from the Department of Health. Calendar year data back to 1912 are recapitulated in Annual Report, Department of Health, State of Hawaii, Statistical Supplement, 1960. Data for 1961 and later years appear in the Statistical Supplements for those years.

11. Mortality data for Hawaii appeared initially in USBC, Mortality Statistics, 1915, Sixteenth Annual Report (1917); natality data, in USBC, Birth, Stillbirth, and Infant Mortality Statistics ... 1929 (Washington, 1932). Beginning with data for 1937, these series were carried in USBC, Vital Statistics of the United States, Part I. Effective with the 1945 volumes, publication of these annual reports was assumed by the Federal Security Agency, Public Health Service, National Office of Vital Statistics. The 1950 report was the first issued by the U. S. Department of Health, Education, and Welfare, Public Health Service, National Office of Vital Statistics. NOVS became the National Vital Statistics Division a decade later.

12. Irene B. Taeuber, "Hawaii," *Population Index*, 28 (April 1962), 98-99.

13. *Ibid.*, p. 100.

14. Romanzo Adams, unpublished and undated manuscript in custody of the Department of Sociology, University of Hawaii, p. 106.

15. *Report of the Minister of Public Instruction ... 1852*, p. 45.

16. *Report of the Minister of Public Instruction ... 1855*, p. 15.

17. *Report of the President of the Board of Education ... 1856*, p. 11.

18. Adams, MS, p. 107.

19. See, however, Adams, MS, p. 108: "From 1890 on, records of births and deaths were kept for all the Islands and, while there is considerable incompleteness, they may be used with some allowance." I have been unable to find these data.

20. See, for example, the different figures for 1867 in the *Report of the Board of Health* for 1868 (p. 11) and 1870 (p. 22) and the discrepancies between Board of Health and Board of Education totals for 1881, reported by Dr. Charles T. Rodgers in the unpublished minutes of the Social Science Association of Honolulu for December 4, 1882. Dr. Rodgers' paper is summarized in Stanley D. Porteus, *A Century of Social Thinking in Hawaii* (Palo Alto, 1962), p. 32.

21. Taeuber, *op. cit.*, p. 100.

22. *Report of the Board of Health ... 1897*, pp. 55-56.

23. *Report of the President of the Board of Health ... 1899*, p. 22.

24. A. Marques, "The Population of Hawaiian Islands. Is the Hawaiian a Doomed Race? Present and Future Prospects," *Journal of the Polynesian Society*, II (Sept. 1893), 260; *Report of the President of the Board of Health, November 10th, 1900 to February 1st, 1901*, p. 7.

25. Report of the President of the Board of Health ... 1884, p. civ.

26. Letter from Anders S. Lunde, Chief, Natality Statistics Branch, National Vital Statistics Division, Public Health Service, Department of Health, Education, and Welfare, April 18, 1963.

27. Annual Report of the President of the Board of Health ... 1920, pp. 10, 99.

28. Letter from Lunde, April 18, 1963.

29. U. S. Department of Health, Education, and Welfare, Public Health Service, National Office of Vital Statistics, "Birth Registration Completeness in the United States and Geographic Areas, 1950. Part I. Data for Each State," Vital Statistics--Special Reports. Selected Studies, 39 (Sept. 21, 1954), 57.

Chapter VII

1. Interracial Marriage in Hawaii (New York, 1937), p. 8; untitled and undated manuscript in custody of the Department of Sociology, University of Hawaii, p. 112.

2. Sources of information on Hawaii-born persons on the Mainland are listed in Robert C. Schmitt, "A Century of Hawaiian Out-Migration," Social Process in Hawaii, 20 (1956), 39.

3. David Malo (translated by L. Andrews), "On the Decrease of Population in the Hawaiian Islands," Hawaiian Spectator, April 1839, pp. 127-128; Polynesian, May 23, 1846 and Oct. 2, 1847; A. Marques, "The Population of Hawaiian Islands. Is the Hawaiian A Doomed Race? Present and Future Prospects," Journal of the Polynesian Society, II (Sept. 1893), 263-267; Ralph S. Kuykendall, The Hawaiian Kingdom, 1778-1854 (Honolulu, 1938), pp. 312, 313, 328; David Kittelson, "Hawaiians and Fur Traders," Hawaii Historical Review, I (Jan. 1963), 16-20.

4. Summarized in HDPR, RR 21 (March 20, 1962), and HDPED, SR 5 (Oct. 14, 1963).

5. _Polynesian_: "Custom House Statistics ..." in issues of Oct. 15, 1859, Jan. 18, 1862, Jan. 10, 1863, and Oct. 17, 1863. Broadside: "Custom House Statistics ..." for years 1866-1871. Collector General: _Custom House Statistics ..._ for years 1872-1884, and _Annual Report of the Collector General of Customs of the Hawaiian Islands ..._ for years 1885-1900. Commerce and Labor: _Fourth Report of the Commissioner of Labor on Hawaii_, Bulletin of the Bureau of Labor, No. 94 (May 1911), pp. 724-725. Governor: U. S. Department of the Interior, _Report of the Governor of Hawaii to the Secretary of the Interior_ for years 1919-1934. Thrum: _Hawaiian Annual_ for years 1912-1927. Health: _Civilian Population, Births, Deaths, and Migration Data of Hawaii by Geographic Area, 1950-1964_ (March 1964) and records.

6. "Components of Population Change, 1950 to 1960, for Counties, Standard Metropolitan Statistical Areas, State Economic Areas, and Economic Subregions," _Current Population Reports_, Series P-23, No. 7 (Nov. 1962), p. 22.

7. Robert C. Schmitt, "Hawaii on the Move," _Paradise of the Pacific_, 65 (Aug. 1953), 25.

8. _Report of the President of the Bureau of Immigration to the Legislative Assembly of 1886_, p. 278.

9. _Labor Problems in Hawaii. Hearings Before the Committee on Immigration and Naturalization, House of Representatives_ (1921), p. 542.

10. Hawaii State Planning Office, _Hawaii's In-Migrants, 1951-58_ (Sept. 30, 1959), and quarterly or annual reports issued by the State Planning Office, Department of Planning and Research, and Department of Planning and Economic Development for 1959-1965.

11. 1960 Census: Summarized in HDPR, RR 21, pp. 15, 19, 20, and

HDPED, SR 13 (Feb. 15, 1964). High school graduates: See RR 21, pp. 3, 8, 12. College enrollment: Summarized in Mildred D. Kosaki, Business Affairs Office, University of Hawaii, "Residence and Migration of Hawaii's College Students, Fall 1958 and 1963," IRP-4, (March 31, 1965). Oahu households: RR 21, pp. 2-3, 4, 7, 12, 17, 18; HRA, Redevelopment and Housing Research, No. 21 (June 1962), Table 4, p. 13, and No. 23 (July 1963), Table 5, p. 15. The same survey included a question on place of birth; see Robert C. Schmitt and Robert A. Souza, Place of Birth of Household Heads on Oahu, 1962 (University of Hawaii, Romanzo Adams Social Research Laboratory, Report No. 38, June 1963). Labor mobility: See HDPR, RR 21, pp. 6-7, and HDPED, SR 31 (June 21, 1965), p. 15. Social Security beneficiaries: HDPR, RR 39 (Feb. 19, 1963), p. 10; HRA, Redevelopment and Housing Research, Supplemental Research Notes for April 1966, pp. 3, 5. Net migration: Ibid., p. 7; Irene B. Taeuber, "Hawaii," Population Index, 28 (April 1962), 107-108, as corrected.

Chapter VIII

1. This section is based largely on Robert C. Schmitt and Rose C. Strombel, "Marriage and Divorce in Hawaii Before 1870," Hawaii Historical Review, II (Jan. 1966), 267-271.

2. SLH 1913, Act 8; SLH 1937, Act 59. For legislation requiring consent of parents or guardian, see SLH 1929, Act 104. For law permitting marriage of a girl at fifteen with court consent, see SLH 1939, Act 122.

3. Laws ... 1878, Chap. XXVI; SLH 1903, Act 22; SLH 1909, Act 25; SLH 1915, Act 192; SLH 1919, Act 10; SLH 1935, Act 27; SLH 1949, reg., Act 174; SLH 1957, Act 72.

4. Couples with children face a one-year waiting period under recent legislation (SLH 1965, Act 52, approved May 8, 1965).

5. 1829: *No Ka Moe Kolohe* (Oahu), Sept. 21, 1829. 1840: *Laws ... 1842*, Chap. X, in Lorrin A. Thurston, ed., *The Fundamental Law of Hawaii* (Honolulu, 1904), p. 48. 1864: *Laws ... 1864-65*, pp. 21-22. 1850: *Penal Code ... 1850*, pp. 200-201. 1851: *Laws ... 1851*, pp. 59-60. 1859 and 1865: *Civil Code ... 1859*, Sec. 762 and 763; *Laws ... 1864-65*, "An Act to Repeal Chapter 10 ...," Sec. 44. 1896: *Laws ... 1896*, Act 50. 1913: *SLH 1913*, Act 86. 1937 and 1949: *SLH 1937*, Act 86; *SLH 1949*, Act 327. See also *SLH 1903*, Acts 28 and 31; *SLH 1913*, Act 8; *SLH 1929*, Act 104.

6. *First Annual Report of the Chief Justice of the Supreme Court* (1853).

7. *SLH 1951*, Act 62.

8. *Missionary Herald*, Feb. 1829, p. 53.

9. *Ibid*., Oct. 1830, p. 312; *Missionary Register*, Feb. 1831, p. 93.

10. *Extracts ...*: Reports for 1832-1844, 1848-1849, and 1851. *Missionary Herald*: Issues of Oct. 1830 (p. 312), March 1832 (p. 74), July 1847 (p. 218), June 1848 (p. 188), Oct. 1849 (p. 362), Dec. 1850 (preliminary figures, p. 398), March 1851 (p. 98), Dec. 1851 (p. 401), Nov. 1852 (p. 324), and Dec. 1853 (p. 372). *Missionary Register*: Issues for Feb. 1831 (p. 93) and Oct. 1832 (pp. 453-454).

11. *Missionary Herald*, March 1832, p. 74; *Missionary Register*, Oct. 1832, pp. 453-454.

12. Ralph S. Kuykendall, *The Hawaiian Kingdom, 1778-1854* (Honolulu, 1938), pp. 140-143.

13. *Report of the Minister of the Interior ... Aug. 1, 1846*, p. 7.

14. *Report of the Minister of the Interior ... April 30, 1847*, p. 9.

15. Report of the Minister of the Interior (1850), pp. 8-9.

16. Report of the Minister of Public Instruction for years 1852-1855; Report of the President of the Board of Education for years 1856, 1858, and 1860; Biennial Report of the President of the Board of Education for 1862 and 1864.

17. Each report carried data for the preceding year or biennium, often with a recapitulation of data for a number of earlier years. These reports were used in preparing the series in Tables 76-78.

18. Report to the Legislature of the Chief Justice of the Supreme Court for 1911-1912 (p. vi) and 1913-1914 (p. xix).

19. Report of the President of the Board of Health ... 1899, p. 22.

20. Data for the period from July 1, 1902 to June 30, 1906 were scattered through the reports, without any indication of the all-island totals.

21. Annual Report, Department of Health, State of Hawaii, Statistical Supplement, 1960, Tables 3 and 4, pp. 6-9.

22. Annual Report of the Board of Health, Territory of Hawaii, for the Fiscal Year Ended June 30, 1937, pp. 87-94.

23. Detailed statistics on divorce for the first six months under Health Department jurisdiction were reported in M. A. Taff, Jr. and Fred M. Colland, Whom Man Hath Put Asunder (Honolulu, Department of Health, Aug. 20, 1952); statistics from 1952 forward appeared in the annual report statistical supplements.

24. Data for 1946, 1947, and 1948 were published in the Federal Security Agency, Public Health Service, National Office of Vital Statistics, Vital Statistics of the United States, 1948, Part I, Supplement for Hawaii (1950), Table 1. Annual figures for later years were carried in succeeding annual issues. The publications were

prepared by the U. S. Department of Health, Education, and Welfare, Public Health Service, National Office of Vital Statistics from 1950 onward. The name of NOVS was changed to National Vital Statistics Division prior to publication of the 1960 reports.

25. U. S. Department of Health, Education, and Welfare, Vital Statistics of the United States, 1960, Vol. III, Marriage and Divorce (Washington, 1964), p. 7-5.

26. Romanzo Adams, Interracial Marriage in Hawaii (New York, 1937), p. 46; Andrew W. Lind, Hawaii's People (Honolulu, 1955), pp. 102-107, and "Interracial Marriage as Affecting Divorce in Hawaii," Sociology and Social Research, 49 (Oct. 1964), 17-26. George K. Yamamoto, "Some Patterns of Mate Selection Among Naichi and Okinawans on Oahu," Social Process in Hawaii, 21 (1957), 42-49. C. K. Cheng and Douglas S. Yamamura, "Interracial Marriage and Divorce in Hawaii," Social Forces, 36 (Oct. 1957), 77-84. Irene B. Taeuber, "Hawaii," Population Index, 28 (April 1962), pp. 97-125, esp. pp. 109-115 and 122, n. 4. Robert C. Schmitt, Age, Race, and Marital Failure in Hawaii (Honolulu, University of Hawaii, Romanzo Adams Social Research Laboratory, Report No. 34, June 1962), and "Interracial Marriage and Occupational Status in Hawaii," American Sociological Review, 28 (Oct. 1963), 809-810; "Demographic Correlates of Interracial Marriage in Hawaii," Demography, 2 (1965), 463-473. Robert C. Schmitt and Robert A. Souza, "Interracial Households and Family Income Differentials," Sociology and Social Research, 46 (Jan. 1962), 203-206, and "Social & Economic Characteristics of Interracial Households in Honolulu," Social Problems, 10 (Winter 1963), 264-268. A number of studies bearing in some measure on this subject are cited in Bernhard L. Hormann, Selected Bibliography on Social Research in Hawaii by Sources (Honolulu, Adams Laboratory, Report No. 37, May 1963).

27. Robert C. Schmitt, "Research Note on Components of Change in Marital Status on Oahu, 1940-1950," Social Forces, 34 (March 1956), 238-240, and "Age Differences in Marriage and Divorce in Hawaii," Sociology and Social Research, 44 (March-April 1960), 266-268.

28. Schmitt, "Demographic Correlates of Interracial Marriage in Hawaii," Demography, 2 (1965), Table 5, p. 468.

29. Biennial Report of the Chief Justice of the Supreme Court to the Legislative Assembly of 1882, p. 4; Biennial Report of the Chief Justice ... 1880, p. 2.

BIBLIOGRAPHY

This bibliography cites some of the more important publications on the demographic statistics of Hawaii. No effort has been made to be exhaustive; readers interested in more detailed listings should refer to the footnotes in this volume or to bibliographies in the books and reports below.

Four classes of work are considered: general demographic studies of Hawaii; general statistical compilations; official census reports; and serial publications on births, deaths, migration, marriage, and divorce.

General demographic studies

Although many general accounts of the population of Hawaii have appeared in print, the five listed below merit special attention:

Romanzo Adams, _The Peoples of Hawaii_. Honolulu: American Council, Institute of Pacific Relations, 1933.

Romanzo Adams, _Interracial Marriage in Hawaii_. New York: Macmillan Co., 1937.

Andrew W. Lind, _An Island Community_. Chicago: University of Chicago Press, 1938.

Andrew W. Lind, _Hawaii's People_. Honolulu: University of Hawaii Press, 1955 and 1967.

Irene B. Taeuber, "Hawaii," _Population Index_, 28 (April 1962), pp. 97-125.

General statistical compilations

The following works provide information not only on Hawaiian demography but also on a number of related social, economic, and governmental topics:

Thrum's Annual. First published as the *Hawaiian Almanac and Annual for 1875* by Thos. G. Thrum, compiler and publisher. After Thrum's death in 1932 this series was continued (as *The Hawaiian Annual for --*) by the Printshop Co., Ltd., terminating with the 1940 edition. Soon thereafter it was absorbed by the Star-Bulletin Press (now known as the Star-Bulletin Printing Co.) and issued as *Thrum's Hawaiian Annual Combined with All About Hawaii, 1940-1941*. In 1948 the title was changed to *All About Hawaii, 1948-49, Combined With Thrum's Hawaiian Annual and Standard Guide*.

Report of the Governor of the Territory of Hawaii to the Secretary of the Interior. Issued annually from 1900 to 1959. Published by the U. S. Government Printing Office, Washington, D. C.

Statistical Abstract of Hawaii, 1962. Prepared by Robert C. Schmitt and published by the Hawaii State Department of Planning and Research (the present Department of Planning and Economic Development) in May 1962.

Official census reports

Major census reports published by the Hawaiian Government and United States Bureau of the Census since

1849 are listed below. Chapters III and IV present more extensive listings.

"Census of the Hawaiian Islands -- From Official Documents -- Taken January, 1849," _Polynesian_, Nov. 10, 1849.

"Report of the Minister of Pub. Instruction, read before the King to the Hawaiian Legislature, April 22, 1850," _Polynesian_, May 4, 1850. Includes census of January 1850.

"Report of the Minister of Public Instruction to the Legislature of 1854," _Polynesian_, April 15, 1854. Includes census data for 1853. Additional information was published in the _Polynesian_ for April 22, 1854.

Biennial Report of the President of the Board of Education to the Legislature of 1862, pp. 23-26 and Table III. Presents 1860 census data.

Biennial Report of the President of the Board of Education to the Legislature of 1868, p. 7 and table following p. 10. Presents 1866 census data.

Biennial Report of the President of the Board of Education to the Legislature of 1874, pp. 16-17 and unpaged table. Presents 1872 census data.

Biennial Report of the President of the Board of Education to the Legislative Assembly of 1880, p. 31 and table after p. 35. Presents 1878 census data.

Census of the Hawaiian Islands Taken December 27th,

1884, Under the Direction of the Board of Education.

Bureau of Public Instruction, *Report of the General Superintendent of the Census, 1890* (1891).

Department of Public Instruction, *Report of the General Superintendent of the Census, 1896* (1897).

U. S. Census Office, *Census Reports, Volume I, Twelfth Census of the United States, Taken in the Year 1900*, *Population, Part I* (1901); *Volume II ...* *Population, Part II* (1902).

U. S. Bureau of the Census, *Thirteenth Census of the United States, Taken in the Year 1910*, *Abstract of the Census ... with Supplement for Hawaii* (1913).

U. S. Bureau of the Census, *Fourteenth Census of the United States, Taken in the Year 1920*, *Volume III*, *Population, 1920, Composition and Characteristics of the Population by States* (1922).

U. S. Bureau of the Census, *Fifteenth Census of the United States: 1930*, *Outlying Territories and Possessions* (1932).

U. S. Bureau of the Census, *Sixteenth Census of the United States: 1940*, *Population, Second Series, Characteristics of the Population, Hawaii* (1943).

U. S. Bureau of the Census, *U. S. Census of Population: 1950*, Vol. II, *Characteristics of the Population*, Parts 51-54, Territories and Possessions (1953).

U. S. Bureau of the Census, *U. S. Census of Popu-*

lation: 1960, Vol. I, Characteristics of the Population, Part 13, Hawaii (1963).

Other official reports

Various serials present official statistics, usually on an annual basis, of births, deaths, migration, marriage, and divorces. The following brief list cites only those serials still in publication. More detailed references, including publications no longer issued, are given in Chapters VI, VII, and VIII.

Annual Report, Department of Health, State of Hawaii, Statistical Supplement. Presents data on births, deaths, marriages, and (since 1951) divorces. Issued annually or biennially, under various titles, since the last third of the nineteenth century. Initially titled Report of the Board of Health to the Legislative Assembly.

Hawaii's In-Migrants. Issued on a quarterly basis through 1963, annually thereafter, by the Territorial Planning Office (1959) and its successor agencies, the State Planning Office (1959-1961), the Department of Planning and Research (1961-1962), and the Department of Planning and Economic Development (1963 forward).

The Population of Hawaii. Issued semi-annually by the Department of Planning and Economic Development since 1963. Includes considerable detail on the estimated components of population change.

INDEX